Using

MICROSOFT®

Excel 97

Using

Using
MICROSOFT®
Excel 97

Que®

Laura Monsen

Using Microsoft® Excel 97

Library of Congress Catalog No.: 97-69800

ISBN: 0-7897-1440-X

99 98 97   6 5 4 3 2 1

Interpretation of the printing code: The rightmost double-digit number is the year of the book's printing; the rightmost single-digit number, the number of the book's printing. For example, a printing code of 97-1 shows that the first printing of the book occurred in 1997.

Screen reproductions in this book were created using Collage Plus from Inner Media, Inc., Hollis, NH.

Contents at a Glance

Table of Contents

Credits

PRESIDENT
Roland Elgey

SENIOR VICE PRESIDENT/PUBLISHING
Don Fowley

PUBLISHER
Joseph B. Wikert

GENERAL MANAGER
Joe Muldoon

MANAGER OF PUBLISHING OPERATIONS
Linda H. Buehler

PUBLISHING DIRECTOR
Karen Reinisch

PUBLISHING MANAGER
Jim Minatel

EDITORIAL SERVICES DIRECTOR
Carla Hall

MANAGING EDITOR
Thomas F. Hayes

ACQUISITIONS MANAGER
Cheryl D. Willoughby

ACQUISITIONS EDITOR
Don Essig

PRODUCT DIRECTOR
Rick Kughen

PRODUCTION EDITOR
Lori A. Lyons

EDITOR
Bill McManus

COORDINATOR OF EDITORIAL SERVICES
Maureen A. McDaniel

WEBMASTER
Thomas H. Bennett

PRODUCT MARKETING MANAGER
Kourtnaye Sturgeon

ASSISTANT PRODUCT MARKETING MANAGER
Gretchen Schlesinger

TECHNICAL EDITORS
Rick Brown
Bill Bruns
Ron Ellenbecker
Brad Lindaas

ACQUISITIONS COORDINATOR
Travis Bartlett

SOFTWARE RELATIONS COORDINATOR
Susan D. Gallagher

EDITORIAL ASSISTANTS
Jennifer L. Chisholm
Jeff Chandler

BOOK DESIGNER
Ruth Harvey

COVER DESIGNER
Sandra Schroeder

PRODUCTION TEAM
Jenny Earhart
Darlena Murray
Nicole Ruessler
Sossity Smith

INDEXER
Greg Pearson

Composed in *Century Old Style* and *ITC Franklin Gothic* by Que Corporation.

*This book is dedicated to **Ron Monsen**. Though his gentle prompting was sometimes met with a lack of appreciation, the encouragement he provided carried me through the writing of this book. Ron made many sacrifices, not the least of which was freeing me from the mundane tasks of everyday life and making candy bar runs at odd hours! His steadfast reminders that there would be an end to the late nights, hard work, and that normalcy would return to our lives, provided me with the extra motivation I needed as the final deadlines approached. Ron is a remarkable and generous man. I am greatly indebted to him for his encouragement, humor, and wisdom.*

About the Author

Laura Monsen is a professional instructor with more than seven years experience teaching computer application classes; the last five of those years have been with Productivity Point International, a leader in computer software training solutions. She teaches a variety of spreadsheet, project management, database, and graphic applications at the PPI site in San Antonio, Texas.

Laura has been a contributing author on several Que computer reference books, including: *Special Edition Using Microsoft Project 98*, *Special Edition Using Microsoft PowerPoint 97*, and *Special Edition Using Microsoft Project 95*. She frequently provides consulting on Excel, Project, and PowerPoint. Laura has a B.A. in Economics from the University of the South, Sewanee, Tennessee.

Acknowledgments

Producing a great computer reference book involves many other people besides the author. **Don Essig** led the team of Que professionals who edited this book. His assistance and flexibility in its production allowed me to focus my attention on writing. Don was responsible for coordinating all the rest. Several other individuals at Que were instrumental in developing this book and deserve my thanks: **Rick Kughen** for his encouragement, good humor, and wonderfully positive attitude; **Bill McManus** and **Lori Lyons**, for attention to detail and valuable editing suggestions.

Together with the production team, a number of other people contributed directly and indirectly to this book. Foremost is my mentor and friend **Dr. Tim Pyron**, without whose help I would never have become an author. Tim introduced me to Excel and to writing. I learned many of the spreadsheet concepts presented in this book from him. And, with his permission, I have incorporated several of his superb spreadsheet examples to help illustrate important Excel features. In addition to teaching me the power of Excel, Tim gave me the opportunity to assist him in editing his own computer reference books, the *Special Edition Using Microsoft Project 95* and the *Special Edition Using Microsoft Project 98, New Edition*. Thank you Tim, for your friendship and guidance.

Another person who contributed greatly to this book is **Ron Stockdreher**. Ron is a Microsoft Certified Trainer in Visual Basic 4.0 and 5.0, and a colleague of mine at the San Antonio office of Productivity Point International, Inc. Ron helped me develop a better understanding of how Visual Basic for Applications could be used by Excel and the other Office programs. His lively teaching style and humor made working with Visual Basic less painful than I expected. My hat's off to the Lord of the Lounge Lizards (you'd have to see his office)!

Finally, there are several people who also deserve my thanks—**Terry Goatley** (for his understanding), **Susan Perry** (for her friendship), and **Edmund Stewart Sr**. & **Carolina Waring Stewart** (who continue to teach me many lessons about life).

We'd Like to Hear from You!

QUE Corporation has a long-standing reputation for high-quality books and products. To ensure your continued satisfaction, we also understand the importance of customer service and support.

Tech Support

If you need assistance with the information in this book or with a CD/disk accompanying the book, please access Macmillan Computer Publishing's online Knowledge Base at:

> **http://www.superlibrary.com/general/support**

Our most Frequently Asked Questions are answered there. If you do not find the answer to your questions on our Web site, you may contact Macmillan Technical Support by phone at **317/581-3833** or via e-mail at **support@mcp.com**.

Also be sure to visit QUE's Web resource center for all the latest information, enhancements, errata, downloads, and more. It's located at:

> **http://www.quecorp.com**

Orders, Catalogs, and Customer Service

To order other QUE or Macmillan Computer Publishing books, catalogs, or products, please contact our Customer Service Department:

> **Phone: 800/428-5331**
> **Fax: 800/835-3202**
> **International Fax: 317/228-4400**

Or visit our online bookstore:

> **http://www.mcp.com/**

Comments and Suggestions

We want you to let us know what you like or dislike most about this book or other QUE products. Your comments will help us to continue publishing the best books available on computer topics in today's market.

Rick Kughen
Product Director
QUE Corporation
201 West 103rd Street, 4B
Indianapolis, Indiana 46290 USA
Fax: 317/581-4663 E-mail: rkughen@que.mcp.com

Please be sure to include the book's title and author as well as your name and phone or fax number. We will carefully review your comments and share them with the author. Please note that due to the high volume of mail we receive, we may not be able to reply to every message.

Thank you for choosing QUE!

Introduction

Excel is one of the most powerful applications available for creating and maintaining spreadsheets. Excel's strength is not in its capability to add numbers or perform simple calculations—you can do these things with a common calculator—rather its strength is in all the additional features available to manipulate data that make Excel a valuable program.

With each new version, Microsoft adds new features and enhances existing ones to make it easier to work with Excel. This version, Excel 97, is a significant upgrade from Excel 5.0 and 95. Improved charting and data entry are among the key enhancements, and new features like additional graphic tools and Internet integration, including Web publishing, have been added. ■

New (and Improved) Features in Excel 97

If you have used other versions of Excel, you will be very pleased with the enhancements and additions in Excel 97:

- **The Internet and World Wide Web**. If you have connectivity to the Internet, Excel provides a plethora of built-in features to make it easy to access information from the Web. With a few mouse clicks, Excel will prompt you for logon information for your Internet service provider, launch your browser, and access a Web site you select. Through the Help menu you can look at (and download) information provided online by Microsoft on the Web. Four topics, like Free Stuff and Online Support, are designed to assist specifically with Excel. Six additional topics are provided to help you get started "surfing the Net."

- **Charting**. The Chart Wizard in Excel has been significantly improved to make creating and enhancing charts even easier than before. Many additional standard chart types and a number of custom chart types have been added. New types include Cone, Pyramid, Cylinder, Bubble, Pie of Pie, and Bar of Pie. Additionally, Microsoft has finally included an option to add a data table to a chart.

- **Workbook Sharing**. Improved features when sharing workbooks include conflict resolution and keeping a "history" of changes.

- **Data Entry**. The New AutoComplete and Pick From List features make it easy to enter repetitive data in lists.

- **Data Formatting**. Many new formatting options are included in Excel 97. Conditional formatting, rotating text, indenting text, and merging cells are among the new options.

- **Data Mapping**. The mapping feature introduced in Excel 95 has been improved in Excel 97.

- **The Office Assistant**. Though it takes a little getting used to, the Office Assistant (replacing the Answer Wizard) is really a valuable tool for locating information in the extensive online help included with Excel 97. Simply type your question in the wizard's search box and the Office Assistant will display a list of related help topics. You will find several references in this book to using the Office Assistant for more information.

- **Specifications and Limits**. Excel 97 worksheets can now hold 65,536 rows of information, up from 16,384. Multiple Undo operations allow you to undo up to 16 of your last actions.

Who Should Read This Book?

This book is designed for people who are currently using Excel (or migrating from another spreadsheet program to Excel) and who want to learn to use Excel more productively and effectively. It was developed to fill a gap between reference books that concentrate on helping people just learning to use spreadsheet programs and those books that are encyclopedias on Excel, exploring every feature of the program and each and every method of working with that feature.

This book is for the person who is currently using Excel but hasn't been able to spend a great deal of time learning to tap its power. This book focuses on the most commonly used Excel features, explaining why you want to use them and then showing you how to use these features. This book does not devote its pages to explaining all the various methods available to accomplish your goal; instead it concentrates on the best methods to expedite using the software.

Although each and every feature in Excel is not discussed in this book, the most common and productive features are presented. This book assumes you have some experience with spreadsheets, a mouse, and Windows. You are not expected to be an expert to use this book, but if you are you will still find valuable "tips and tricks" within these pages.

How This Book Is Organized

This book is divided into five main sections: maximizing your productivity with Excel features, creating and modifying charts, analyzing spreadsheet data, manipulating lists of data, and using Excel with other windows applications, mainframe computers, and the Internet.

Part I: Unleashing the Power of Excel

In this section, you focus on Excel features and tools that will help you get the most from your spreadsheets, using some of the most popular Excel features:

- Learn to design effective spreadsheets.
- Create totals quickly.
- Discover the importance of Excel's grouping feature to manipulate multiple worksheets simultaneously.
- Explore common worksheet functions that can help you determine the monthly payment on a car loan or calculate how much money you will have if you invest or save $100 a month for five years. Learn to use functions to check data entry or assist in making decisions.
- Create calculations to summarize data in multiple worksheets and workbooks.
- Use Excel's built-in templates or create your own templates to replace everyday forms. Store the data in completed forms in a database.

Part II: The Visual Impact of Excel

Creating and manipulating charts is the focus of this section. Excel has an excellent charting capability. Following are just a few of the ways Excel helps you chart your data:

- Multiple chart styles allow you to select the best chart type to display your data.
- Create a chart with one keystroke.
- Enhance the appearance of your charts by using eye-catching formats.
- Create charts that can compare more than one type of data.
- Explore the new Bar in a Pie and Pie in a Pie variations of the Pie chart.
- Create picture charts and charts from outlined worksheets.

Part III: Finding Answers with Excel

This section discusses the analytical and auditing features in Excel:

- Evaluate and locate data using functions like IF and VLOOKUP.
- Use Goal Seek and Scenario commands to perform what-if analysis.
- Locate, troubleshoot, and avoid errors in worksheets by auditing your formulas.
- Learn to interpret and correct worksheet error messages. Resolve circular reference errors.
- Add comments to cells that document procedures, or provide instructions on what will avoid worksheet errors.

Part IV: Making Your Point with Excel

This section contains six chapters that concentrate on only one thing—creating and manipulating lists of information. A list is a worksheet that contains information about many items, such as all orders received or the expenses for every employee. Excel provides many tools for manipulating a variety of lists:

- Learn to design a list type of worksheet.
- Expedite list data entry.
- Reorganize the data in your lists by sorting a list alphabetically, numerically, or using a custom sort order.
- Create subtotal and grand total calculations effortlessly.
- Use functions designed specifically for lists and databases.
- Discover how to view part of a list of information, based on criteria you specify.
- Create charts based on filtered data, which automatically update when you change or remove the filter.
- Summarize and consolidate lengthy lists of Excel information through pivot tables. Once consolidated, the information can be analyzed more easily.

Part V: Excel and the Outside World

This book concludes with chapters that illustrate how to reach outside Excel to exchange data with other windows applications, mainframe computers, and the Internet, as well as learning to use Visual Basic for Applications in Excel. Following are just a few of the areas in which Excel can help you be part of today's global community:

- Bring data into Excel from databases like Access, use Excel productively with the other Office 97 products, share data with the Internet or internal intranets, and learn the basics of Visual Basic for Applications (VBA).
- Retrieve data from external sources, such as Access, to analyze and manipulate the data using built-in Excel tools, such as pivot tables. Microsoft Query is used to retrieve the data.
- Move and copy data between Windows applications.
- Link and embed data from Excel worksheets into Word documents or PowerPoint slides.

■ Attach Excel files to e-mail messages in client applications such as Outlook or cc:Mail.

■ Use the features of the innovative Binder application to work with files created in different applications as if they are a single "bound" document. Within one window you can work with documents created in any Office 97 application.

■ Exchange data over networks like standard home or office networks, company intranets, and the Internet including the World Wide Web.

■ Import and export data between Excel and other personal computer programs (like Lotus 1-2-3 FoxPro, and dBASE) and mainframe computers.

■ Learn how Visual Basic for Applications can be used to automate tasks in Excel.

Conventions Used in This Book

Certain text formats, margin icons, and other conventions are used in *Using Microsoft Excel 97* to help you use this book more easily. The following typefaces are used to distinguish specific text:

Type Appearance	Meaning
bold	Information that you type.
italic	New terms or phrases when they are first defined. Also used in Visual Basic.
underlined characters	Indicates keyboard shortcuts for menu and dialog box commands.
special type	Visual Basic code and text that appears on-screen.

Text appearing in uppercase represents a function name, such as AVERAGE; file format extensions such as .XLS; and cell references such as A1.

Generally, keys appear in this book just as they appear on the keyboard—for example, Enter or Tab. When two keys are used together, a plus sign (+) appears between them, such as Ctrl+Home.

Cross-references like the one here directs you to related information in another part of the book:

▶ **See** "Designing Effective Spreadsheets," **p. 9**

 Icons representing buttons on Excel toolbars are displayed next to paragraphs that reference the button. The Chart Wizard button from the Standard toolbar appears to the left of this paragraph.

 TIP Additional, helpful information that will make a procedure easier to perform or a feature easier to use will be displayed in this format.

N O T E Additional, useful information will be displayed in this format. Notes often can help you avoid problems or understand concepts. ▪

CAUTION

Warnings of potential problem areas will be represented in this format.

PART

Unleasing the Power of Excel

CHAPTER 1

Essential Excel— Increasing Your Efficiency

Perhaps you have learned Excel on your own, attended a class, or are switching to Excel from another spreadsheet program. Though you are probably familiar with the basic ways to create, enhance, and print spreadsheets, you'll find this chapter focuses on accomplishing these tasks productively. ■

Design spreadsheet layout

The way you design your worksheet layout affects how Excel sorts your data and calculates your formulas.

Expedite data entry

You will spend less time on data entry and have more time to analyze the data you enter using the AutoComplete, Pick From List, and AutoFill features in Excel.

Create totals quickly

The AutoSum button calculates totals in your entire worksheet and, at the same time, can calculate the multiple totals and grand totals.

Use WordArt and AutoFormat for a professional look

You can enhance your worksheets with the new WordArt feature. Choose from 16 predesigned formats by using AutoFormat.

Open, save, and print files

You can open files created in previous versions of Excel or convert files from Lotus 1-2-3 and Corel Quattro Pro. Print all or part of your worksheet.

Identifying the Parts of the Excel Screen

Several new features have been added to the Excel 97 screen (see Figure 1.1). The menu bar and toolbars contain a move handle to reposition the bars. The toolbar buttons are more animated; a border appears when the mouse is positioned over a button. An Edit Formula button has been added to the Formula Bar to aid in changing formulas. Tips that were once available only for toolbar buttons have been added to identify different parts of the screen, such as Name Box, Edit Formula button, and Minimize Window button. Knowing the different parts of the Excel 97 screen will improve your use of the program.

FIG. 1.1

The items identified in this figure will be referenced throughout this book.

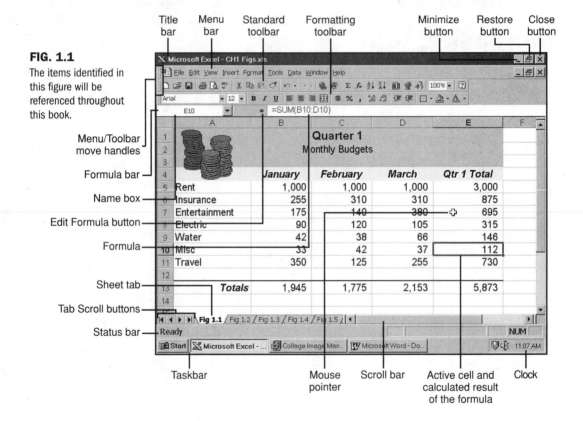

Designing Effective Spreadsheets

Taking time to design your spreadsheet *before* you start entering data will save you time (and headaches) in the end. Consider carefully the different aspects of the worksheet layout when creating your design. Worksheet titles are followed by one or more empty rows. Headings border the data and can appear either above the data, to the left of the data, or in both places. The data is entered next to or below the heading(s). One or more rows should separate the data from the formulas. Figure 1.2 displays an optimal spreadsheet layout.

FIG. 1.2

A good worksheet design will help avoid errors as you use the more powerful Excel features.

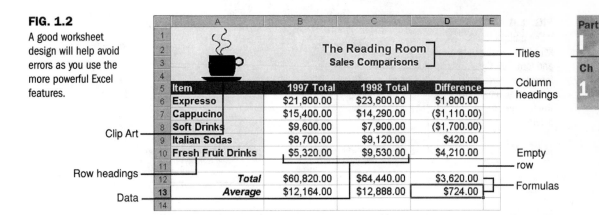

You should always leave a blank row between your data and your formulas, and include the empty row in your formulas, when you create them. This design layout is important for several reasons:

- *Inserting New Rows.* With the worksheet layout shown in Figure 1.3, when a new row of data is inserted at the bottom of the list, the formulas are not updated automatically. Each time you add a new row of information, the formulas have to be modified to include the reference to the new row.

FIG. 1.3

The formula results aren't updated automatically when there isn't a blank row between the data and formulas.

Monthly Budget					Monthly Budget		
	January	February				January	February
Rent	1,000	1,000			Rent	1,000	1,000
Insurance	255	310			Insurance	255	310
Utilities	90	120			Utilities	90	120
Misc	33	42			Misc	33	42
Totals	1,378	1,472			Travel	350	125
					Totals	1,378	1,472
Before inserting a new row of information					**After** inserting a new row of information, the Totals did not change		

However, if you include an empty row between your data and your formulas, as in Figure 1.4, when you insert new information, the formulas are recalculated automatically.

- *Sorting Data.* Figure 1.5 shows a list of monthly budget expenses, where the formulas start immediately below the last expense (no empty row is inserted before the Totals row). Notice what happens with the Totals row when the list is sorted by expense name, using the Ascending Sort button on the Standard toolbar. This problem is easily avoided by inserting an empty row prior to the Totals row, as demonstrated in Figure 1.6.

FIG. 1.4

When a blank row is kept between the data and formulas, the formula results are updated automatically when a new row is inserted.

Monthly Budget				Monthly Budget		
	January	*February*			*January*	*February*
Rent	1,000	1,000		Rent	1,000	1,000
Insurance	255	310		Insurance	255	310
Utilities	90	120		Utilities	90	120
Misc	33	42		Misc	33	42
				Travel	350	125
Totals	1,378	1,472				
				Totals	1,728	1,597

| <u>Before</u> inserting a new row of information | | | | <u>After</u> inserting a new row of information, the Totals are automatically updated | | |

FIG. 1.5

The sort results include the Totals row in the list of expenses when the row containing the formulas immediately follows the data.

Monthly Budget				Monthly Budget		
	January	*February*			*January*	*February*
Rent	1,000	1,000		Insurance	255	310
Insurance	255	310		Misc	33	42
Utilities	90	120		Rent	1,000	1,000
Misc	33	42		*Totals*	288	352
Travel	350	125		Travel	350	125
Totals	1,378	1,472		Utilities	90	120

| <u>Before</u> sorting the list | | | | <u>After</u> sorting the list, the Totals are included in the sort | | |

FIG. 1.6

When a blank row is kept between the data and the formulas, sorting the expense list doesn't affect the Totals row.

Monthly Budget				Monthly Budget		
	January	*February*			*January*	*February*
Rent	1,000	1,000		Insurance	255	310
Insurance	255	310		Misc	33	42
Utilities	90	120		Rent	1,000	1,000
Misc	33	42		Travel	350	125
Travel	350	125		Utilities	90	120
Totals	1,728	1,597		*Totals*	1,728	1,597

| <u>Before</u> sorting the list | | | | <u>After</u> the sort, the empty row provides a buffer between the Totals and the expenses | | |

TIP The AutoSum button on the Standard toolbar is widely used to create quick totals. When you select the cell where you want the total to appear, the AutoSum highlights the numbers it believes you are trying to total. If you use numbers or dates for your column (or row) headings, such as 1998, AutoSum will attempt to include the heading in your formula. This happens because the heading is a number, not text. There are two ways to avoid this problem: You can insert an apostrophe (') in front of the number so that Excel reads the heading as text (a label) rather than as a number, or you can insert a blank row (or column) between the heading and the data. When AutoSum finds a blank or text in a column or row, it stops highlighting.

Convenient Methods for Entering Data into Worksheets

There are two types of data used in Excel—constant values and formulas. *Constant values* include text, numbers, dates, and time (essentially everything but formulas), and are displayed in the cell when you type them. *Formulas* are calculations, the results of which appear in the cells; the formula that calculates the results appears in the Formula Bar (refer to Figure 1.1). This section focuses on efficient and effective methods for entering and editing constant values. Look ahead to the section in this chapter, "Working with Formulas," and to Chapter 3, "Formulas and Functions," for more information on creating formulas in Excel.

 T I P A quick way to enter the current date or time in a spreadsheet is with keyboard shortcuts. To enter the current date, press and hold the Ctrl key, and then press the colon/semicolon key (Ctrl+;). To enter the current time, press and hold the Ctrl and Shift keys, and then press the colon/semicolon key (Ctrl+Shift+;).

The current date and time are based on your computer's internal clock. To adjust the clock, double-click the clock on the right side of the Taskbar (refer to Figure 1.1).

When you have a series of data to enter into your worksheet, it may be more convenient to select the cells you want to enter the data into, before you enter the data. You can use the selected cells to control data entry; the active cell automatically moves to the next cell in the selected range after each data entry is made.

There are several quick techniques you can use, either with the mouse or with the keyboard, to select multiple cells or several ranges of cells:

▪ *A Range of Cells*

Mouse: Position the mouse pointer on the first cell you want to select. Press and hold the mouse button as you drag the mouse pointer from the first cell in the range to the last cell in the range of cells you want to select. Alternatively, you can select the first cell in the range, hold down the Shift key, and click the last cell in the range. Using either method, the cells you select will be highlighted in black, with a heavy boarder surrounding the cells. The first cell in the selection will not be highlighted in black to indicate that it is the *active cell* of the range—the first cell where data will be entered.

Keyboard: Use the arrow keys on your keyboard to position the active cell indicator (the heavy boarder around the cell) on the first cell in the range of cells you want to select. Hold down the Shift key while you use the arrow keys to extend the range. The cells you select will be highlighted in black, with a heavy boarder surrounding the cells. The first cell in the selection will not be highlighted in black to indicate that it is the *active cell* of the range—the first cell where data will be entered.

▪ *Several Ranges of Cells*

Mouse: To select several ranges, you can use the dragging method described in the preceding bullet for selecting a single range. Select the first range of cells, and then hold down the Ctrl key as you select each additional range. Each individual range will be become highlighted as it is selected.

Keyboard: Select the first range using the keyboard method previously described. Next, press Shift+F8 once, which will cause ADD to appear in the status bar; this is a keyboard indicator that you can add another range to the selection. Then use the arrow keys to move the active cell to the beginning of the next range. Hold down the Shift key and use the arrow keys to select the next range. Each time you want to highlight another range, you will have to begin with Shift+F8.

After the cells you want to enter data into are selected, you can begin entering the data. The active cell automatically changes or "moves" to the next cell in the selected range after each data entry is made; the cells remain highlighted as you type. After data has been entered into all the selected cells, the active cell changes back to the beginning of the range.

After you have selected the cells, use only the keyboard keys, described in Table 1.1, to move around in the selected cells. Using any other keyboard keys, such as the arrow keys, turn off the cell highlighting.

Table 1.1   Movement Keys Used with Selected Cell Ranges

Active Cell Movement	Key(s)
Down	Enter
Up	Shift+Enter
Right	Tab
Left	Shift+Tab

In Figure 1.7, two ranges of cells are selected—one listing general expenses and another listing all travel expenses. The cell for Insurance in January is the active cell in Figure 1.7.

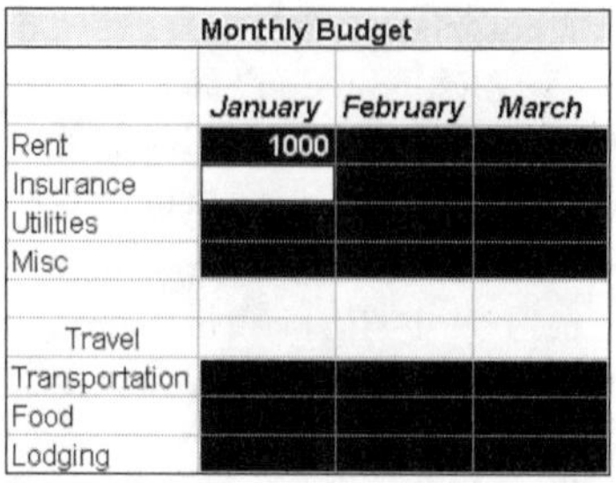

FIG. 1.7

Select multiple cells for quick and controlled data entry.

Monthly Budget			
	January	February	March
Rent	1000		
Insurance			
Utilities			
Misc			
Travel			
Transportation			
Food			
Lodging			

When you press Enter, the next cell down becomes the active cell by default. However, you can redirect this movement to the right, left, or up by going to the Options dialog box and choosing Tools, Options, and then selecting the Edit tab. Use the Direction drop-down list arrow in the

Move Selection After Enter box to change the direction you want the active cell to move when you press Enter.

- The Enter key on your keyboard's numeric keypad is a convenient means of moving the active cell when you are entering numbers.

- If more than one range of cells is selected, the keys listed in Table 1.1 will cycle through all the cell ranges. In Figure 1.7, when the Misc entry for March is completed by pressing the Enter or Tab key, the active cell will move to the Transportation cell for January.

- If you use an arrow key to move between cells when entering data, the active cell will move in the direction of the arrow, but this action removes the highlighting from the selected cells.

Using AutoComplete to Enter Data Quickly

In Excel, the AutoComplete and Pick From List features make it easier to enter repetitive data. AutoFill is used to enter a series of data or numbers, such as Quarter 1, Quarter 2, and so forth.

If you have repetitive text entries in a particular column, AutoComplete can help you enter the text quickly. As you type characters in a cell, AutoComplete checks up the column from the active cell to the point where it encounters a blank cell. If there is another text entry that matches the characters you have typed, AutoComplete fills in the remaining characters.

For example, suppose that you have a series of entries like *Cairo*, *Calcutta*, *Calgary*, and *Canberra* in a column. Each entry differs after the first 2 letters, *Ca*. For the next entry, if you type **Can**, AutoComplete fills in the remaining letters of the city *Canberra*. If Canberra is not the entry you want, you can continue to type your entry. If Canberra is the entry you want, you can press Enter to proceed with the next entry. In this example, if you type **ca**, where the letter *c* is not capitalized, AutoComplete will duplicate the capitalization used in the first occurrence of Canberra. AutoComplete is a terrific feature in Excel for expediting data entry, especially when the entries differ after the second or third letter.

N O T E   AutoComplete does not work with numbers.

Pick From List

If many entries in a column begin with identical characters, it is easier to select the entry you want by using the Pick From List command. Like AutoComplete, Pick From List does not work with numbers. To select an entry from a list, right-click the cell to activate the shortcut menu, choose Pick From List, and then select your entry. You also can use Ctrl with the down arrow on your keyboard to activate the Pick From List command.

Using AutoFill

With the AutoFill feature, you can automatically complete a sequence of information, such as labels, in your worksheet. For example, when Quarter 1 is entered into a cell, the entries Quarter 2, Quarter 3, and Quarter 4 can be created quickly using AutoFill. The Fill Handle appears as a dot in the lower-right corner of the active cell. When you position your mouse pointer on the Fill Handle, the pointer changes to a thin, black plus sign (see Figure 1.8).

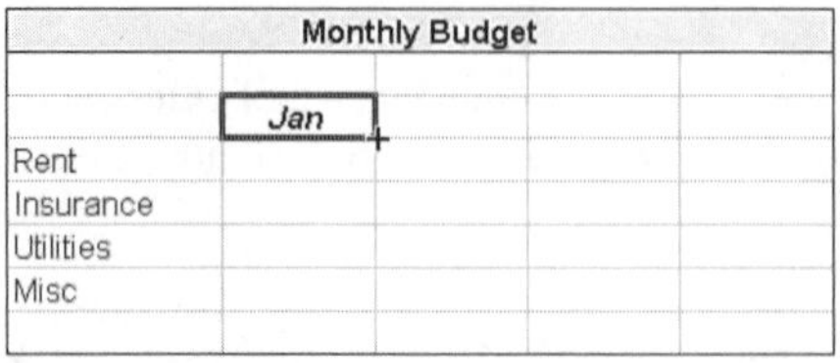

FIG. 1.8

The Fill Handle appears only on the active cell.

AutoFill is capable of performing two functions—it can complete a series of entries, and it can copy the contents of a cell to adjacent cells. When AutoFill is used, the formatting on the data in the initial cell will be transferred to the new cells. In Figure 1.8, January is abbreviated to Jan and is formatted with bold and italic styles. When the Fill Handle is used to create the headings for February and March, they will be abbreviated, with bold and italic (see Figure 1.9), just like the original cell containing Jan.

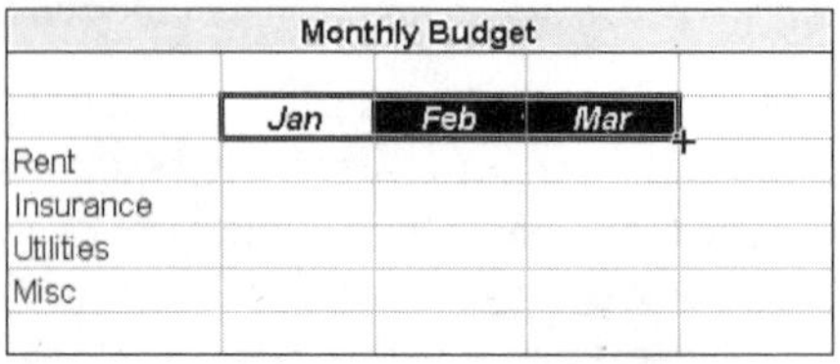

FIG. 1.9

The Fill Handle is a quick way to add headers and labels, or copy data.

Table 1.2 shows the way in which AutoFill will complete a series. Selecting multiple cells (shown separated by commas in Table 1.2) is required with numbers or when you want to create a series that skips entries. For example, although 1998 represents a year to us, it represents a number to Excel. In order for Excel to understand you want an ascending series of numbers —1998, 1999, 2000—you have to provide Excel with an example of the series.

Table 1.2 Completing a Series with AutoFill

Selected Cell Entries	Series Created	Comments/Explanation
9:00	10:00, 11:00, 12:00	Hourly time
9:00, 9:30	10:00, 10:30, 11:00	
Mon	Tue, Wed, Thu	Days of the week, abbreviated
Monday	Tuesday, Wednesday	Days of the week, spelled out

Selected Cell Entries	Series Created	Comments/Explanation
Jan, Apr	Jul, Oct, Jan	Quarterly months, abbreviated
Jan-98, Apr-98	Jul-98, Oct-98, Jan-99	Quarterly months and years, abbreviated
15-Jan, 15-Apr	15-Jul, 15-Oct	Quarterly date and month, abbreviated
Qtr1	Qtr2, Qtr3, Qtr4, Qtr1	Quarters
Q2	Q3, Q4, Q1	Quarters
1st Period	2nd Period, 3rd Period	Sequential number, followed by text
Room 1	Room 2, Room 3, Room 4	Text followed by sequential number
1995, 2000	2005, 2010, 2015	Numbers, increasing by 5
1, 2	3, 4, 5, 6	Numbers, increasing by 1 (sequential)
1, 3	5, 7, 9, 11	Numbers, increasing by 2
100, 75	50, 25, 0, -25, -50	Numbers, decreasing by 25

See the "Copying Formulas" section later in this chapter for information on using the Fill Handle with formulas.

Editing Cell Contents

There are several Excel features essential to editing data. You can replace or remove the content of a cell, reverse multiple actions, or have Excel correct commonly mistyped words.

There are two ways to edit your data quickly—editing directly in the worksheet cell, referred to as *in-cell editing*, or editing in the Formula Bar. To edit directly in the cell, you can either double-click the cell or press F2 to edit a specific part of the entry. To change the entire cell contents, simply type the new entry over the old entry. To edit using the Formula Bar, select the cell and click once in the Formula Bar.

Two elements exist in a cell—the data and the formatting. When the Delete key is used on a selected cell, only the data is removed, leaving the formatting in the cell. The next time data is entered into the cell, the formatting which remained in the cell is applied to the new data. To clear both the data and the formatting, choose Edit, Clear, All.

 A new feature of Excel 97 is the capability to undo multiple actions. The Undo tool on the Standard Toolbar now has a drop-down arrow that enables you to see the specific actions you will be undoing. The maximum number of actions you can undo is 16.

AutoCorrect

AutoCorrect recognizes common typographical mistakes and automatically corrects them as you type. You can add to AutoCorrect words that you frequently mistype or abbreviations for words that you want Excel to complete. To access the current list of words, choose Tools, AutoCorrect (see Figure 1.10).

FIG. 1.10

In the AutoCorrect dialog box, you can set the AutoCorrect options (and exceptions), and add or delete items.

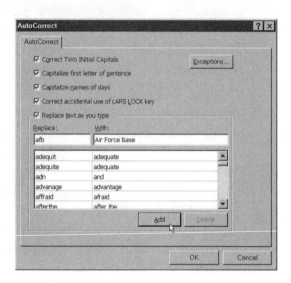

 T I P Using AutoCorrect to store abbreviations for long phrases or passages will save you a lot of typing. In the AutoCorrect dialog box (see Figure 1.10), type a unique sequence of characters in the Replace box. Select the With box and type the phrase or passage you want to appear when the abbreviation is typed. Make sure you type it exactly as you want it to appear, including uppercase and lowercase letters. For example, the letters *afb* can be replaced with *Air Force Base* and *sf* with *San Francisco*.

Working with Formulas

Number crunching is one of the main uses of spreadsheets. You can create simple calculations that add up a series of numbers, calculate the difference between two numbers, or figure the percentage a specific item is of all items combined. Additionally, Excel has a list of more than 320 functions that can be used to perform complex calculations, such as determining how much money you will have (including the compound interest earned) if you invest $100 a month for five years, or looking up the cost for a product in a price list to incorporate the cost in an invoice or order form.

There are a few items to remember when creating formulas:

■ Formulas begin with an equal (=) symbol.

- Formulas can contain as many as 1,024 characters.
- The results of a formula appear in the worksheet; the formula that calculated the results appears in the Formula Bar.
- Use cell references in formulas whenever possible.

When you need to include a cell reference in a formula, it often is easier to point to the cell than it is to type in the cell reference. Using a pointing method will help avoid typing mistakes.

To add cell references to formulas by using a pointing method, follow these steps:

1. Select the cell where you want the answer to appear.
2. Type an = (equal symbol) to begin the formula.
3. To include a cell reference, click the cell with the mouse or use the arrow keys on your keyboard to select the cell. A marquee (flashing set of dotted lines) appears around the cell you select and the reference appears in the cell where the formula is being built.
4. Type in the next part of your formula, such as an arithmetic operator, and continue building the formula.
5. Press Enter or click the Enter button (green check) in the Formula Bar to complete your formula. The result of the formula displays in the worksheet and the formula appears in the Formula Bar.

 If you need to work with an Excel function, the Paste Function button (formerly known as the Function Wizard) on the Standard toolbar will help you use the functions quickly and (almost) effortlessly.

▶ **See** "Common Worksheet Functions," **p. 57**

Order of Operations for Calculations

Sometime in the past, someone created a *pneumonic*—a shorthand way to remember the order in which arithmetic calculations are performed. This pneumonic is *PEMDAS*, which is explained in Table 1.3.

Table 1.3   Order of Operations

Remember	Pneumonic	Arithmetic Operator
P	Please	( ) Parentheses *[Highest Priority]*
E	Excuse	^ Exponents (carat)
M	My	* Multiplication (asterisk)
D	Dear	/ Division (forward slash)
A	Aunt	+ Addition (plus)
S	Sally	– Subtraction (dash)

The following examples are illustrations of how Excel calculates formulas using the order of operations:

$5 + 8 / 2 = 9$ Division calculates before addition

$(5 + 8) / 2 = 6.5$ Parentheses calculate before division

In Excel calculations, multiplication and division have the same priority, and addition and subtraction have the same priority. When these types of calculations are included in the same formula, the calculation is performed from left to right, as follows:

$6 / 2 * 3 = 9$ Division then multiplication

$2 * 3 / 6 = 1$ Multiplication then division

$4 - 2 + 3 = 5$ Subtraction then addition

$2 + 3 - 4 = 1$ Addition then subtraction

Copying Formulas

The calculations you perform in a spreadsheet often are similar, following a repeating pattern. For example, in Figure 1.11 the difference between the sales for 1997 and 1998 for each beverage item is being calculated. Regardless of the item, the pattern is the same—1998 sales minus 1997 sales. When there is a pattern Excel can follow, you can create the first calculation and copy the formula to the other cells, using the Fill Handle (see Figure 1.11).

N O T E Copying formulas works only if cell references are used in the formulas. ■

The Fill Handle, which was discussed earlier in this chapter in the "Using AutoFill" section, can perform two functions: complete a series Excel can recognize, and copy cell contents. When AutoFill is used, the formatting on the formula in the initial cell will be transferred to the new cells where the formula has been copied.

When copying formulas, it is important to understand the difference between relative and absolute cell referencing.

FIG. 1.11
After you create the first formula, it can be copied to adjacent cells.

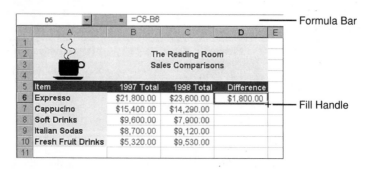

Formula Bar

Fill Handle

Item	1997 Total	1998 Total	Difference
Expresso	$21,800.00	$23,600.00	$1,800.00
Cappucino	$15,400.00	$14,290.00	
Soft Drinks	$9,600.00	$7,900.00	
Italian Sodas	$8,700.00	$9,120.00	
Fresh Fruit Drinks	$5,320.00	$9,530.00	

The Reading Room
Sales Comparisons

Relative Cell Referencing

Relative cell referencing occurs when you copy a formula and the references automatically adjust. In Figure 1.11, when the formula for Expresso is copied down the list to the other beverage items, the cell references will adjust to perform the calculation on the row in which each item appears. For example, the initial formula created in row 6 for Expresso reads =C6-B6, the 1998 sales of Expresso minus the 1997 sales of Expresso (see the Formula Bar in Figure 1.11). When this formula is copied to the remaining rows, the cell references will change to reflect the row they are copied to. Because Italian Sodas are listed in row 9, the formula for Italian Sodas will be =C9-B9.

Absolute Cell Referencing

Occasionally, you will need one of the references in the formula to remain constant when you copy it to another cell or cells. In these situations, you will use a code to freeze the cell reference so that it does not adjust when the formula is copied. This is known as *absolute cell referencing*.

In the worksheet shown in Figure 1.12, a formula has been created to determine what percentage each beverage's total sales comprise the grand total for the year. In this example, the formula has determined that the sales for Expresso ($21,800) is 36% of the total sales for 1998 ($60,820). The formula for Expresso is =B6/B12. When the formula was copied, all the references adjusted (relative cell referencing) based on the pattern of the original formula—one cell to the left divided by the cell located one column to the left and six rows down.

When the formula used for Expresso is copied to the rows below it, an error message occurs indicating a division-by-zero error. In Figure 1.12, the cell containing the first error message, for Cappuccino, is selected. The formula for Cappuccino appears in the Formula Bar as =B7/B13. The first part of this formula, B7, is correct because that cell represents the Cappuccino total sales figure for 1998. However, relative cell referencing causes the second cell referenced to be the empty cell *below* the grand total, B13, rather than the actual grand total. To keep the reference to the grand total fixed on B12, a code has to be added to the original formula for Expresso. When added to the first formula, it can then be copied to the remaining items. The code used by Excel to freeze a cell reference is the dollar symbol ($).

To add the dollar symbols quickly, follow these steps:

1. Select the cell where the original formula was created—cell C6 in Figure 1.12.

2. In the Formula Bar, click once in the middle of the cell that you want to freeze (B12).

3. Press the F4 function key once. It will highlight the cell reference in the Formula Bar and add a dollar symbol in front of both the row and column indictors (see Figure 1.13)

4. Press Enter or click the Confirm button (green check) in the Formula Bar to complete the change to the formula.

5. Use the Fill Handle to copy the corrected formula to the remaining items.

▶ **See** "Common Arithmetic Formulas," **p. 57**

FIG. 1.12

With relative cell referencing, the formulas won't be calculated properly in a Percent of Total calculation.

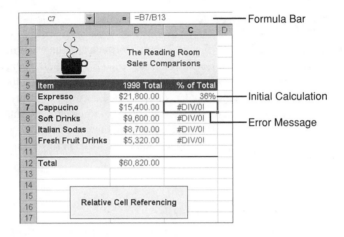

FIG. 1.13

Absolute cell referencing is used when you need to freeze a cell reference to copy the formula.

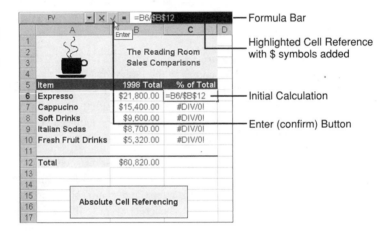

Quick Ways to Total Columns and Rows

 Because adding rows or columns is a very common need with spreadsheets, there is an Excel function used to add multiple cells, called SUM. This function is accessed by clicking the AutoSum button on the Standard toolbar, which helps create totals in your spreadsheets quickly. The AutoSum function can be used in several different ways:

- To total one column or row

- To total multiple columns or rows

- To total multiple columns and multiple rows, and provide a grand total

When adding up a column or row, you select only the cell in which you want the answer to appear. Selecting more than one cell causes AutoSum to perform differently, which is the topic of the next two sections, "Totaling Multiple Columns or Rows" and "Totaling Multiple Columns and Rows with a Grand Total."

As with any other Excel calculation, you first select the cell in which you want the answer to appear. When you select the AutoSum button, it proposes a range of cells to add. If the cells are not the ones you want to add, you can select the correct cells with your mouse. To complete the AutoSum, click the Enter (green check) button in the Formula Bar, or press Enter.

 TIP A quick way to confirm the AutoSum, especially if it proposes the correct range you want, is simply to click the AutoSum button again.

Before you use the AutoSum button, it's important that you understand how it works. By default, when you use AutoSum, the order in which it views your spreadsheet is as follows:

- AutoSum first looks *above the active cell* for numbers to add. When it finds an empty cell or text, it stops and displays the cell references it proposes to add.

- If there is an empty cell or text immediately above the active cell, AutoSum then looks *to the left of the active cell* for numbers to add. When it finds an empty cell or text, it stops and displays the cell references it proposes to add.

- If AutoSum encounters empty cells immediately above and to the left of the active cell, or if it encounters only one cell of numbers to the left of the active cell, it will once *again look above the active cell* in search of numbers to calculate.

- If there are multiple empty cells, the priority is for AutoSum to continue to look above the active cell. For example, if AutoSum encounters only one empty cell to the left, and multiple empty cells above, AutoSum will propose to calculate the sum of the cells above the active cell.

Using Figure 1.14 as an illustration, if the active cell is C14 (1996 Total by Year), AutoSum will encounter an empty cell (C13) above the active cell and text to the left of the active cell. AutoSum then will once again look above the active cell (C14) and propose to add cells C8 through C13.

If the active cell is D14 (1997 Total by Year), AutoSum will encounter an empty cell (D13) above the active cell and only one number to the left of the active cell (1996 Total). AutoSum once again will look above the active cell (D14) and propose to add cells D8 through D13.

If the active cell is E14 (1998 Total by Year), AutoSum will encounter an empty cell (E13) above the active cell and will propose to add C14 and D14, the Totals for 1996 and 1997. This calculation will not provide the same answer as you would receive by adding the 1998 column. Thus, you would reject AutoSum's proposal by selecting the appropriate cells with your mouse.

NOTE In Figure 1.14, there are empty rows between the column headings and the sales numbers, and between the sales figures and the Total by Year. The reasons you should include empty rows in these locations is explained in an earlier section, "Designing Effective Spreadsheets."

Totaling Multiple Columns or Rows

When you select multiple cells and use the AutoSum button, Excel assumes you know what you're doing! AutoSum does not propose a range of cells to total—instead, it performs a sum based on the location of the first cell in the selected group and then copies the formula to the remaining cells in the selection. For example, in Figure 1.15, cells C14 through E14 are selected. AutoSum will calculate the total for C14 and copy the formula to D14 and E14.

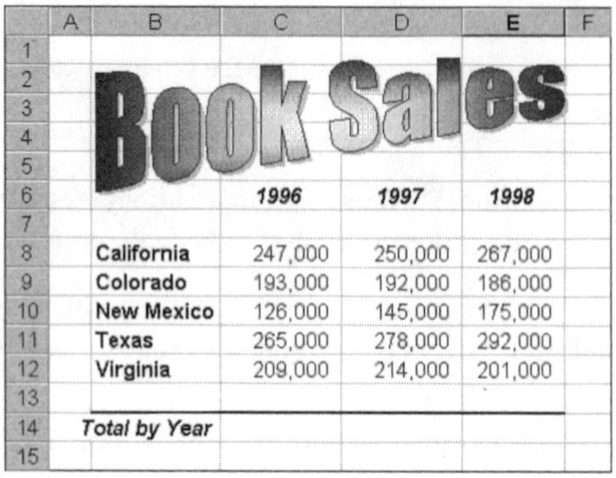

FIG. 1.14
The cells that AutoSum proposes depends on which cell is the active cell.

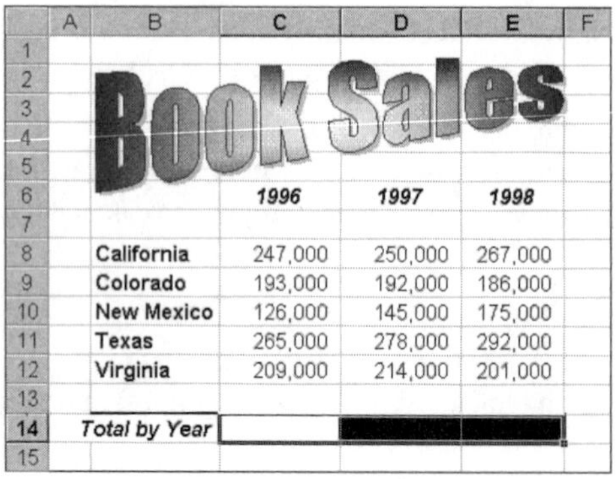

FIG. 1.15
AutoSum can perform multiple totals at the same time.

Totaling Multiple Columns and Rows with a Grand Total

In Figure 1.16, by selecting the sales data and the cells in which you want the totals to appear, you quickly can perform all of the calculations in your spreadsheet. You also can get a grand total at the intersection of the rows and columns that you have selected. In Figure 1.16, this grand total will appear in cell F14. Because multiple cells are selected, these calculations are performed immediately.

▶ **See** "Automatic Worksheet Subtotals," **p. 187**

Moving and Copying Data with Ease

Of the many different ways to move and copy data, one of the most convenient methods is *drag and drop*. By using your mouse, you can drag cells to another part of the same worksheet, to a different worksheet, or even to a different application such as Microsoft Word.

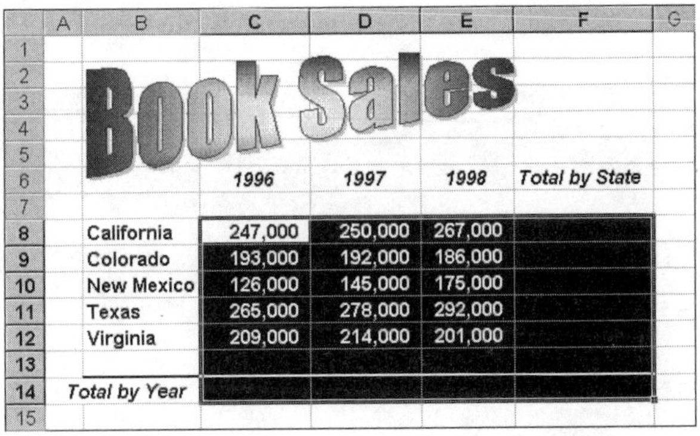

FIG. 1.16
AutoSum can quickly create the totals by year and state, as well as a grand total.

	1996	1997	1998	Total by State
California	247,000	250,000	267,000	
Colorado	193,000	192,000	186,000	
New Mexico	126,000	145,000	175,000	
Texas	265,000	278,000	292,000	
Virginia	209,000	214,000	201,000	
Total by Year				

Book Sales

The cells you are moving or copying are referred to as the *source* cells. The destination of these cells is referred to as the *target* cells or *document*. To use drag and drop, you must be able to see both the source and the target (see Figure 1.17). You can configure your screen to see both the source and the target by performing one of the following actions:

- If the target destination is another worksheet in the same workbook, choose Window, New Window. Select the target worksheet in the new window and choose Window, Arrange. Select Windows of Active Workbook to display both windows side by side on the screen.

- If the target destination is another workbook, that workbook must be open to perform the drag and drop. With both the source and target workbooks open, choose Window, Arrange, and then select Tiled to display all open workbooks on the screen.

- If the target destination is another application, the application must be open to perform the drag and drop. With both applications open, right-click the Task Bar and choose either Tile Horizontally or Tile Vertically. The open applications will be displayed together on the screen.

To move or copy by using the drag-and-drop method, follow these steps:

1. Display both the source and target documents as described above.

2. Select the cells to be moved or copied.

3. Position the mouse on a border of the highlighted cells until the mouse becomes a white pointing arrow.

4. To move the selected cells, hold down the mouse button and drag the cells to the target document. A gray outline, which represents the highlighted cells, indicates the position to which the cell will move in the target document.

   Copying the selected cells is almost identical to moving the cells, except that you must hold down the Ctrl key while dragging the mouse to copy them. A plus sign (+) is attached to the white-arrow mouse pointer when the Ctrl key is held down. Always release the Ctrl key *after* you have released the mouse button or else you will perform a move instead of a copy.

In Figure 1.17, the Quarter 1 Totals are being copied into the Annual Budget.

FIG. 1.17
Copying data from one
spreadsheet to another
is easy with drag and
drop.

Source Document
Target Document
Mouse Pointer

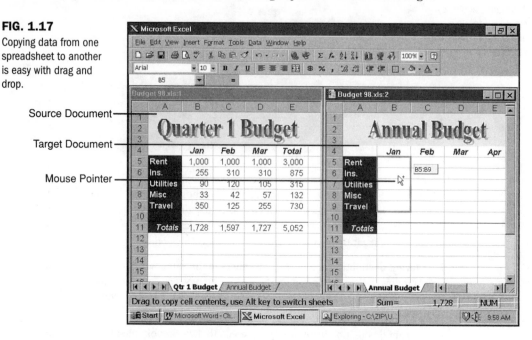

N O T E Use the traditional Edit, Cut/Copy and Edit, Paste commands to move and copy data if you
are uncomfortable with using the mouse to drag and drop. ▓

 If the Annual Budget shown in Figure 1.17 reflected the quarterly totals only, instead of listing each
month, you could not use drag and drop to copy the totals from Quarter 1 to the Annual Budget
worksheet. Drag and drop would copy the formulas, not just the results. See the section "Calculations
Across Worksheets and Workbooks," in Chapter 4 to create formulas that link the source and target
documents.

Using WordArt to Format Worksheets

The WordArt feature, new in Excel 97, enables you to create dynamic-looking text for
worksheet titles. In Figure 1.17, the Quarter 1 Budget and Annual Budget titles were created
with WordArt. Choose Insert, Picture, WordArt to display the WordArt Gallery. Choose one of
the styles and select OK. The Edit WordArt Text dialog box appears. Type in the text for your
title. You can change the font, size, or add bold or italic to the text. When you select OK, the
text appears in your worksheet, along with the WordArt Toolbar (see Figure 1.18). From the
WordArt toolbar, you can change the text, choose a different shape the text makes, format the
colors of the text, or choose a completely different style from the gallery.

FIG. 1.18
Whenever WordArt text is selected in your worksheet, the WordArt toolbar appears.

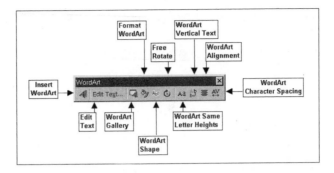

Using AutoFormat

It can be very time consuming to select individual formats for the cells in your worksheet. AutoFormat provides 16 predefined formats for worksheets. To use AutoFormat, you first must select the cells you want to change. To access the AutoFormat command, choose Format, AutoFormat. Select one of the names in the Table Format list, which will display the formats in the Sample area. If you want to remove some of the formats before applying the AutoFormat to your worksheet, choose Options to eliminate the formats you do not want (see Figure 1.19). After you have selected the name of the format and have specified which options you would like, choose OK to apply the AutoFormat.

FIG. 1.19
Copying data from one spreadsheet to another is easy with drag and drop.

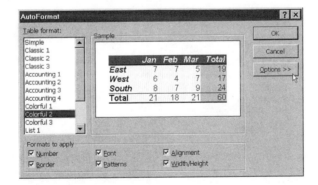

Conditional Formatting

A powerful new number-formatting feature has been added to Excel 97, which makes it easy to format a cell based on the data in the cell. For Excel to know how to format the cell, you must specify the conditions for each format. Conditional formatting is especially useful for highlighting the results of formulas.

The worksheet shown in Figure 1.20 calculates the percentage change in book sales between 1997 and 1998. For this example, if the percentage change in book sales is a negative number, that cell will be displayed with light gray shading. If the percentage change is between 0 and 5 percent, the cell will not change. If the difference is between 5 percent and 15 percent, the number representing the percentage change will be displayed in bold font. Finally, if the difference is 15 percent or higher, the number will be displayed in bold and will be colored red.

FIG. 1.20

The Book Sales spreadsheet as it appears before conditional formatting is applied.

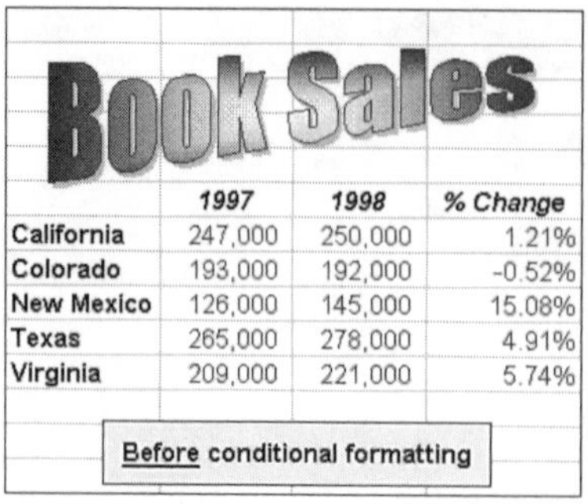

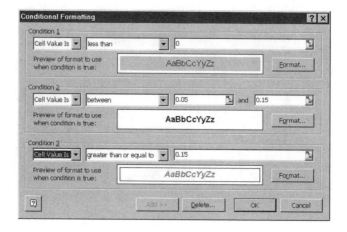

	1997	1998	% Change
California	247,000	250,000	1.21%
Colorado	193,000	192,000	-0.52%
New Mexico	126,000	145,000	15.08%
Texas	265,000	278,000	4.91%
Virginia	209,000	221,000	5.74%

Before conditional formatting

To apply conditional formatting, follow these steps:

1. Select the cell you want to format.

2. Choose Format, Conditional Formatting, which displays the Conditional Formatting dialog box (see Figure 1.21).

FIG. 1.21

The Conditional Formatting dialog box provides for three separate conditions.

3. Choose one of the eight conditional operators. In Figure 1.21, the operators shown are Less Than (Condition 1), Between (Condition 2), and Greater Than Or Equal To (Condition 3).

4. In the box (or boxes) to the right of the conditional operators, type in values or choose cell references.

5. To select a format when the condition is met, choose Format. Select the font style, font color, underlining, borders, shading, or patterns that you want to apply, then select OK.

6. If desired, choose the Add button to specify another condition and repeat steps 3–5. Up to three conditions may be used.

7. Choose OK to accept the conditions.

In Figure 1.22, the conditional formatting shown in Figure 1.21 has been applied to all the % Change cells. The % Change for Colorado has gray shading because the formula result is a negative number. The % Change for New Mexico is displayed in bold and colored red because the formula result is greater than 15 percent. The % Change for Virginia is in bold because the formula result was between 5 percent and 15 percent. Note that when the % Change number is between 0 and 5 percent (for which there is no condition), the formatting that already exists in the cell remains.

FIG. 1.22
The Book Sales worksheet after conditional formatting is applied.

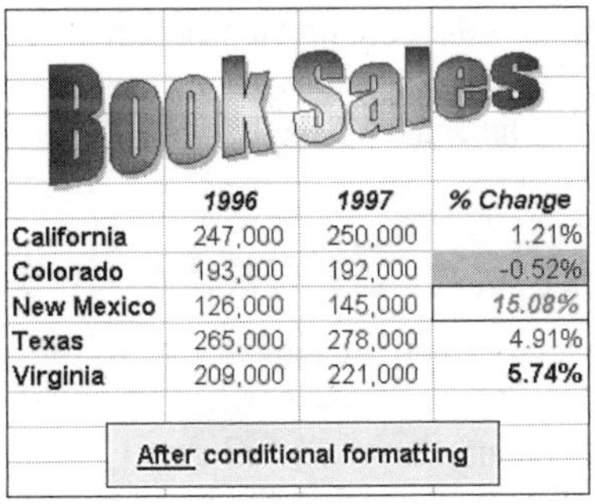

	1996	1997	% Change
California	247,000	250,000	1.21%
Colorado	193,000	192,000	-0.52%
New Mexico	126,000	145,000	15.08%
Texas	265,000	278,000	4.91%
Virginia	209,000	221,000	5.74%

After conditional formatting

If conditional formatting is added to a cell that has a formula, when the formula is copied, the conditional formatting is copied also.

Conditional formatting is particularly useful for highlighting data entry errors and for performing analyses. With Conditional Formatting, the font style, font color, cell borders, and cell background color or pattern can be changed to accentuate numbers in your spreadsheet.

Opening Files Created with Other Applications

Working with your files in Excel is very similar to the way you work with files in your word processor, graphics package, or database. Most file management actions begin with the File menu.

If you have spreadsheet files from earlier versions of Excel, the files will open in Excel 97. However, upon saving the file, a message will ask whether you want to save the file in the new (Excel 97) file format. If you save the file in the new format, Microsoft Excel Workbook, it will no longer be compatible with the earlier version in which the file originated.

If you need to save a file so that it can be used in Excel 5.0 or 95 (also known as 7.0), you will need to use the File, Save As command and select the Microsoft Excel 5.0/95 Workbook format. If you need the file to be available in Excel 5.0 and 97, or 95 and 97, choose the Microsoft Excel 97 & 5.0/95 Workbook format. This creates a file that is readable by all of these formats.

Excel 97 can open files created in either Lotus 1-2-3 or Quattro Pro that use the file extensions .wk1, .wk3, .wk4, .wq1, or .wb1. To open a file from another spreadsheet program, choose File, Open. From the Open dialog box, choose the location of the file and change the Files of Type to the appropriate file type. Select the file name and choose Open.

Preview Your Files Before Opening Them

 In the Open dialog box, there is a button on the toolbar that will enable you to preview the selected file to make certain it is the file you want to open. The preview feature is not automatic—a preview will appear in the Open dialog box only if the Properties for the file indicate a preview is available. In Excel 97, the preview option is turned off for all files.

To make a preview available, you must select the preview option in the Properties dialog box for *each* file you want to have available. To access the Properties dialog box, choose File, Properties. At the bottom of the Summary tab, check Save Preview Picture.

Creating New Folders While Saving Files

 In the Save As dialog box, there is a button on the toolbar that will allow you to create a new folder before you save a file. This is particularly useful when you realize, in the middle of saving a file, that you want to place the file in a new folder. Before choosing the Create New Folder button, use the Save In drop down list box and select the location where you want the new folder to be placed. Then use the Create New Folder button. You will be prompted for the new folder's name. After the new folder has been created, double-click the new folder so that it appears in the Save In list box. You can now save the Excel file in the new folder.

Saving a Workspace

If you frequently work with the same set of files, saving those files as a workspace will provide a convenient way to open all the files at one time. This is especially true if some of the files are located on your computer's hard drive and others are located on a network drive. Additionally, if the files are displayed together on-screen in a particular arrangement, the workspace tracks this information as well. Choose File, Save Workspace to save the list of open files (and their arrangement) as a workspace file. When the workspace file is opened, all the workbooks in the workspace are opened and arranged as they were when the workspace file was created.

Printing Worksheets

The number one rule to remember when printing is to preview before you print. To preview your active worksheet, use the Preview button on the Standard toolbar or choose File, Print Preview.

Page Orientation, scaling, margins, alignment, headers, footers, and gridlines can be controlled through the Setup button in the Preview screen. A few print options can't be changed while you are previewing your document; these include specifying a print area, print titles, or displaying comments in your printout. To adjust these three items, you must access the Setup dialog box before you preview. Choose File, Page Setup to access the Setup dialog box.

Frequently, you may want to print several ranges of cells, skipping some rows or columns. Figure 1.23 shows an example in which months have been selected for printing but the quarterly summaries have not been selected. When you select several ranges, Excel prints each range on a separate page. To have these ranges appear on one printed page, you first must hide temporarily the rows or columns you don't want to print. In Figure 1.23, this would mean hiding columns where the quarterly totals are being displayed, such as columns E and I.

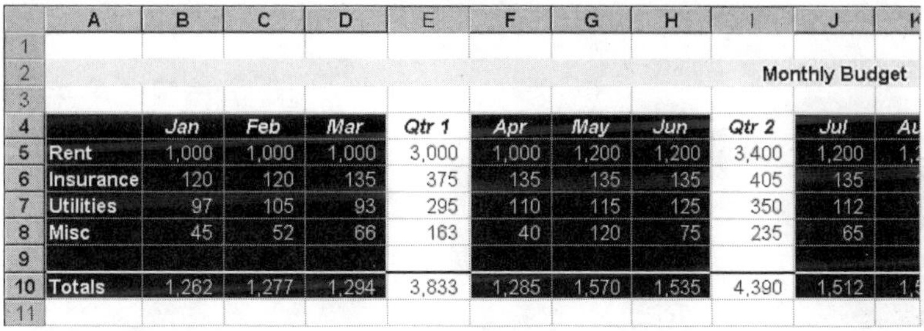

FIG. 1.23

When you don't want to print the entire worksheet, select only the ranges you want to print.

	A	B	C	D	E	F	G	H	I	J	K
1											
2										Monthly Budget	
3											
4		Jan	Feb	Mar	Qtr 1	Apr	May	Jun	Qtr 2	Jul	Au
5	Rent	1,000	1,000	1,000	3,000	1,000	1,200	1,200	3,400	1,200	1,
6	Insurance	120	120	135	375	135	135	135	405	135	
7	Utilities	97	105	93	295	110	115	125	350	112	
8	Misc	45	52	66	163	40	120	75	235	65	
9											
10	Totals	1,262	1,277	1,294	3,833	1,285	1,570	1,535	4,390	1,512	1,
11											

To hide columns temporarily, select any cell in the column and choose Format, Column, Hide. After the columns are hidden, you can select the cells you want to print and proceed with establishing your print settings. The printout will print the cells on one page.

TIP The trick to unhiding a column is to select the column headings on either side of the hidden column. If column E had been hidden in Figure 1.23, for example, you would select column D and drag the selection to column F. After the columns on either side of the hidden column are selected, choose Format, Column, Unhide.

By default, Excel prints only the active worksheet. You can print multiple sheets by using grouping or you can print a portion of a worksheet by using range names.

▶ **See** "Printing Multiple Worksheets," **p. 33**

CHAPTER 2

Using Worksheets and Workbooks

Excel provides numerous commands and features that can help optimize your use of worksheets and workbooks. These features include grouping worksheets to perform common actions, altering the screen display, and naming cell ranges.

You can group together worksheets so that they are identical in their appearance and purpose. For example, suppose you need to create a file that tracks monthly expenses, with one worksheet for each month. Instead of creating each worksheet separately, or even creating one worksheet and copying the information to the other monthly worksheets, you can create them all at the same time, through Excel's grouping feature.

Range names are often used in formulas and functions to make the calculations easier to understand. One big advantage of using range names is they use absolute cell reference values. ■

Using Excel's group feature

Add or remove multiple worksheets from the workbook, print more than one worksheet at a time, or spell check all the worksheets in a workbook at once.

Moving and copying worksheets with ease

Move and copy worksheets within the same workbook or between workbooks quickly by using drag and drop.

Making the screen display work for you

Use Zoom, Freeze Panes, Arrange, and Outline to yield the most from your screen display.

Displaying worksheets from the same workbook together on the screen

Create additional windows of the same workbook to display worksheets side-by-side to compare information from multiple worksheets.

Identifying worksheets and cells through names

Make the worksheet tabs more meaningful by giving them substantive names. Learn how naming ranges of cells can be used to move quickly around a large file, select specific cells for printing, and aid you in building formulas.

Grouping Worksheets

The group feature in Excel is used to speed up worksheet tasks. The group feature involves selecting multiple worksheets, and then performing an action that you want applied to all the selected worksheets. These group actions include:

- Inserting and deleting multiple worksheets.

- Moving and copying multiple worksheets, either in the same workbook or between workbooks.

- Entering and formatting data to create identical worksheets or forms. For example, you might use this feature to modify a workbook that tracks monthly budgets by using individual sheets for each month. By using these features, you can quickly change the layout, labels, and formulas so that they are identical in each worksheet.

- Checking the spelling in multiple worksheets.

- Printing multiple worksheets at the same time.

When working with multiple worksheets, it is helpful to be acquainted with the worksheet tab scrolling buttons (see Figure 2.1). These buttons enable you to scroll the worksheet tabs. The first button scrolls to the beginning of the worksheet tabs. The second button scrolls one worksheet tab to the left. The third button scrolls one worksheet tab to the right. The last button scrolls to the end of the worksheet tabs.

FIG. 2.1

The worksheet tab scrolling buttons do not select the worksheets— they merely scroll the worksheet tabs into view.

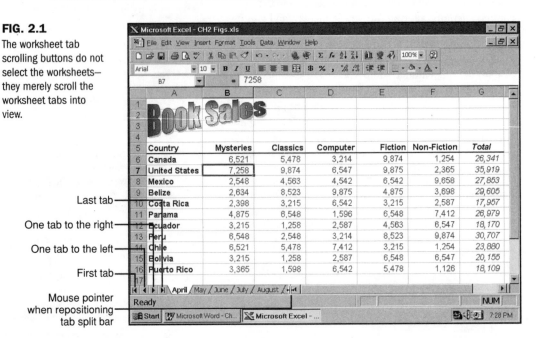

You can control the number of worksheet tabs visible on-screen by repositioning the tab split bar. When you point your mouse on the tab split bar, the mouse pointer changes to a black split pointer, as shown in Figure 2.1. Drag the tab split bar to the right to increase the number of worksheet tabs displayed. Drag the tab split bar to the left to decrease the number of worksheet tabs displayed.

When you move the tab split bar, the horizontal scroll bar shrinks or expands to accommodate the corresponding increase or decrease in the number of worksheet tabs visible. To return the tab split bar to its original position, double-click the tab split bar.

Before you can take advantage of the group feature, you must learn to select multiple worksheets:

1. Select the first tab you want to include in the group. If you want to select the months in the second quarter in Figure 2.1, you start by selecting April.

2. To select consecutive worksheets, hold down the Shift key and click the tab of the last sheet that you want to include in the group. In Figure 2.2, April, May, and June are selected.

   To select nonconsecutive worksheets, hold down the Ctrl key and click each individual sheet tab that you want included in the group.

3. The title bar indicates that the Group mode is active.

FIG. 2.2
Each worksheet tab selected will be white; those not selected will be gray.

Group mode indicator —

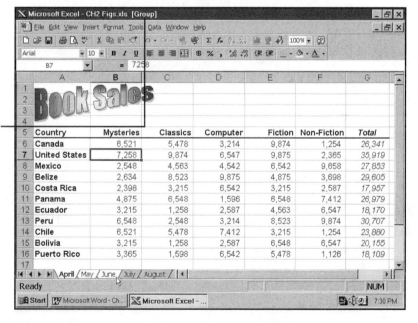

TIP If the worksheet you want to select is not visible, either use the tab scrolling buttons (refer to Figure 2.1) to scroll the worksheet tabs, or move the tab split bar to the right.

To deselect individual sheets, press Ctrl and click the sheet tab that you want to deselect. To deselect all sheet tabs (exit Group mode), right-click any selected sheet tab and choose <u>U</u>ngroup from the shortcut menu.

Inserting and Deleting Worksheets

You can add or remove worksheets as needed in your workbook file. The default number of worksheets in a *new* workbook is three, while the number of worksheets a workbook can hold is limited only by the memory available on your computer. When inserting worksheets, the following information is useful:

- The number of worksheets selected will be the number of worksheets added. If three worksheets are selected, three new worksheets will be added to the workbook.

- You must select consecutive worksheets to insert more than one worksheet at a time. Refer to the previous section, "Grouping Worksheets," for instructions on selecting multiple, consecutive worksheets.

- The position of the selected worksheet(s) determines the position at which the new worksheets will be inserted. New worksheets will be inserted in the position of the active worksheet(s). The active worksheet(s) move to the right.

- Excel uses consecutive numbers for each worksheet. When new worksheets are inserted, the next higher number that has not been used during the active session will be the default name on the worksheet tab. Naming your worksheet tabs is covered in the later section, "Renaming Worksheets."

To insert new blank worksheets, follow these steps:

1. To insert a single worksheet, select the worksheet in the position you want the new worksheet to appear. To insert multiple worksheets, select the number of worksheets you want to add.

2. Choose <u>I</u>nsert, <u>W</u>orksheet. The number of worksheets you select represents the number of worksheets that will be added to your workbook.

T I P   Sometimes you need to create a new worksheet that is very similar to an existing worksheet. Instead of inserting a worksheet and copying the data from an existing worksheet to the newly inserted worksheet, it is quicker to create a new worksheet by copying an existing worksheet. The section "Copying Worksheets," later in this chapter, provides the steps to accomplish this.

N O T E   To insert a worksheet based on a template, right-click the worksheet tab and choose <u>I</u>nsert from the shortcut menu. The Insert dialog box is displayed. Choose a template and click OK. The Worksheet template, listed on the General tab of the dialog box, inserts blank worksheets. The other tabs contain worksheet and workbook templates. ▓

▶ **See** "Saving Time by Using Excel's Built-in Templates," **p. 87**

You cannot undo the insertion of worksheets. To remove unwanted worksheets, you have to delete them.

To remove worksheets from a workbook, you first must select the worksheets you want to delete. The worksheets do not have to be in consecutive order for you to select and delete them. Refer to the earlier section, "Grouping Worksheets," for instructions on selecting multiple worksheets.

After the worksheets are selected, choose Edit, Delete Worksheet. A warning message appears, indicating the worksheet(s) will be permanently deleted. Choose OK to remove the worksheet(s).

Part
I
Ch
2

CAUTION

You can't undo the deletion of worksheets. However, you can close the workbook file without saving the changes. The deletion, and any other changes you made since you last saved the file, will be ignored. When you open the file again, it will appear as it did the last time the file was saved.

If you have activated the Autosave feature in Excel, the workbook may be saved before you have a chance to close it. For this reason, you should select the Autosave option, which prompts you before the file is saved.

N O T E To change the default number of worksheets in a workbook, choose Tools, Options. In the Options dialog box, select the General tab. Use the Sheets in New Workbook option to change the default number of worksheets that appear when you create a new workbook. The default number of worksheets can range from 1 to 255. Changing the default number affects only *new* workbooks you create; it does not impact any existing workbooks. Unused worksheets are saved with the file and increase the file size. ▪

Rearranging Worksheets

After inserting or deleting worksheets, you may want to rearrange the order in which the worksheet tabs appear. Whenever you move worksheets, Excel displays two symbols to indicate the worksheets are being moved. The first symbol is a white page icon attached to your mouse pointer. If more than one worksheet is selected, the symbol appears as three pages (regardless of the number of worksheets selected). A black downward-pointing triangle indicates exactly where the worksheet tabs will be moved. Figure 2.3 shows both symbols, as the worksheets Santa Fe and Monterrey are being moved (note that Excel enables you to move nonconsecutive tabs at the same time).

To rearrange worksheet tabs, follow these steps:

1. Select the worksheet(s) to move.
2. Position the mouse pointer over a selected worksheet and drag the worksheet tab(s) to the new position. Use the black triangular point as a guide to position the worksheet(s).
3. When you release the mouse, the worksheet(s) will move.

FIG. 2.3

You can reposition worksheet tabs for consecutive or nonconsecutive worksheets.

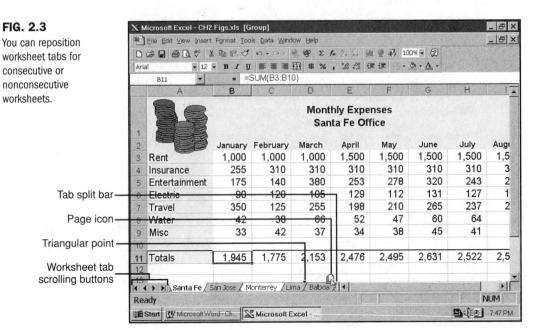

If you need to move worksheets to a position not visible on-screen, the worksheet tabs will automatically scroll. If you drag the mouse pointer into the worksheet tab-scrolling buttons, for example, the worksheet tabs scroll toward the beginning of the list of tabs. Likewise, if you drag the mouse pointer into the tab split bar, the worksheet tabs scroll toward the end of the list of tabs.

Copying Worksheets

Copying worksheets is very similar to moving worksheets. Like moving, whenever you copy worksheets, Excel displays two symbols, a white page icon attached to your mouse pointer and a black downward-pointing triangle. Additionally, to indicate that a copy is taking place—as opposed to a move—Excel puts a plus sign (+) in the middle of the page icon. As with moving a worksheet, the triangle is designed to indicate exactly where the worksheet tabs will be copied. To copy worksheet(s), use these steps:

1. Select the worksheet(s) to copy.
2. Position the mouse pointer over a selected worksheet. Hold down the Ctrl key and drag the worksheet tab(s) to a new position. A plus sign (+) appears in the page icon. Use the black triangular point as a guide to position the worksheet(s).
3. Release the mouse button, and then the Ctrl key; a copy of the worksheet(s) will be created.

CAUTION

If you release the Ctrl key before you release the mouse button, Excel *moves* the worksheet(s).

Excel doesn't allow worksheets in the same workbook to have the same name. Therefore, when you *copy* a worksheet, Excel names the new worksheet WorksheetName (2). For example, if you copy a worksheet named January, the copy is named January (2). See the section, "Renaming Worksheets," later in this chapter for instructions on naming your worksheet tabs.

As when a worksheet is moved, if you need to copy worksheets to a position that is not visible on-screen, the worksheet tabs will automatically scroll.

Part
I
Ch
2

Moving and Copying Worksheets Between Workbooks

Just as you can move and copy worksheets within a single workbook, you also can move and copy worksheets between workbooks. In order to use the drag-and-drop technique described in the previous two sections, you first must display both workbooks on-screen.

To move or copy worksheets from one workbook to another, follow these steps:

1. Open both the source and target (destination) files.

2. Choose <u>W</u>indow, <u>A</u>rrange to display the Arrange Windows dialog box, as shown in Figure 2.4.

3. The <u>T</u>iled option is selected. Choose OK to display all your open workbooks side by side on-screen. More information for the other options in this dialog box appears later in this chapter, in the section "Viewing Multiple Worksheets."

FIG. 2.4

There are four basic arrangements available in this dialog box. The Tiled option is a good choice when you want to view several open files at once.

After the files are displayed on-screen, the procedures to move and copy the worksheets are identical to those detailed in the previous two sections. To move a worksheet, position the mouse pointer on the worksheet tab in the source workbook. Drag the mouse to the new position in the target workbook. To copy a worksheet, position the mouse pointer on the worksheet tab in the source workbook. Click Ctrl and drag the mouse to the new position in the target workbook. In Figure 2.5, the worksheet Calgary is being copied from the International Sales workbook to the North American Sales workbook.

Multiple sheets can be moved and copied as well. Use the techniques described in the earlier section, "Grouping Worksheets," to select multiple worksheets.

FIG. 2.5
Make sure you look for the black triangular point to position the worksheets in the target (destination) workbook.

Target (destination) workbook

Source workbook

Page icon with plus sign indicating the worksheet is being copied

Triangular point

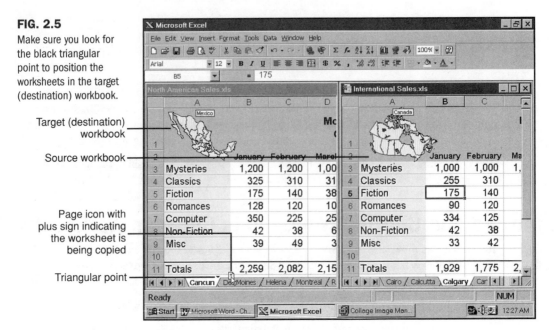

Creating Identical Worksheets

One of the best uses of Excel's grouping feature is to create multiple, identical worksheets at the same time. For example, suppose you need a workbook to track expenditures or sales, where each worksheet lists information for a particular month. The layout, and most of the titles, headings, and formulas will be identical in each worksheet. Instead of creating each worksheet separately, or even creating the first worksheet and copying it, you can use Excel's grouping feature to enter the data and create the copies all at the same time, as follows:

1. Select the tabs for all the worksheets in which you want to enter identical information or formats.

2. Enter and format the data on the active worksheet, including the calculations you want performed, as shown in Figure 2.6.

   Because the worksheets are grouped, changes you make to a cell in the active sheet are reflected in the corresponding cells on all other selected worksheets. This includes any data (such as titles, headings, and values) entered into the worksheet, formats applied to the data, and formulas that you create.

3. If the values will be different in each worksheet, select the cells containing the values and press Delete. The values will be cleared from the cells, but all formatting remains, such as currency symbols and commas. Make sure you don't select the cells containing formulas; otherwise, you will have to recreate the formulas. The values have been cleared in the worksheet shown in Figure 2.7.

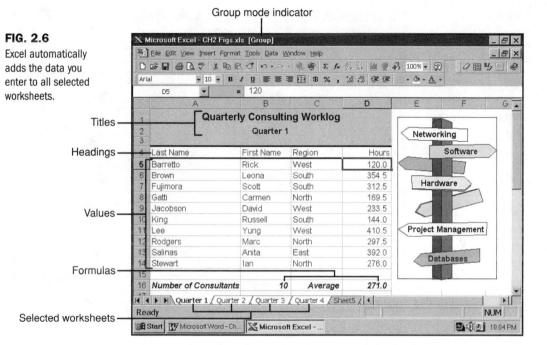

FIG. 2.6

Excel automatically adds the data you enter to all selected worksheets.

4. After you create the worksheet that contains the styles and formatting that you want to carry through to all the worksheets in your workbook, simply right-click a worksheet tab and choose Ungroup from the shortcut menu.

5. Select the individual worksheets to enter or edit specific data as necessary.

Once ungrouped, the changes you apply to a worksheet appear only in that sheet. Anytime an identical change is needed in several worksheets, such as inserting a row to include a new expense item, you can group the worksheets together again and make the change so that the item appears in the same location in each worksheet.

The grouping feature in Excel is extremely beneficial when you want to create a number of identical worksheets from scratch, or edit worksheets laid out identically. If you already have an existing worksheet that you want to duplicate, the grouping feature will not help you create additional, identical worksheets. Instead, you can quickly copy the data from the existing worksheet to the corresponding cells on other worksheets by using the Fill Across Worksheets command:

1. Select the worksheet that contains the data to be copied, as well as the worksheets to which you want to copy the data.

2. Click the worksheet tab that contains the data you want to copy, to make it the active tab of the selected group.

3. Select the cells to be copied and choose Edit, Fill, Across Worksheets. The Fill Across Worksheet dialog box appears.

4. You can choose to fill All, Contents, or Formats. After you make your choice, click OK.

FIG. 2.7
The cells containing values, which will differ from worksheet to worksheet, have been cleared.

Group mode indicator

Selected worksheets

Formulas

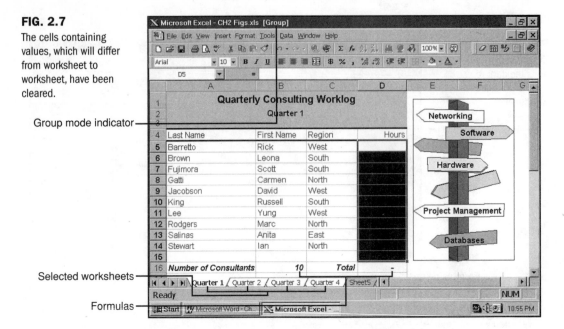

Spell Checking Multiple Worksheets

By default, Excel will check the spelling of all selected worksheet(s). If only one worksheet is selected, then only that worksheet will be checked. If multiple worksheets are selected, the spelling will be checked in all the selected worksheets.

To spell check more than one worksheet, use the grouping feature to select those worksheets.

When spell checking, if a single cell is selected, Excel checks the spelling of the entire worksheet(s). If more than one cell is selected, Excel checks the spelling only in the selected cells. If multiple worksheets are selected, and you have more than one cell in the active worksheet selected, only those cells, and the corresponding cells in the other selected worksheets, will be checked.

 After you select the worksheets (and cells) to be checked, click the Spelling button on the Standard toolbar. The Spelling dialog box appears, as shown in Figure 2.8.

If you have used the spell check feature in other Microsoft applications, such as Microsoft Word or Microsoft PowerPoint, you will find that it is virtually identical in all Microsoft Office programs. Words are checked against a main dictionary and a custom dictionary. The main dictionary contains thousands of words, which cannot be changed by the user. The custom dictionary is designed to hold words that you want to add as correctly spelled words, because they don't appear in the main dictionary. Excel uses both dictionaries to check spelling.

FIG. 2.8
If you anticipate using a word frequently, select the Add button to add it to the custom dictionary.

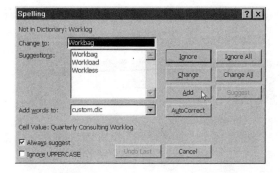

Many proper names have been added to the main dictionary. Names of places, such as Tampa, Taos, Trinidad, and Tonga, now appear in the dictionary. Names of people, such as Eloise, Esther, Edgar, and Eddie, also are included.

However, you may find that in Excel (or other Microsoft Office programs), you regularly use certain proper names, acronyms, abbreviations, and words from foreign languages that don't appear in the main dictionary. You can add these words to the custom dictionary when you spell check your file. Select the Add button in the Spelling dialog box (refer to Figure 2.8) when you want to add a word to the dictionary that it does not recognize.

Excel's AutoCorrect feature is designed to correct common typing and misspelling errors. As you type, AutoCorrect changes "adn" to "and" and changes "acheive" to "achieve." Additionally, you can add new AutoCorrect entries to the list to correct additional words that you often mistype. When a word that you often misspell or mistype is identified while you are spell checking your file, type the correct spelling in the Change To text box of the Spelling dialog box. Use the Suggest button if you are not sure of the spelling. From the Suggestions list, choose the correct spelling. When you choose AutoCorrect, your misspelled word and the correct spelling will be added to the list of automatic corrections.

After you complete the spell check, exit Group mode by right-clicking any selected sheet tab, and then choose Ungroup from the shortcut menu.

Whenever possible, add words to the custom dictionary in all lowercase letters. This enables Excel to recognize the word, whether it appears in lowercase, mixed case, or all uppercase.

Printing Multiple Sheets

Excel's default setting is set to print only the selected worksheet(s). To print more than one worksheet, you first need to select the desired worksheets by using the techniques described earlier in this chapter, in "Grouping Worksheets."

 As described in Chapter 1, "Essential Excel—Increasing Your Efficiency," you should always preview before you print. In the Print Preview screen, the status bar will indicate how many printed pages there will be. Use the Next button to view each page. Any changes you make using the Setup, such as the orientation of the printouts or whether gridlines should be printed, will be applied to all of the selected worksheets.

Part
I

Ch
2

When you select the Print button from the Preview screen, the Print dialog box appears, as shown in Figure 2.9.

FIG. 2.9
You can return to the preview screen by selecting the Preview button at the bottom of the Print dialog box.

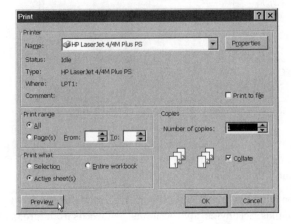

To print only the selected worksheets, leave the Print What option on Active Sheet(s). To print all of the worksheets in the workbook, choose Entire Workbook. After you choose what to print, click OK.

 N O T E If you use the Print button on the Standard toolbar, all selected worksheets will be sent directly to the printer. If you previously changed the page setup options, such as page orientation, headers, and footers, the settings for each worksheet are used when it is printed. Otherwise, the default settings are used. ■

To deselect all sheet tabs and exit Group mode, right-click any selected sheet tab and choose Ungroup from the shortcut menu.

▶ **See** "Printing Worksheets," **p. 9**

Changing the Zoom Magnification

The Zoom command is used to reduce or enlarge the display of cells in the active worksheet. Zoom is a convenient way to get either an overall perspective of your worksheet or a close-in view of specified cells. The default magnification is 100 percent, with a range from 10 percent to 400 percent. Changing the magnification changes only the screen display, and has no impact on how the worksheet appears when printed.

Zoom provides several predefined magnification percentages, while also enabling you to enter your own custom percentages. Additionally, the Zoom feature allows you to magnify the display to a group of selected cells. The zoom magnification can be different for each worksheet. By using the grouping feature, you can set a magnification for several worksheets at once.

Perhaps the data in the worksheet is one column or row beyond the screen display. Reduce the magnification to 95 percent or 90 percent to display the hidden column or row on the screen. Zoom also can be useful when you are creating and modifying a chart. If you select the cells around a chart and use the Zoom Selection option, it increases the magnification to make the chart appear as large as possible on-screen.

▶ **See** "Modifying Charts," **p. 117**

To change the Zoom magnification, select the arrow next to the Zoom percent list box, and then choose either one of the predefined percents, or type in a custom percentage and press Enter. To zoom into a group of selected cells, you first must select the cells, then choose the Zoom arrow and click Selection. When the file is saved, the zoom magnification you selected is saved with the worksheet.

Part
I

Ch
2

Freezing Row and Column Headings

With large worksheets, scrolling to the right or scrolling down to see additional data causes the headings, or labels, to roll off the screen. It is possible, by using the Freeze Panes command, to freeze row and column headings. The headings will always appear on-screen, even when you scroll to see additional data.

Freezing panes affects only the screen display, and has no impact on how the worksheet appears when printed. Freezing is a permanent part of the worksheet. When you save the file, the headings remain frozen until you unfreeze the panes.

The cell you select—the active cell—is the key to where the freezing takes place. Freezing always takes place above and to the left of the active cell. Use the following guidelines for freezing panes:

- *To freeze one or more columns.* Select the cell in row 1 that is in the column immediately to the right of the column(s) you want to freeze. For example, to freeze columns A and B, select cell C1.

- *To freeze one or more rows.* Select the cell in column A that is in the row immediately beneath the row(s) you want to freeze. For example, to freeze rows 1–3, select cell A4.

- *To freeze both columns and rows.* Select the cell immediately to the right and beneath where you want the freezing to take place. For example, to freeze column A and rows 1–4, select cell B5.

To freeze the headings in rows or columns, follow these steps:

1. Select the appropriate cell, as described in the preceding bulleted list.

2. Choose Window, Freeze Panes. A darkened border appears where the panes have been frozen. If your file has been formatted with borders, you may not be able to see the borders that have been added. These borders are for display purposes only and do not appear when you print the worksheet.

In Figure 2.10, the headings have been frozen at cell B3 and the display has been scrolled to the right to show columns H through N. The headings in column A still remain on-screen.

FIG. 2.10

Only one Freeze Panes command can be active on a worksheet. To change the location where the panes are frozen, you first must remove the existing freeze command.

Freeze Panes indicator —

Freeze Panes indicator —

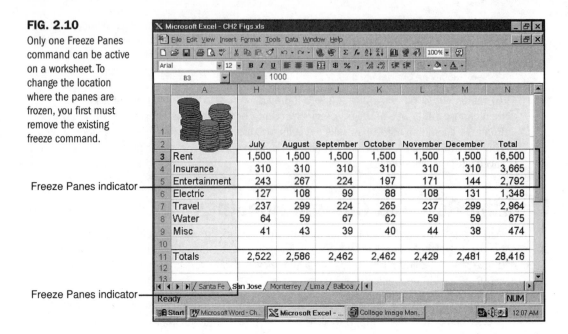

To unfreeze rows or columns, choose <u>W</u>indow, Un<u>f</u>reeze Panes. You do not have to select a particular cell to unfreeze panes.

Viewing Multiple Worksheets

When trying to compare, copy, or move information between several files, it is easier if both files are on-screen at the same time. The Arrange command is designed specifically for this purpose. Each workbook will appear in its own window.

The fewer files you arrange on-screen, the larger each window is for viewing data. The optimum arrangement is two to four files. If you have more than four files open, consider closing one or more of the files that you don't need to arrange.

To display all your open files on-screen, choose <u>W</u>indow, <u>A</u>rrange. The Arrange Windows dialog box appears. After you make your selection, choose OK.

There are five options in the Arrange Windows dialog box:

- ■ *Tiled*. This option displays the open workbooks in a patchwork tile pattern. If you have an even number of open workbooks, half the windows appear on the left and half on the right. If the number of open workbooks is odd, the right side displays the additional workbook. Figure 2.11 shows three files in a tiled arrangement.

- ■ *Horizontal*. All workbooks are displayed across the entire screen, left to right, showing many columns, but only a few rows.

- *Vertical.* All workbooks are displayed down the entire screen, top to bottom, showing many rows, but only a few columns. See Figure 2.12 for an example of three files in the vertical arrangement.
- *Cascade.* All workbooks are displayed with the titles cascading down, one window on top of another.
- *Windows of Active Workbook.* This option is used to display several worksheets of the same workbook, where each worksheet appears in a separate window. The next section of this chapter discusses this option in more detail.

Part

I

Ch

2

FIG. 2.11
The Window Arrange command always places the active workbook in the upper-left corner.

Active window

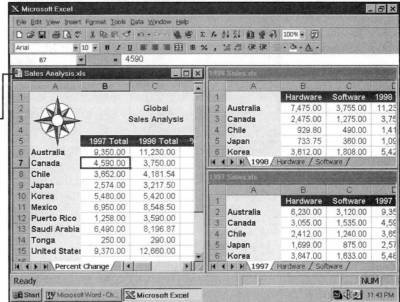

Displaying Worksheets in Separate Windows

Occasionally, you may want to display several sheets from the same book, side by side. To do this, you need to create another window for the active file. The original window displays the file name as FILENAME.XLS:1, and the second window of the active workbook is named FILENAME.XLS:2. This is not a copy of the workbook; the same file is being displayed in two windows. In order for you and Excel to distinguish between the two windows, a number is assigned temporarily to each window.

To make this concept clearer, imagine you are looking out a window from the back of your home, where you see a tree in the center of the backyard. If you move to another window in your home, your view may be slightly different, but you will still will see the tree. Even though you have two windows, it's still the same tree. If you plant flowers around the tree, you can see them from either window.

FIG. 2.12

The active window always has a colored title bar and active scroll bars. The inactive window(s) has dimmed title bar(s) and no scroll bars. Simply click a window to make it the active window.

Active window

Inactive window

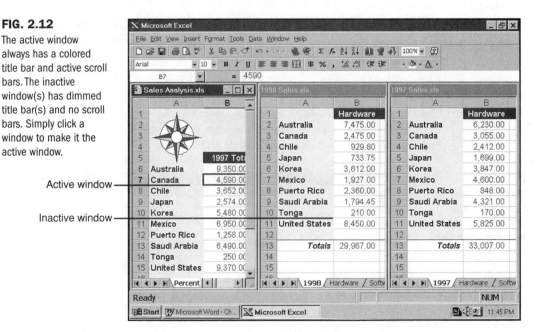

Although Excel might seem more difficult to understand than this tree example, it's really much the same. In Excel, if you create a second window for a file, then you have two windows displaying the same file. If you change data in one window, the change will be visible in the other window. The purpose of having your workbook displayed in two windows is to show data from different parts of the workbook at the same time.

To create a second window for a workbook, and to display the two windows side by side, use these steps:

1. Display the workbook for which you want to create a second window—make sure it is the active file.

2. Choose Window, New Window. A second window for the active workbook appears, as denoted by the title bar.

3. Choose Window, Arrange. The Arrange Windows dialog box appears (see Figure 2.13).

FIG. 2.13

Two windows are arranged side by side, regardless of whether they are arranged tiled or vertical.

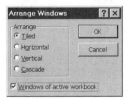

4. If this file is the only open file, choose one of the arrangement options.

   If other files are open, choose <u>W</u>indows of Active Workbook. This will display only the two windows you have created for the active file, temporarily hiding the other files.

5. Select OK. The two windows will be displayed side by side. Figure 2.14 displays an example of this arrangement.

NOTE You must remember to turn off the Windows of the Active Workbook option when you want to arrange the other files you have open again. ■

Part

I

Ch

2

In Figure 2.14, the Calgary and Canberra worksheets from the International Sales file are displayed on-screen, making it easy to compare the sales figures.

FIG. 2.14

Whenever you use the Window, <u>A</u>rrange command, the active file appears on the left. To make the other window active, click anywhere in the window.

Active window

Close button

Inactive window

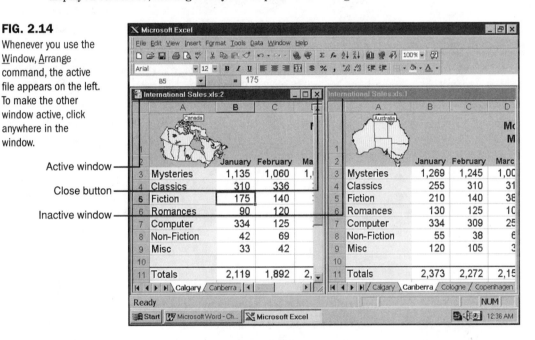

When you no longer need to display the two windows, you can close one of the windows of the active file. Use the close button in the upper-right corner of the window you want to close.

Outlining Worksheets

Excel's Outlining feature is designed to be used with worksheets that contain *groups*— detailed information with corresponding formulas at regular intervals. The formulas in each group are the basis for the outline. You can collapse the details to display just the formulas, providing a quick summary of the worksheet, or expand the outline to show all the detailed information. Groups can be outlined in both rows and columns.

Outlining a worksheet makes it easy to hide the detail information in a large worksheet and quickly see the summary data. You can print the worksheet with the outline collapsed, to create a summary report. Additionally, charts can be created from a collapsed outline.

▶ **See** "Creating Charts from Outlined Worksheets," **p. 137**

Figure 2.15 shows a worksheet that has its detailed information divided into quarters and regions. The columns are grouped by months, with January, February, March, and Qtr 1 comprising the first group; the months provide the details summarized in the Qtr1 total. Likewise, the rows are grouped by regions, with Canada, United States, Mexico, and North America Total as the first group in the rows.

FIG. 2.15

The background fill color in this figure is used to accentuate the groups; it is not necessary to format cells with a background fill color to use the outline feature in Excel.

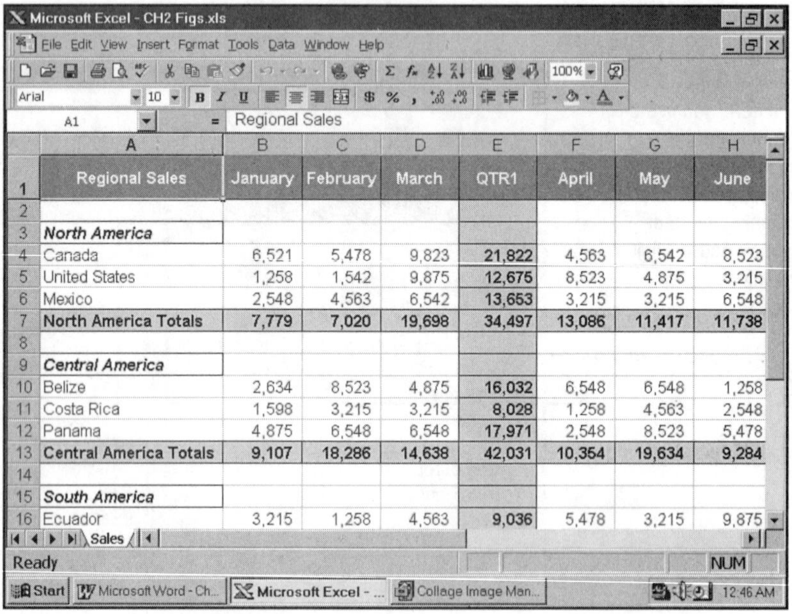

Outlines can display up to eight levels of information. A worksheet can contain only one outline. Several Excel commands automatically outline your worksheet—subtotals, consolidation, and scenario reports.

▶ **See** "Automatic Worksheet Subtotals," **p. 187**

▶ **See** "Conducting a What-if Analysis with Scenarios," **p. 151**

Worksheets can be outlined either manually or automatically. To use the outlining feature in Excel, your worksheet has to meet the following conditions:

■ The worksheet must contain rows or columns of formulas that summarize the detail data. Examples of summary formulas are SUM and AVERAGE.

■ The cell references in the formulas must "point" in a consistent direction, with summary rows placed consistently above or below their related detail data and summary columns to the left or right of their corresponding detail data. If the worksheet mixes the direction in which the data is summarized, you have to manually create the outline.

■ When an outline is collapsed, the rows and columns throughout the entire worksheet are hidden. Data in the detail rows and columns that is not part of the outline will also be hidden.

▶ **See** "Using the SUM Function," **p. 57**

▶ **See** "Using the AVERAGE Function," **p. 57**

By default, the Auto Outline feature looks for summary formulas that are to the right of the detail columns and below the detail rows. If the outline has the summary rows and columns in different positions, use the Data, Group and Outline, Settings command to modify these assumptions.

Figure 2.16 displays the Settings dialog box. If the summary rows are above their corresponding detail rows, remove the check from the Summary Rows Below Details check box. If the summary columns are to the left of their corresponding detail columns, remove the check from the Summary Columns To Right of Detail check box. The formulas must summarize in the directions specified in the Settings dialog box for the outline to work correctly.

FIG. 2.16

The default options in the outline Settings dialog box.

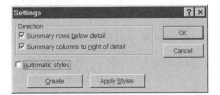

If you select a single cell in the worksheet and use the Auto Outline command, the entire worksheet is outlined. To outline only part of the worksheet, click any cell in the group that you want to select, and then use the keyboard shortcut Ctrl+Shift+* (asterisk). This shortcut highlights the current region until it reaches blank rows and columns. If you have blank rows in your list, you need to select the cells manually. You can also create a range name for the cells if you will be selecting them frequently. The steps necessary to create a name for a group of cells is discussed later in the section, "Using Range Names."

To automatically outline a worksheet, follow these steps:

1. Select any single cell to outline the entire worksheet, or select a range of cells for which you want to create an outline.

2. Choose Data, Group and Outline. From the submenu, select Auto Outline.

3. Your worksheet will be reformatted, similar to the worksheet displayed in Figure 2.17.

4. Use the outline symbols and numbers, described next, to collapse and expand the outline.

FIG. 2.17

Excel automatically places outline symbols around your worksheet to make it easy to collapse or expand the outline.

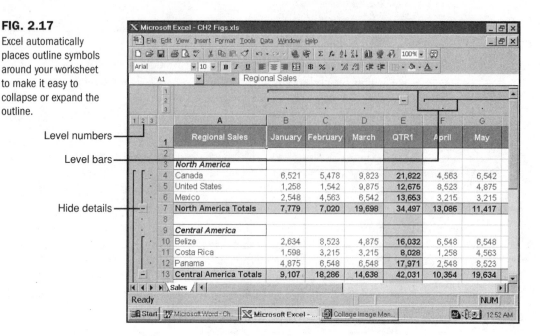

Use the following outline symbols to collapse and expand the outline:

- *Level numbers.* You can display specific levels of outline information by clicking these numbers. One set of numbers is for the row levels, the other for the column levels. In Figure 2.18, clicking the row-level 2 number collapses the outline to display the regional totals. Specifically, you can see all the groups at levels 1 and 2 (but not 3) of the outline.

- *Level bars.* These bars span the ranges referred to in the formulas. One endpoint of the bar is over the formula itself, the other endpoint is over the last cell referred to in the formula.

- *Hide details.* The minus (-) signs are used to hide rows or columns of information, collapsing individual groups.

- *Show details.* The plus (+) signs are used to display hidden rows or columns of information, expanding individual groups.

To remove an outline from your worksheet, choose Data, Group and Outline, Clear Outline.

Renaming Worksheets

Providing useful worksheet names is easy. You can change the names of the worksheet tabs by following these simple steps:

1. Double-click the tab you want to rename; the current name will be highlighted.

2. Type the new name, and press Enter.

FIG. 2.18
You can manually create or remove groups within your worksheets by using the Data, Group and Outline command, and then selecting either the Group or Ungroup options.

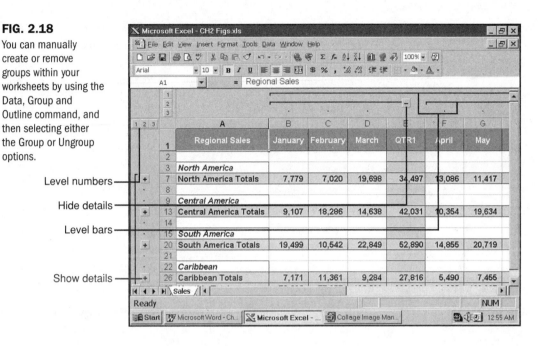

Level numbers

Hide details

Level bars

Show details

Part

I

Ch

2

Worksheet names have the following properties:

- *Maximum Length.* Up to 31 characters can be used in the name. A space is counted as a character.
- *Multiple Words.* You can use spaces in the name so that several words can be used to name a worksheet, such as 1998 Expense Report.
- *Mixed Case.* Uppercase, lowercase, and mixed case are permitted in worksheet names.
- *No Duplicates.* You cannot use a name more than once in a workbook.

Using Range Names

Range names are names that you give to one or more cell references that describe the cell or range. These names can be used to move around a large worksheet or workbook, to select only part of a worksheet for printing, and in formulas.

A descriptive name in the formula makes it easier to understand the formula. The formula =AVERAGE(1998Sales) is easier to identify than =AVERAGE(B6:F16).

The following are guidelines to use when creating range names:

- Use a letter or an underscore for the first character in a range name—the remaining characters can be letters, numbers, periods, and underscores.
- The maximum length of a range name is 255 characters.
- Range names cannot contain spaces. Use the underscore or periods to separate words— for example 1998_Sales or Amount.Due.

■ Names can contain uppercase and lowercase letters, though Excel does not distinguish between them. Therefore, you cannot create two names—Expenses and expenses—in a workbook, even if they are for different worksheets in the workbook.

■ Range names that are the same as a cell reference, such as F111 or B52, are not allowed. If you must have a name that is like a cell reference, use an underscore as the first character of the name (_F111).

■ Range names are absolute cell references. An absolute cell reference is useful especially in formulas to "freeze" the cell references.

▶ **See** "Absolute Cell Referencing," **p. 9**

To create a range name, follow these steps:

1. Select the cell or cells you want to name.
2. Click the Name Box on the left side of the Formula Bar, as shown in Figure 2.19.
3. Type the range name, using the guidelines above, and then press Enter.

There is no limit to the number of range names you can create in a workbook.

FIG. 2.19
Range names cannot contain spaces; use the underscore (_) or period (.) in a range name to create the illusion of a space in the name.

Name box

Formula bar

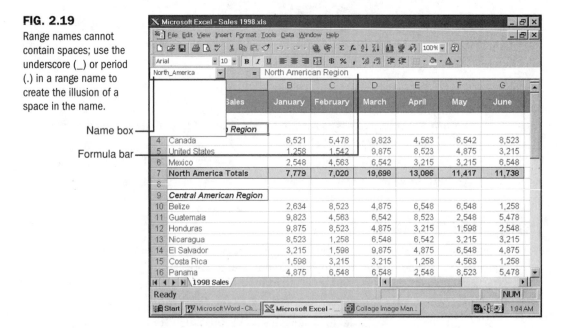

Moving Around Using Range Names

In a very large worksheet, you can use range names to move quickly from area to area, thus avoiding endless scrolling in the worksheet. You need to name only a single cell for each major area of the worksheet to take advantage of this use for range names.

Select a cell in the first major area of the worksheet, like a label or heading. Using the Name Box, provide the cell with a name as described in the previous section. Repeat the process for as many areas of the worksheet as needed.

After you have created the names, select the range name from the Name Box to move to the desired area within your workbook.

Using Range Names to Print Part of a Worksheet

By default, Excel prints the entire active worksheet. If you routinely need to print only a portion of a worksheet, use a range name to identify the portion you want to print:

1. Create the range name for the cells you want to print.

2. Select the range name from the Name Box on the Formula Bar. The cells in the range will be highlighted.

3. Choose File, Print. The Print dialog box is displayed, as shown in Figure 2.20.

4. From the Print What area of the dialog box, choose Selection.

5. To preview the range before you print, choose Preview. To print the range without previewing it, choose OK.

FIG. 2.20

It is a good idea to preview before you print, to make sure the data and the print page settings are what you intend.

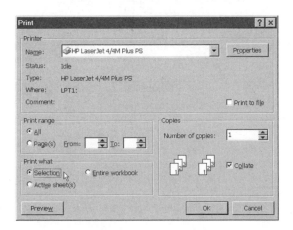

N O T E If you choose the Print button on the toolbar, your entire worksheet is printed, not just the range you have selected. This occurs because the default setting in the Print What area of the Print dialog box is to print the Active Sheet(s); that is, your entire worksheet. You must change the option in the Print dialog box to print only the selection. ■

▶ **See** "Printing Worksheets," **p. 9**

Using Range Names in Formulas

Instead of using cell references in formulas, you can substitute range names. For example, in Figure 2.21, a formula has been created to calculate what percentage of total sales an individual item encompasses. To copy the formula, an absolute cell reference for cell B12 is normally used. For the sales of Expresso, the formula is =B6/$B$12. However, you can use a range name for the cell reference, because by default, range names use absolute cell references. Range names make formulas easier to read. If a range name of 1998_Total is created for cell B12, the formula—with a range name substituted for the absolute cell reference, $B$12—will be =B6/1998_Total.

▶ **See** "Absolute Cell Referencing," **p. 9**

▶ **See** "Accessing Range Names," **p. 57**

▶ **See** "Using Formulas to Look Up Information in Lists," **p. 151**

FIG. 2.21
Range names frequently are used with Excel functions.

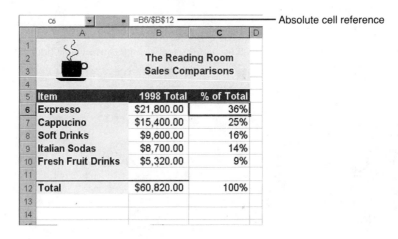

Absolute cell reference

Formulas and Functions

One of the most fundamental uses of worksheets is to perform calculations. The simplest calculations involve addition, subtraction, multiplication, or division. More complex calculations can be created "from scratch" or by using the more than 320 predesigned functions to quickly create common, but intricate, calculations.

Examples of simple calculations include formulas for adding a series of numbers, calculating the difference between two numbers, or figuring the percentage of a total. Examples of complex calculations include determining how much money you will have (including the compound interest earned) if you invest $100 a month for five years, or looking up the cost of a product in a price list to incorporate the cost in an invoice or order form.

This chapter explores a wide range of common formulas and functions. ■

Common Arithmetic Formulas

Excel calculations can be divided into two types—those that use functions and those that do not use functions. Generally, the formulas that do not use functions are simple addition, subtraction, multiplication, or division calculations.

TIP When creating any type of calculation, it is easiest if you first create the formula in words and then substitute the words with the appropriate cell references. For example, to calculate your take-home pay, you could create this formula:

= Annual Salary – Taxes

Using this method to create formulas makes it easier to understand what you are calculating. You will see this technique used throughout this chapter.

Although there are a number of arithmetic calculations available in Excel, three formulas are used most frequently with worksheets: Amount Change, Percent Change, and Percent of Total.

Suppose you want to know how much you spent on Utilities this year and then want to compare that amount to what you spent last year? Or, suppose you want to compare this month's sales for a particular item with last month's sales for that same item?

The Amount Change formula calculates the *amount* of increase or decrease for a particular item between any two periods of time. Similar to the Amount Change calculation, the Percent Change formula calculates the *percentage* increase or decrease for a particular item between two periods of time. Another valuable formula is the Percent of Total calculation, which determines the percentage an item makes up of the total percentage for all items. For example, you can determine what percentage of your total worldwide sales is made by Canadian sales, or what percentage of your total expenditures is spent on entertainment expenses.

TIP The help screens in Excel provide several examples of common formulas and functions. Ask the Office Assistant for a list of example files by typing in **examples** in the Office Assistant search box. Choose "Examples of common formulas" from the results list.

Amount Change

The Amount Change calculation determines the increase or decrease in *amount* between two periods of time such as years, quarters, or months. "Amount" often refers to currency, such as Dollars ($), Pounds (£), or Yen (¥), but it also can mean quantity—the number of a particular item. For example, in Figure 3.1, the difference between global sales for 1998 and 1997 is being calculated.

The Amount Change formula is subtraction—the value represented in the most recent timeframe minus the value represented in the older timeframe. To create the Amount Change calculation used in Figure 3.1, start with the following generic formula:

= 1998 – 1997

In Figure 3.1, the Amount Change for Australian sales between 1997 and 1998 is 1,880.00. In the Formula Bar, the specific formula for Australia is =C6–B6.

FIG. 3.1

Use the Amount Change calculation to compare the change in sales or number of items sold between two periods of time.

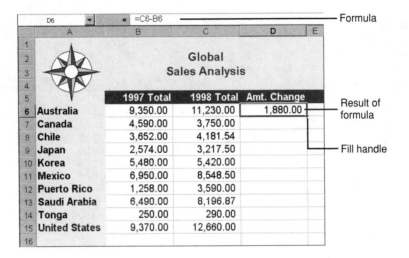

After this first calculation is created, it can be copied to the other cells by using the Fill Handle.

▶ **See** "Copying Formulas," **p. 9**

Percent Change

When you need to determine the percentage increase or decrease between two periods of time, the Percent Change calculation is handy. As with Amount Change, Percent Change works with any two timeframes, such as years, quarters, or months. In the worksheet shown in Figure 3.2, the percentage difference between the sales for 1998 and 1997 is being calculated. To create the Percent Change calculation used in Figure 3.2, start with the following generic formula:

= (1998 – 1997)/1997

The Percent Change formula entails both subtraction and division—the value for the most recent timeframe minus the value for the older timeframe, divided by the value for the older timeframe. In this calculation, the subtraction must be calculated before the division. Because the natural order of arithmetic operations calculates division before subtraction, parentheses are used to force Excel to calculate the subtraction first.

▶ **See** "Order of Operations for Calculations," **p. 9**

N O T E The first part of the Percent Calculation is, in fact, the Amount Change calculation. Therefore, the formula for Percent Change also can be worded as the Amount Change divided by the value of the older timeframe. So, if your worksheet includes a column that calculates the Amount Change, you can reference the Amount Change column in your Percent Change formula. Parentheses are not needed in this case. ■

In Figure 3.2, the Percent Change for Australia is 20.11%. The formula has been copied to the other cells by using the Fill Handle.

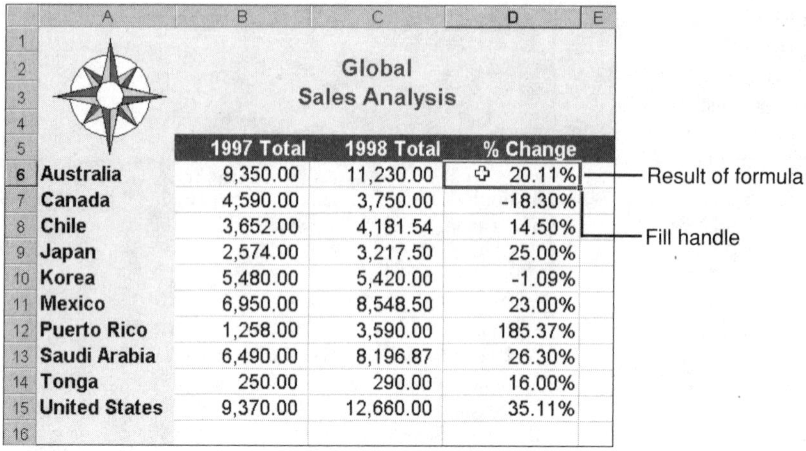

FIG. 3.2
The Percent Change calculation yields the percent increase or decrease in the items.

Result of formula

Fill handle

Percent of Total

Another worthwhile formula is Percent of Total, which determines what percentage the value of an item constitutes of the total values for all items. For example, what percentage are travel expenses of your total monthly expenditures. Percent of Total is calculated based on the values for each item within a single timeframe. To perform the Percent of Total calculation, you first must calculate a total for the list of items—for example, total monthly expenditures.

▶ **See** "Quick Ways to Total Columns and Rows," **p. 9**

The Percent of Total formula is calculated through division. The specific item's amount for the pertinent timeframe is divided by the total amount for all items during the same timeframe. In Figure 3.3, the Percent of Total is calculating what percentage of the total sales for 1998 are attributed to Australia's sales. To create the Percent of Total calculation used in Figure 3.3, start with the following generic formula:

= 1998 Item Total/Grand Total

If you intend to copy the formula, the reference to the Grand Total must be made an absolute cell reference. Use the F4 function key to change the reference before you copy.

▶ **See** "Absolute Cell Referencing," **p. 9**

In Figure 3.3, the Percent of Total for Australia is 18.38%. In the Formula Bar, the specific formula for Australia is =B6/$B$17. The dollar symbols ($) make the reference to the grand total absolute. The formula is ready to be copied.

FIG. 3.3

Use the Percent of Total calculation to determine how much a given item constitutes of the total for all items.

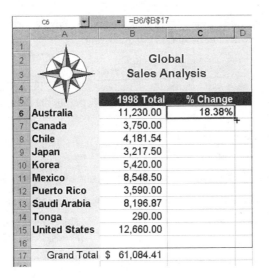

 TIP When creating calculations, use the point method to select the cells you want to include in your formula instead of typing in the cell references. This can help avoid any errors made by typing the incorrect cell reference. See "Working with Formulas" in Chapter 1 for more information on pointing to cells while creating formulas.

Common Worksheet Functions

Because creating complex formulas "from scratch" is time-consuming, Excel provides more than 320 predefined functions to quickly create common, but intricate, calculations. Functions are formulas that perform specific calculations.

Suppose you have a list of employee information and you want Excel to indicate on what date an employee has been with the company five years or more because the employee will then be eligible for more annual vacation time. You can create a formula using the IF function, which checks the date the employee was hired and alerts you when the employee has been with the company for five or more years. Specifically, an IF function performs a test. If the results of the test are "true," then one action is taken. If the results of the test are "false," then another action is taken. In the current example, the test is comparing the employee's hire date with today's date. If there are five or more years between the dates, an alert will be displayed. If there are less than five years, nothing will happen.

Functions all have the same syntax:

= Function Name (Argument, Argument, ...)

The syntax for all functions begins with the function name, followed by an opening parenthesis, followed by the arguments for the function, concluding with a closing parenthesis. Arguments are separated by commas.

Part
I

Ch
3

Arguments can be a reference to a single cell or to a range of cells. Arguments can also be calculations (including functions) and range names—for example:

=Sum(B2,B10:B17,D5*G5,January_Sales)

Some functions require that the arguments be displayed in a particular order. The PMT (payment) function is one such function that requires the arguments be in a specific order (see Table 3.1).

▶ **See** "Using Range Names," **p. 33**

Table 3.1 A Sampling of the Functions Available in Excel

Function Name	Example	Example Comments
AVERAGE	=AVERAGE(B6:B12,C6:C12)	Calculates the average of two ranges of cells, B6 to B12 and C6 to C12.
MAX	=MAX(D4,G3*G4)	Displays whichever is larger, the data in cell D4 or the result of multiplying G3 and G4.
SUM	=SUM(Qtr_1)	Totals the cells included in the Qtr_1 range name.
PMT	=PMT(B4,B5,B6)	Calculates the monthly payment for a house or a car loan—where B4 is the monthly interest rate, B5 is the number of months on the loan, and B6 is the amount borrowed.

Because there are so many functions in Excel, nine categories have been created to help you locate specific functions. The function categories are as follows:

Financial	Date & Time
Math & Trig	Statistical
Lookup & Reference	Database
Text	Logical
Information	

TIP

There are many sources of information that can be used to look up the 320+ functions available in Excel 97. Among the best are the following:

- Use the comprehensive online help to discover more about functions in Excel 97. Choose <u>H</u>elp, <u>C</u>ontents and Index. On the Index tab, type **functions** and double-click **overview**. Choose one of the function categories.

- Que's *Special Edition Using Microsoft Excel 97* is a good reference book that offers a detailed listing of Excel 97 functions.

- Excel 97 comes packaged with several programs, called *Add-Ins*, which provide optional commands and features to Microsoft Excel. Because most of these features are not widely used, they must be "added in" to Excel. The Analysis ToolPak is an add-in program that includes a number of data-analysis tools such as: Covariance, Exponential Smoothing, F-Test, Histogram, and Regression Analysis. To add the Analysis ToolPak to Excel, choose Tools, Add-Ins. Select Analysis ToolPak and choose OK.

Using the Paste Function Command

Instead of memorizing complex function syntax, Excel provides the Paste Function command so that you can create functions rapidly, while avoiding syntax errors. The Paste Function command steps you through the process of selecting a function and providing the necessary arguments. There are several advantages to using the Paste Function command instead of typing the function syntax:

- The Paste Function adds all the necessary function names and arithmetic symbols (equal, comma, and parenthesis) for you—No more error messages about missing commas or parenthesis!

- Any time you need help with a particular function or argument, the Office Assistant is available to describe the function or argument.

Part
I
Ch
3

Categories of Functions

As mentioned earlier in this chapter there are nine categories of functions in Excel, which are grouped by type. In addition to these categories, there are two other categories available under Paste Function—Most Recently Used and All. The Most Recently Used and All categories provide alternative ways to locate functions. When you first use The Most Recently Used category, it lists some of the most common functions for you, because obviously you have yet to use a function. Thereafter, every time you use a function, that function will appear at the top of the Most Recently Used list.

The All category is an alphabetical list of every function in Excel. When you are uncertain to which category a function belongs, use the All category as a starting point in your search for the function.

To create a function by using the Paste Function command, follow these steps:

1. Select the cell in which you want the calculated answer to appear.

2. Click the Paste Function button on the Standard toolbar. The Paste Function dialog box appears (see Figure 3.4).

3. Choose one of the categories in the Function Category list box. In Figure 3.4, the Financial category is selected.

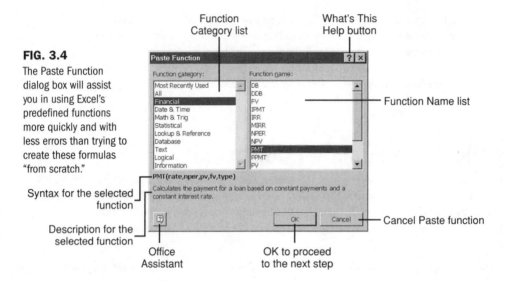

FIG. 3.4

The Paste Function dialog box will assist you in using Excel's predefined functions more quickly and with less errors than trying to create these formulas "from scratch."

Function Category list

What's This Help button

Function Name list

Syntax for the selected function

Description for the selected function

Office Assistant

OK to proceed to the next step

Cancel Paste function

4. Choose a function from the names in the Function Name list box. The syntax and description for the selected function appear below the Function Category list box. In Figure 3.4, the PMT (payment) function is selected. A description of the selected function appears toward the bottom of the dialog box.

5. Select OK and the Formula Palette will appear, detailing the arguments for the function (see Figure 3.5).

   Arguments appearing in Bold are required. Those not in Bold are optional.

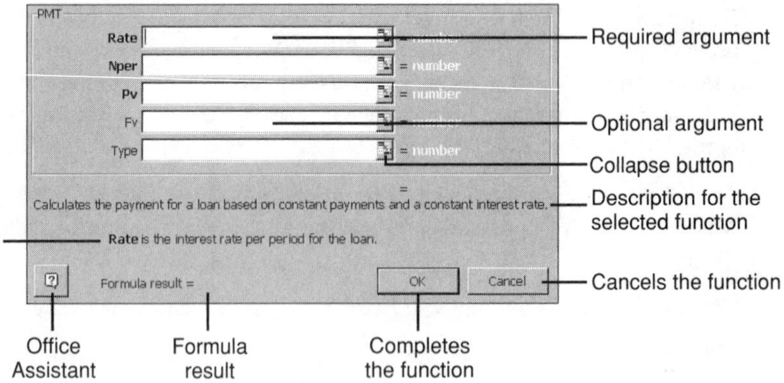

FIG. 3.5

The Formula Palette box will lead you through the specific syntax required for the function that you select.

Required argument

Optional argument

Collapse button

Description for the selected function

Cancels the function

Description for the selected argument

Office Assistant

Formula result

Completes the function

6. The first argument, Rate, is selected—note the flashing cursor in the Rate entry box. A description of the function and the selected argument appear near the bottom of the Formula Palette box.

7. Select the cell or cells in your worksheet that contain the data for the first argument, or manually type the cell references.

8. If necessary, select the next argument by pressing the Tab key or clicking with your mouse. Do not use your Enter key, as that is equivalent to selecting OK, which concludes creating the function.

9. After you have completed all the desired arguments, choose OK. The result of the function appears in the worksheet and the function appears in the Formula Bar.

 TIP If the Formula Palette box is blocking the data you want to select, use the collapse button for the argument (refer to Figure 3.5) to temporarily hide most of the Formula Palette box while you are selecting cells. There is a collapse button located at the far right side of the entry boxes for each argument.

Choose the collapse button again to show all of the Formula Palette box. You also can move the box out of your way—position your mouse pointer on any part of the gray background of Formula Palette box and drag.

 When you need to edit a function in your worksheet, choose the Edit Formula button located in the Formula Bar. The Formula Palette will display.

Accessing Range Names

Range names are particularly useful when you are developing calculations using functions. By definition, range names are absolute cell references, something frequently needed with functions.

Using range names in formulas can ease the process of creating and updating calculations. See the section "Using Range Names in Formulas" in Chapter 2 for more information on how to create range names and some of their other uses.

The Name Box on the Formula Bar can be used to create and select range names. Figure 3.6 shows the Name Box listing the range names already created for this worksheet.

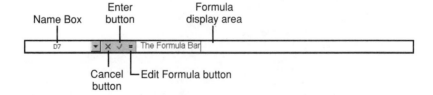

FIG. 3.6

The Formula Bar in Excel 97.

The previous section discussed how to use the Paste Function command to create functions in Excel. When Paste Function is active, the Name Box is not available. A possible list of worksheet functions is substituted in its place on the Formula Bar, as shown in Figure 3.7.

While you can use the traditional menu method (Insert, Name, Paste) to include range names in functions, it is not particularly convenient. If you plan to use range names frequently in your formulas, add the Paste Names command as a button to one of your active toolbars. This way, the list of range names is easy to access.

Part
I

Ch
3

FIG. 3.7
The Name Box on the
Formula Bar is replaced
by the function drop-
down list when the
Formula Palette is
displayed.

Function drop down ─┐

Formula Palette box ──

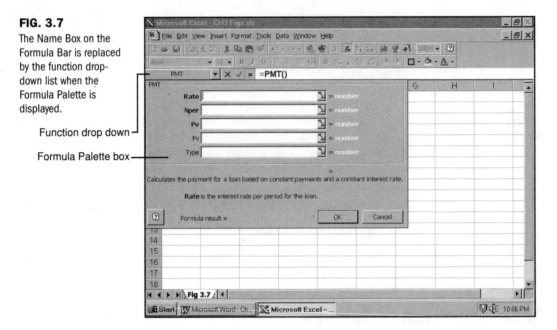

To add the Paste Names button to a toolbar, follow these steps:

1. Choose Tools, Customize; the Customize dialog box appears.

2. Select the Commands tab, and then choose Insert from the Categories list.

3. Scroll down the Commands list and choose the Paste… command. Note the icon image in front of the Paste command (see Figure 3.8).

FIG. 3.8
The Paste command can
be added to a toolbar
for easy access to your
worksheet range names.

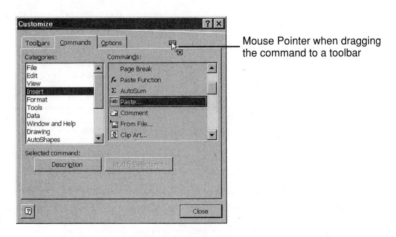

Mouse Pointer when dragging
the command to a toolbar

4. Drag the Paste command to any active toolbar; the icon image will appear on the toolbar button.

5. Choose Close to exit the Customize dialog box.

6. You now can use the Paste Names button to paste range names into functions.

> **See** "Using Range Names," **p. 33**

> **See** "Absolute Cell Referencing," **p. 9**

Using the SUM Function

The *SUM* function *adds* all the numbers in a range of cells. There can be up to 30 arguments in the SUM function; the arguments can be listed in any order. Arguments were discussed in detail in the "Common Worksheet Functions" section, earlier in this chapter.

The syntax for SUM is:

=SUM(argument,argument, ...)

Because adding up columns (or rows) of numbers is a very common calculation, Excel provides a button on the Standard toolbar to access the SUM function, called Auto Sum, in addition to using the Paste Function command to access it.

Chapter 1 discussed in detail how to use the AutoSum function button on the Standard toolbar to create totals in your worksheets. This section focuses on using the SUM function through the Paste Function command to create more complex totals.

> **See** "Quick Ways to Total Columns and Rows," **p. 9**

Figure 3.9 displays a monthly expense list with quarterly totals. The total expenses for the year by adding quarterly totals together, needs to be determined.

FIG. 3.9

Notice the formula in the Formula Bar is using range names instead of cell references.

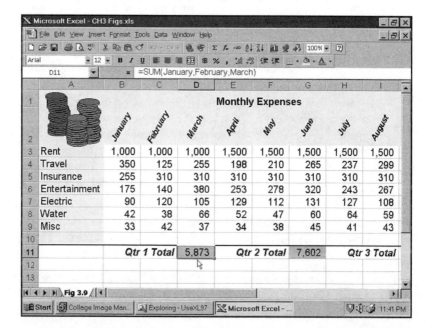

To calculate the total expenses for the year, after you have selected where you want the answer to appear, click the Paste Function button. Choose the SUM function from either the Most Recently Used category or the Math & Trig category and click OK to display the Formula Palette (see Figure 3.10).

N O T E When the SUM function is accessed, it proposes a range of cells to total, just like the AutoSum button does on the toolbar. Simply select the first cell or range of cells to replace the proposal made in the first argument box in the Formula Palette. Refer back to the section "Quick Ways to Total Columns and Rows" in Chapter 1 for more information on using the AutoSum button. ■

FIG. 3.10

The Formula Palette for the SUM function.

Collapse button —

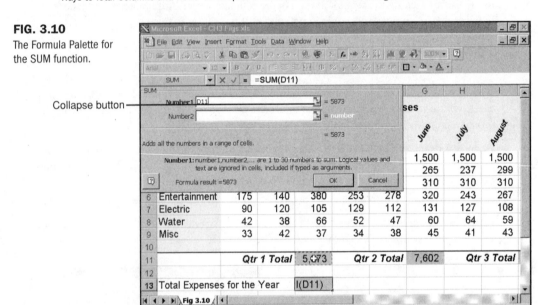

To insert the cell reference for the Qtr 1 total, select the Qtr 1 total directly in the worksheet. If the Formula Palette box is blocking the cell you want to select, use the collapse button for the argument to temporarily hide most of the Formula Palette box (refer to Figure 3.10). There is a collapse button located at the far right side of the entry boxes for each argument. Choose the collapse button again to show the Formula Palette box. You also can move the Formula Palette box by positioning your mouse pointer on any part of the gray background of the Formula Palette box and then dragging it.

Select the next argument by pressing the Tab key or by clicking with your mouse in the next argument entry box. Then choose the cell that contains the Qtr 2 total. Continue until all four quarterly totals are selected. Choose OK to complete the function.

The SUM function also can be used to create totals across multiple worksheets or workbooks. Chapter 3 explains how to accomplish this very powerful use of the SUM function.

▶ **See** "Calculations Across Worksheets and Workbooks," **p. 75**

▶ **See** "Linking Worksheets," **p. 75**

Using the AVERAGE Function

The *AVERAGE* function calculates the *arithmetic mean* of a list of numbers. For example, if the numbers being averaged are 10, 15, 20, and 35, Excel will add the numbers (totaling 80) and divide by the number of numbers (4) to derive an average, or mean, of 20.

There can be up to 30 arguments in the AVERAGE function, and the arguments can be listed in any order. If the term *argument* is unfamiliar to you, see the section titled "Categories of Functions," earlier in this chapter.

The syntax for AVERAGE is:

=AVERAGE(argument,argument,…)

If a cell is empty, it will not be included in the average; however, if a cell contains a zero, it will be averaged in with the other values in the calculation.

In the worksheet displayed in Figure 3.11, the average number of hits for the Little League Baseball team needs to be calculated.

Part

I

Ch

3

FIG. 3.11

To determine the average number of hits for the team, we need to average both columns of numbers.

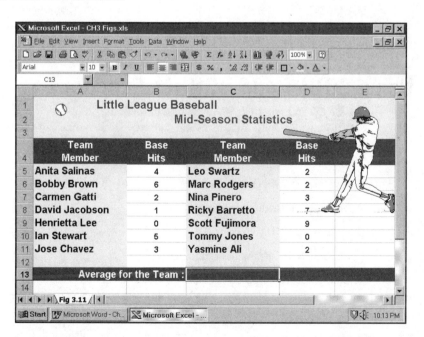

To calculate the average number of hits so far this season, begin the calculation by selecting the cell in which you want the answer to appear and then click the Paste Function button. Choose the AVERAGE function from either the Most Recently Used category or the Statistical category. Then select OK to display the Formula Palette (see Figure 3.12).

FIG. 3.12

The Formula Palette for the AVERAGE function.

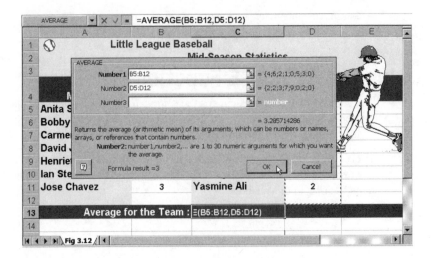

Select the cells for the first column of numbers by highlighting the cells directly in the worksheet. Press the Tab key or click with your mouse to select the second argument box and choose the second group of cells in the worksheet. Choose OK to complete the function.

Like the SUM function, AVERAGE also can be used across multiple worksheets or workbooks. Look ahead to the section "Calculations Across Worksheets and Workbooks" in Chapter 4 for more information.

Using COUNT and COUNTA Functions

Use the *COUNT* and *COUNTA* functions to *count* the number of entries in a group of cells. The COUNT function counts numbers and dates; COUNTA counts all non-blank cells including numbers, dates, text, and error values. There can be up to 30 arguments in either function, and the arguments can be listed in any order.

The syntax for COUNT is:

=COUNT(argument,argument,…)

The syntax for COUNTA is:

=COUNTA(argument,argument,…)

Neither COUNT nor COUNTA include blank cells in their calculations. The COUNT function can be found in the Most Recently Used and Statistical categories. The COUNTA function is located in the Statistical category.

In Figure 3.13, the number of orders received thus far this month is being calculated. The COUNTA function has been selected and the Formula Palette displayed. The range name "Orders" has been inserted as the first argument.

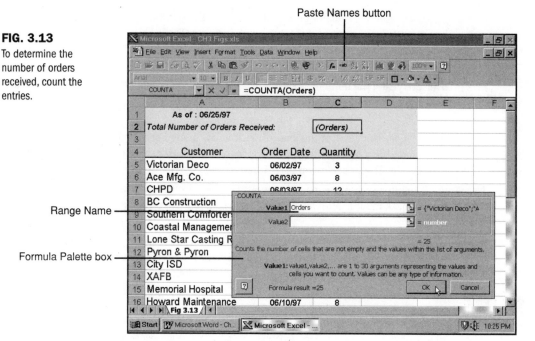

FIG. 3.13
To determine the number of orders received, count the entries.

Paste Names button

Range Name

Formula Palette box

On the Standard Toolbar, the Paste Names button is selected to insert the "Orders" range name. This button was added to the toolbar to make it easy to work with the list of range names. See the section "Accessing Range Names," earlier in this chapter, for instructions on adding this tool to one of your toolbars. You also can use Insert, Name, Paste to include a range name in a function.

▶ **See** "Using Range Names," **p. 33**

Using the PMT Function

The *PMT* function is used to calculate the *payment* on a loan or annuity. Unlike the functions previously discussed, the arguments for PMT are specified and must appear in a certain order. The syntax for PMT is:

=PMT(rate, nper, pv, fv, type**)**

Arguments appearing in bold are required; those not in bold are optional. In the PMT function, the *fv* and *type* arguments are optional.

Whenever you work with a function that includes predefined arguments, it is important that you know what those arguments mean before proceeding with the function. The Office Assistant will provide you with comprehensive descriptions of all arguments. For PMT the arguments are:

- ■ **rate**   The interest rate per period. If the annual interest rate is 9.5 percent, the quarterly interest rate is 9.5 percent divided by four quarters. The monthly interest rate would be 9.5 percent divided by 12 months. The rate argument is required.

- ■ **nper**   The number of payment periods or installments. If a loan is to be paid monthly over five years, the number of payment periods is 5 multiplied by 12. If it is a thirty-year loan, the number of payment periods is 30 multiplied by 12. The nper argument is required.

- ■ **pv**   The present value of the loan—how much is being borrowed. If you are borrowing the money, this number will be positive; if you are lending the money, this number will be negative. The pv argument is required.

- ■ **fv**   The future value of a loan or annuity. Usually with a loan, fv will be zero (the loan will be paid back in full). With an annuity, it will be a positive number. The fv argument is optional.

- ■ **type**   The timeframe within which the payment is due. If this argument is omitted or zero, payments are due at the end of the period. If set to one, the payments are due at the beginning of the period. The type argument is optional.

 T I P   When working with functions in the Financial category, it is important that you remember to use positive numbers for money received (like a mortgage loan or cash withdrawal) and negative numbers for money paid (loan payments or savings deposits). Naturally, if you're the lender, loan payments would be positive and cash withdrawals would be negative.

In Figure 3.14, the monthly payment is being calculated for a home mortgage loan. The PMT function has been selected and the Formula Palette displayed. The cells in the worksheet that contain the rate, nper, and pv data have been selected for the appropriate arguments. The interest rate and number of years in which to pay off the mortgage have been converted to months.

PMT calculates the principle and interest portions of a loan. When buying a house or car, you will need to factor in the taxes and insurance, too.

N O T E   Excel provides an excellent illustration of using the PMT function to create a mortgage data table. The data table calculates various loan payments associated with different interest rates. Choose <u>H</u>elp, <u>C</u>ontents and Index to display the Help Topics dialog box. ■

After this first calculation is created, it can be copied to the other cells by using the Fill Handle.
▶ **See** "Copying Formulas," **p. 9**

Using the FV Function

The *FV* function is used to calculate the *future value* of a savings or investment account. As with PMT, the arguments for FV are specified and must appear in a certain order. The syntax for FV is:

=FV(rate, nper, pmt, pv, **type)**

FIG. 3.14
Use the PMT function to
determine the monthly
payment on a loan.

Interest rate converted
into months

Number of periods
converted into months

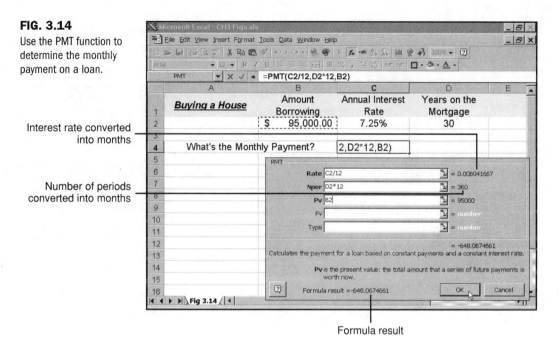

Formula result

Arguments that appear in bold are required; those not in bold are optional. In the FV function, the *pv* and *type* arguments are optional.

The financial functions share similar arguments. For descriptions of the FV arguments, see the previous section on PMT. Remember that the interest rate and number of payment periods need to be represented in the same time unit as the payment. If you are contributing to a savings program twice a month (24 times a year), the annual interest rate is divided by 24 to determine the interest rate per period. The number of years you are contributing is multiplied by 24 to determine the number of times you make a contribution.

In the worksheet shown in Figure 3.15, a calculation is being performed to find out how much will be saved (with interest) after 15 years of payments if the monthly contribution is $75.00. The FV function has been selected and the Formula Palette displayed. The cells in the worksheet that hold the rate, nper, and pmt data have been selected for the appropriate arguments. The interest rate and number of years over which the contributions will be made have been converted to months.

Notice the result in the bottom of the Formula Palette box in Figure 3.15. If you invest $75.00 per month at 11.5 percent interest, you will have $35,738.71 after 15 years. If you hide the money in your house each month (perhaps in a mattress?) instead of investing it or placing it in a savings account, after 15 years you will accumulate $13,500.00 ($75.00 multiplied by 180 months). The $22,238.71 difference is a result of the compounded interest.

Part

I

Ch

3

FIG. 3.15

Use the FV function to determine the future value of your money when you invest or save.

Interest rate converted into months

Number of periods converted into months

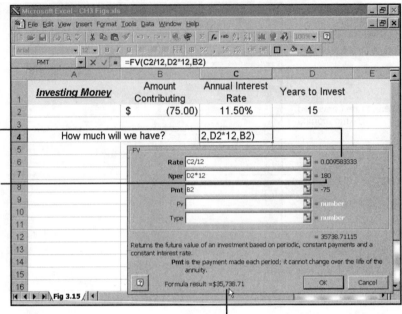

Formula result

CHAPTER 4

Combining Functions and Linking Formulas

Using functions together

Learn to nest functions, one inside another, to create powerful calculations.

Linking sheets and books through formulas

Create worksheet formulas that summarize all of your data and build links between sheets and books.

Chapter 3 covered performing simple calculations by using common formulas and functions. In this chapter, you learn to create functions that are used inside other functions—known as *nesting* functions. You also learn to create calculations that link data across multiple worksheets and workbooks. ■

Nesting Functions

As you work more with functions, you will probably find it useful to create functions that use other functions. When one function is used inside another function, it is referred to as *nesting functions*. An example of nesting functions is:

=MAX(SUM(B12:B15),SUM(C12:C15))

Here you are requesting Excel to display whichever sum is larger—the sum of cells B12 through B15 or the sum of cells C12 through C15—the larger sum will appear as the answer to the MAX function.

Nesting functions is particularly common when working with IF functions. Recall from Chapter 3 that the syntax for IF is:

=IF(logical_test, value_if_true, value_if_false)

The following examples demonstrate IF functions with other functions nested as part of the IF function arguments.

In the following example, the SUM function is nested inside the IF function, and is used in both the logical_test and the value_if_true arguments:

=IF(SUM(B12:B15)<SUM(C12:C15),SUM(C12:C15),"ERROR")

If the sum of cells B12 through B15 is less than the sum of cells C12 through C15, then the sum of cells C12 through C15 is calculated; otherwise, ERROR is displayed.

The OR function is used in the logical_text portion of the IF function in the following example:

=IF(OR(B12="San Antonio",B12= "Austin"),C12*5%,C12*4%)

In this case, if B12 contains the text "San Antonio" or "Austin," the value_if_true argument (C12*5%) is performed. If some other city name appears, then the value_if_false calculation is performed (C12*4%).

The logical_test in the next example contains both the OR and the IS functions:

=IF(OR(ISTEXT(C3),ISBLANK(C3)),"New Account",E3/C3)

If cell C3 contains text or is empty, the phrase New Account will appear; otherwise, a division is calculated.

The VLOOKUP function is used in both the value_if_true and value_if_false arguments in the following example. Table1 and Table2 are range names:

=IF(C3>=5000,VLOOKUP(C3,Table1,3,False),VLOOKUP(C3,Table2,3,False)

In this scenario, if the number in cell C3 is 5,000 or greater, then the number is looked up in Table1; if the number is less than 5,000, then the number is looked up in Table2. In both cases, the corresponding number in column 3 of the VLOOKUP table_array will be returned. Exact match lookups are being performed.

IF functions can be placed inside of other IF functions. In the next example, a second IF function is the value_if_false argument for the first IF function:

=IF(D4<0,"Contact Rep",IF(D4>=30%,"Bonus Due",""))

In the previous example, the logical_test is to determine whether cell D4 is negative. If it is negative, then Contact Rep is displayed. If it is not negative (then it must be zero or positive), another test is being performed. This second IF function is the value_if_false of the first IF function. In the second IF, we are checking to see whether D4 is 30 percent or greater. If it is, then Bonus Due is displayed. If it is not (D4 is between 0 and 29 percent), then nothing is displayed.

To make it easier to understand this example, look at the following syntax:

=IF(Test1,True1,IF(Test2,True2,False2))

The second IF function is the False1. When IF functions are nested inside of other IF functions, writing the syntax as shown in this example can make it easier to understand.

N O T E   A maximum of seven IF functions may be nested.

Calculations Across Worksheets and Workbooks

One advantage of having multiple sheets in a book is the capability to create calculations across the sheets. For example, suppose you have a workbook devoted to expenses for 1998, in which each sheet in the book lists the expenses for a single month. There is a sheet for January, another for February, and so on, for all 12 months of the year. In addition, there will be another sheet that tracks the cumulative expenses for the year. To create the cumulative calculations, you will need to refer to cells in the other sheets. Through the calculations, the sheets are linked together. Changes made to the monthly expenses are reflected in the year-to-date cumulative expenses.

When formulas and functions contain references to other sheets in the same book, the references include the worksheet name, followed by the cell reference. The worksheet name always appears with an exclamation point after the name—for example:

SHEET!CELL

January!B12

January!B12:B15

When formulas and functions contain references to other sheets in different books, the references include the workbook name, worksheet name, and then the cell reference. The workbook name always appears inside square brackets—for example:

[BOOK]SHEET!CELL

[Expenses98]January!B12

[Expenses98]January!B12:B15

Part

I

Ch

4

N O T E If the book or sheet name is multiple words, you will see apostrophes (') surrounding the words. This is Excel's way of identifying that several words make up a name. For example:

'Jan 98'!B12

'[Expense Information 1998]January'!B12

Linking Worksheets

Although creating links between worksheets can be used in a variety of situations, the most common situation is where information from individual sheets is linked into a summary sheet.

Creating calculations that link data across multiple sheets is very similar to creating calculations in a single sheet:

- When the data is updated, the formulas are recalculated—regardless of where the data is located—on the same sheet as the formula or on a different sheet than the formula.
- As with calculations in a single sheet, the Formula Bar displays the calculation as each component of the formula is built.

When creating calculations across sheets and books, the manner in which the sheets are laid out impacts the way you approach creating the calculations. In some cases, using an identical design for both sheets can expedite building the calculations, saving you a significant amount of time!

▶ **See** "Grouping WorkSheets," **p. 33**

▶ **See** "Creating Identical Worksheets," **p. 33**

Chapter 1 discussed how to create formulas by selecting the cell rather than typing in the cell reference. It often is easier to point to the cell and it avoids making typing mistakes.

▶ **See** "Working with Formulas," **p. 9**

Figure 4.1 demonstrates a worksheet designed to show Net Profit. Net Profit is calculated as Sales minus Expenses. Because the sales and expense information is contained in other sheets in the file, a calculation will be created to link these sheets to the Net Profit sheet.

To link multiple sheets in a simple calculation, follow these steps:

1. Select the cell in which you want the answer to appear. In Figure 4.1, this is cell B6.

2. Begin the formula or select the function by using the Paste Function button. In the example used in Figure 4.1, because a subtraction equation is being created, the formula begins by typing an = (equal) symbol.

3. Select the sheet tab that contains the first piece of data that you want to include in the formula. In this example, the Sales sheet will be selected.

4. Select the required cell(s). Select cell B6, the sales figure for California (see Figure 4.2). Notice that the name of the sheet and the cell reference appear in the Formula Bar.

FIG. 4.1

To create calculations across multiple sheets in a workbook, start in the cell in which you want the answer to appear.

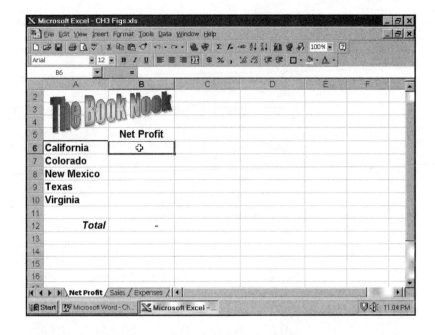

FIG. 4.2

The sheet name is included in the formula to identify where the data was obtained.

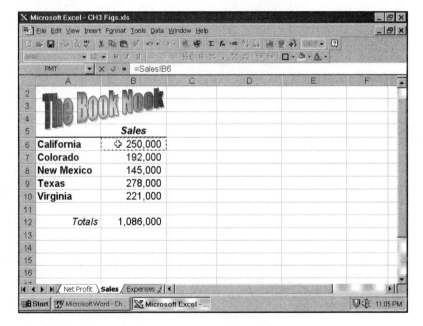

5. Type the next component of the formula. In this example, it is a – (minus) sign.

6. Repeat steps 3, 4, and 5 until the formula is complete. Select the Expenses sheet and choose cell D7 (see Figure 4.3).

Part

I

Ch

4

7. Verify the formula in the Formula Bar. The formula in Figure 4.3 is :

=Sales!B6–Expenses!D7

FIG. 4.3

As you build the
formula, use the
Formula Bar to make
sure it is building the
formula you want.

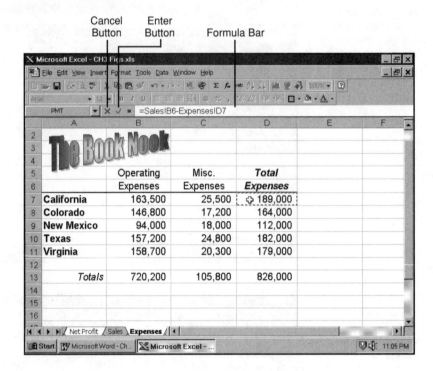

8. Press Enter or click the Enter button (green check) in the Formula Bar to finish the
formula. In the present example, the formula will be copied to the remaining states.

▶ **See** "Copying Formulas," **p. 9**

There are, of course, other more intricate examples of calculations being used across
worksheets. Figure 4.4 shows a spreadsheet designed to track cumulative expenses for 1998.
Notice the sheet tabs; they begin with Jan (January) and end with Dec (December) and Year
To Date.

In this example, a simple SUM calculation for Rent in Calgary will be created in the Year To
Date worksheet. The formula will then be copied to the other expenses and cities. Each
monthly expense sheet is laid out identically, meaning that in each sheet, the Rent for the
Calgary office is located in cell B3.

To link multiple sheets that are laid out identically, follow these steps:

1. Select the cell in which you want the answer to appear. In Figure 4.4, this is cell B3.

FIG. 4. 4

This file illustrates the most common use of linking, in which information from individual sheets is linked into a summary sheet.

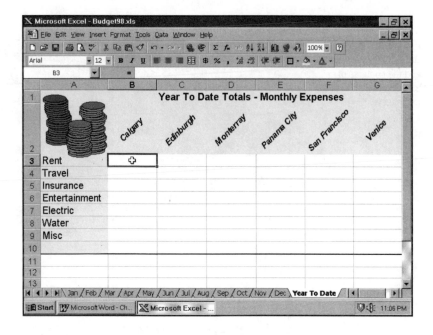

2. Begin the formula or select the function by using the Paste Function button. Because you are creating a SUM, use the AutoSum button on the Standard toolbar.

3. Select the first sheet tab to display the sheet that contains the cell or cells you want to include in your formula. For this example, select the Jan sheet. The Formula Bar will display the formula as it is built.

   Because the sheets are laid out identically, select multiple consecutive sheets by holding down the Shift key and clicking the last sheet in the group. In this example, hold the Shift key and click the Dec sheet to include the January through December worksheets.

4. Select the required cell(s). In the present example, select cell B3—Rent for Calgary. In Figure 4.5, notice the formula in the Formula Bar.

5. Verify the formula in the Formula Bar. The formula in Figure 4.5 is :

   =SUM('Jan:Dec'!B3)

6. Press Enter or click the Enter button (green check) in the Formula Bar.

N O T E If you are using a function and the sheets are not laid out identically, or you need to select sheets that are not consecutive, you will have to select each sheet and cell separately. After the first sheet and cell are selected, type a comma, which will appear after the cell reference in the Formula Bar. Continue to select the necessary sheets and cells, making sure you use a comma before continuing to the next sheet, until you reach the last sheet. After the last sheet and cell have been selected, press Enter or use the Enter button on the Formula Bar to finish the formula. ■

Part

I

Ch

4

FIG. 4.5

The SUM function will add the contents of cell B3 from each of the 12 worksheets.

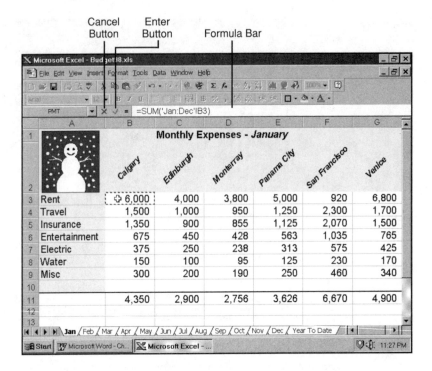

Sometimes you simply will want the contents of a cell to appear in another sheet or book. The data can be copied by using the traditional copy/paste commands. However, if the data changes in the original location, it will not change in the destination location when you use copy/paste. If you want the data to change in the destination location when the original changes, the data will have to be linked. To accomplish this, first select the cell in which you want the data to appear in the target worksheet. Type = (equal) to begin the link. Select the cell in the source worksheet from which the data will come. Press Enter or click the Enter button (green check) in the Formula Bar.

Linking Workbooks

When linking workbooks, the workbook containing the original data is referred to as the *source*. The workbook that receives the linked data is called the *target*. The formula that creates the link is sometimes referred to as the *external reference formula*.

To ensure that the links made between books remain intact, the following guidelines should be used when working with linked books:

- *Opening linked books.* Source workbooks should be opened before target workbooks.
- *Closing linked books.* Source workbooks should be closed before target workbooks.
- *Moving the source cell.* If both the source and target workbooks are open, Excel adjusts the formula to reflect the new location when the source cell is moved. However, if only

the source workbook is open when the source cell is moved, the target workbook will continue to use the old reference for the source cell. This will result in incorrect calculations or error messages. The only exception to this result is if a range name is used for the source cell instead of a cell reference. When the target workbook is opened, it looks for the range name, which now refers to different cells.

- *Renaming the source sheet or book.* If both the source and target workbooks are open, Excel adjusts the formula to reflect the new name for the sheet or book when the source sheet or book is renamed. However, if only the source workbook is open when the source sheet or book is renamed, the target workbook will continue to use the old reference for the source sheet or book. This will result in incorrect calculations or error messages.

- *Deleting the source sheet or book.* Naturally, this will result in an error message in the target book.

The steps to create links between books are very similar to the steps followed to create links between sheets, which are described in previous sections of this chapter. Follow these steps to create links between books:

1. Open both the source and target workbooks.
2. Make the target workbook the active file and select the cell in which you want the answer to appear.

3. Begin the formula or select the function by using the Paste Function button.
4. When building the formula, at the point where you need the cell reference from the source workbook, choose <u>W</u>indow and select the name of the workbook from the list of open files. If you are using a function, the Paste Function box will stay on the screen as you build your formula.
5. Select the worksheet and cells you want to include in your formula. You can see the formula being built in the Formula bar.

TIP Whenever you include a cell reference from another workbook in a formula, the cell reference is automatically made absolute by inserting the $ symbol code in front of the column letter and row number. If you intend to copy the formula in the target book, the reference needs to be changed to a relative cell reference. Press the F4 key three (3) times to convert the cell reference from absolute to relative.

6. If you need to select multiple sheets in the source workbook, select the first sheet tab. If the sheets are laid out identically, you can select multiple consecutive sheets by holding down the Shift key and clicking the last sheet in the group.

   If the sheets are not laid out identically, or you need to select sheets that are not consecutive, you will have to select each sheet and cell separately. After the first sheet and cell are selected, type in a comma, which will appear after the cell reference in the Formula Bar. Continue to select the necessary sheets and cells, making sure that you use a comma before continuing to the next sheet, until you reach the last sheet.

7. If you need to select cells in other workbooks and are using the Paste Function box to build a formula, select the next argument box and repeat steps 4, 5, and 6.

8. After the last sheet and cell have been selected, or you have typed in the last component of the formula, press Enter or use the Enter button (green check) on the Formula Bar to finish the formula.

▶ **See** "Relative Cell Referencing," **p. 9**

▶ **See** "Grouping Worksheets," **p. 33**

Opening Linked Workbooks

Whenever you open a file that has links to other workbooks, if the source workbook is open, the links are immediately updated. If the source file is not open, Excel will ask you whether you want to update the links (see Figure 4.6). If you select Yes when queried about the links, Excel will access the source file and perform any necessary updates. If you choose No, the data that was in the book when it was last saved appears in your target file. In either case, the source file does not open.

FIG. 4.6

Excel displays this
message when you open
a file that contains links.

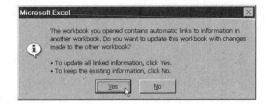

If there is a series of files that contain links, you should open these files in sequence. Suppose a Worklog file is the source file for a Payroll file, which in turn is the source file for the Monthly Budget file. The hours that employees have worked is fed into the payroll, where taxes and take-home pay are calculated. The taxes and payroll are fed into the budget for the month, which summarizes all the expenses for the month.

In this scenario, the Worklog file should be opened first, followed by the Payroll file, followed by the Monthly Budget file. If the Monthly Budget file is opened first, it will look only to the Payroll file (its source file) for any changes to the linked data. If changes have been made to the Worklog file, the Monthly Budget file will not see those changes because it is linked only to the Payroll file.

Changing and Updating Links

If a link to the source workbook is lost or needs to be changed, you do not have to recreate the formula. To reestablish links to a workbook or to link the target workbook to a different source, use the following steps:

1. Open the target workbook.

2. Choose Edit, Links. The Links dialog box will appear.

3. A list of the workbook's source files is displayed (see Figure 4.7). If the source file is not open, the full path to locate the files is listed.

FIG. 4.7

The Links dialog box is used to change the source document for links in a file.

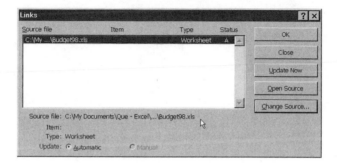

4. Use the Change Source button to select a different source file or to reestablish the link to the source file, when the source file has been renamed or moved.

Part

I

Ch

4

CHAPTER 5

Working with Templates

Use Excel's predesigned templates

Excel provides 10 built-in templates that you can customize to fit your specific requirements. Helpful notes and tips embedded in the templates assist you in working with and customizing the templates.

Create your own templates

Design custom workbooks or worksheets tailored to your specific tasks and projects. Any spreadsheet you create repeatedly is a good candidate for a template.

Customize the default workbook and worksheet templates

Whenever a new book is created or a new sheet is inserted, they are based on the default *autotemplates* in Excel. You can change the formats or contents of the new, blank workbook that opens when you start the program or ask for a new file or sheet by modifying the existing autotemplates or designating alternative autotemplates.

A *template* is a special type of workbook file that is used as a master, or blueprint, for creating other Excel workbooks. There are two kinds of templates—ordinary templates and autotemplates. *Ordinary templates* are workbooks or worksheets that you create to serve as the basis for other similar workbooks. *Autotemplates* are used when you want to change the default formats for new, blank workbooks or worksheets.

Documents created from a template are identical to the template, containing all the elements of the template. These elements include the: number of sheets; layout; data; formulas; cell formats; range names; sheet names; print options; graphics; macros; worksheet controls; and Visual Basic modules.

Templates are useful for establishing default settings, such as the default headers and footers that print with the workbook. You can also use a template when you need to create a workbook or worksheet repeatedly. For example, templates are handy when you want to create company expense forms, client invoices, or budget reports.

Templates also can expedite the creation of routine workbooks. For example, you can create a monthly expense-report form with all the necessary formatting and formulas built in. If saved as a template file, when you need to submit an expense form each month, the template provides the basis for the report. Tax records for a home business is another example. You can create a workbook which tracks your business expenses and tax information for the year. The workbook can be designed where the information for each month is stored on its own worksheet, and there is an additional worksheet to display cumulative, or year-to-date, information. See Chapter 4 "Combing Functions and Linking Formulas," for more information on creating cumulative worksheets. ■

Saving Time by Using Excel's Built-In Templates

Because many Excel users frequently require common spreadsheets, such as an expense report, Microsoft Excel includes 10 predesigned template files. These templates represent some of the most frequently used spreadsheets. Table 5.1 lists each of these templates.

Table 5.1 The Built-In Templates Included with Microsoft Excel

Template Name	Description
Business Planner	A series of spreadsheets designed to analyze current financial status and forecast future cash flow. Includes several sheets and charts: a Data Sheet, Balance Sheet, Income Statement, Cash Flow Sheet, Income Chart, and an Asset Chart.
Car Lease Advisor	A tool to determine the best options when considering a vehicle lease.
Change Request	A form to monitor problems with a product or process. Includes a feature to add data from each change request to a database.
Expense Statement	A form to track employee expenses. Contains categories for accommodations, travel, fuel, meals, phone, entertainment, and "other." Includes a feature to add data from each expense report to a database.
Invoice	A form to generate customer invoices. Includes a feature to add data from each invoice to a database.
Loan Manager	A form to calculate loan payments, which includes an amortization schedule.
Personal Budgeter	A series of spreadsheets to organize personal finances. Includes several sheets—Income, Utilities, Insurance, Living Expenses, Entertainment, Credit Cards, Budget Summary, and a Budget Graph.
Purchase Order	A form to track orders placed with vendors. Includes a feature to add data from each purchase order to a database.
Sales Quote	A form to prepare sales quotes for customers. Includes a feature to add data from each quote to a database.
Time Card	A form to track time spent on various projects during a given timeframe. Includes a feature to add data from each time card to a database.

Each built-in template contains macros. Whenever a file containing macros is accessed in Excel, a warning is displayed. This is a new feature in Microsoft Excel 97. The warning alerts you that the file contains one or more macros and reminds you that macros may contain viruses (see Figure 5.1). This warning appears whenever you create a workbook by using one of the built-in templates. Choose <u>E</u>nable Macros to proceed with creating the new workbook.

N O T E Excel cannot detect viruses in your files. The virus alert message is just a warning that has been added to the Office 97 products since most viruses are found in macros. In order to protect your computer and files from viruses, you should purchase software designed specifically to detect and remove viruses. I highly recommend Symantec Norton AntiVirus, available through most stores which sell software. Their web site is **www.symantec.com**. ■

FIG. 5.1

The virus alert message appears whenever you attempt to open a file that contains macros.

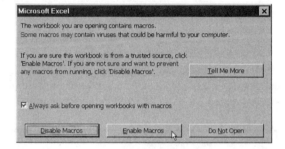

There are three features in each built-in Excel template to help you work with the templates: a toolbar, template-specific help, and embedded comments.

However, not all buttons appear on every template toolbar—the toolbars have many of the same buttons. Table 5.2 illustrates and describes the buttons that appear on the built-in template toolbars.

Part
I

Ch
5

Table 5.2   Toolbar Buttons Available with the Built-In Templates

Toolbar Button	Description
	Size to Screen/Return to Size
	Hide CellTips/Display CellTips (CellTips are embedded comments)
	Document a Cell
	Template Help

continues

Table 5.2 Continued

Toolbar Button	Description
	Display Example/Remove Example
	Assign a Number
	Capture Data in a Database
	Split and Freeze Panes
	Bring Up a Calculator

Each built-in template toolbar includes the Template Help button. Whenever you create a new workbook from a template, this button will explain how to use the template. In Figure 5.2, a new workbook has been created based on the built-in Invoice template.

FIG. 5.2

Built-in Excel templates come with custom toolbars, template-specific help, and embedded comments.

Embedded Comment—

Customize Button—

Template Toolbar—

Template Help Button—

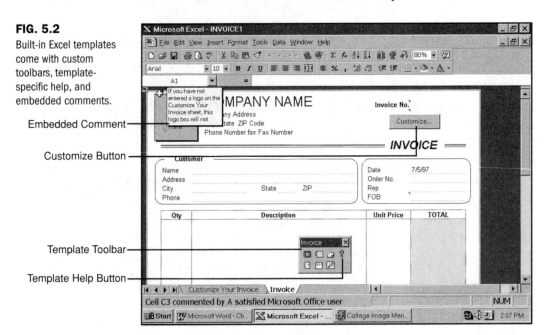

Each built-in template has comments embedded in the template to provide you with information about the parts of the template that require explanation. Position your mouse pointer near the triangular comment marker to see the comment. In Figure 5.2, the comment for the Logo is displayed.

T I P Sometimes the comment boxes are not large enough to display the entire comment, as is the case with the Logo comment in Figure 5.2. You can view the entire comment by first selecting the cell in which the comment resides and then choosing Insert, Edit Comment. Scroll within the box to read the entire comment. Many of the built-in templates have hidden the gridlines. All comment indicators appear in the upper-right corner of the cell to which the comment is attached.

The built-in templates are accessed through the New command on the File menu. The New dialog box displays a series of tabs that identify the templates available in Excel 97 (see Figure 5.3).

FIG. 5.3
Which tabs are listed in the New dialog box depends on how Excel 97 was installed and whether you have created any custom template folders.

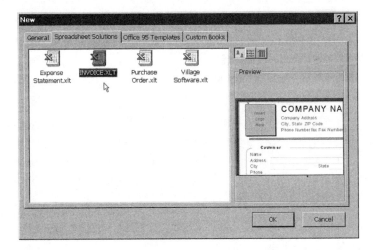

The General tab lists the Workbook template, which is used as the default template for new workbooks. Excel 97 templates appear in the Spreadsheet Solutions tab, which contains the three most popular templates: Expense Statement, Invoice, and Purchase Order. Additionally, a marketing template is listed for Village Software, the company that created these built-in templates for Microsoft. The seven remaining built-in templates do not appear automatically.

The Office 95 Templates tab also may be listed in the New dialog box if you have upgraded from Microsoft Excel 95. The Excel 95 versions of the built-in templates (and any templates you created in Excel 95) will be listed in the Office 95 Templates tab.

All of the built-in templates from Excel 95 have been updated for Excel 97. There are two ways to display the other Excel 97 built-in templates, which are listed in Table 5.1. One way is to copy them from the Office 97 CD. They are in the following folder location on the CD:

Valupack\Templates\Excel

These templates need to be copied to the MSOffice\Templates\Spreadsheet Solutions folder on your hard drive. The Help file (VSTMPLT.HLP) is shared by all the spreadsheet solutions and must be placed in the MSOffice\Excel directory.

Part
I

Ch
5

If you have access to the Internet, another method of obtaining the latest templates is through the World Wide Web. Choose "Microsoft on the Web" from the Help menu and select Free Stuff.

To create a new workbook based on a built-in template, follow these steps:

1. Choose File, New. The New dialog box appears.
2. Choose the Spreadsheet Solutions tab for the most current version of the built-in templates, or choose another tab where the template you want is listed.
3. Double-click the template, or select the template and choose OK to open it.
4. The macro virus warning message appears (refer to Figure 5.1). Choose Enable Macros. A new workbook appears that is based on the template.

Each built-in template has an option to modify the template to include your company name and logo. You also can change the font and add your own comments.

To modify a predefined template, follow these steps:

1. Display the template you want to modify.
2. Choose the Customize button, located in the upper-right corner of the template.
3. Make the necessary changes. The customize sheet provides notes to assist you.
4. Choose the Lock/Save Sheet button to prevent accidental changes to the customization you have made. You will have the choice of locking the existing template or locking and saving the template you modified as a new template file.
5. Choose OK. If you select the lock and save option, you will be prompted for a name and location for the new template. Make sure you save the template in the Spreadsheet Solutions folder for easy access.

Some of the built-in templates include a feature that enables you to add data to a database each time you complete the template form. The data is added as a new record in a database that is associated with the template. If you want to use the Template Wizard to place data in an Excel list, see "Using a List as a Database" in Chapter 11.

For more information about the Template Wizard, see "Using the Template Wizard with Data Tracking," later in this chapter.

 Use the Excel help screens or Office Assistant to search for additional information pertaining to the built-in templates and the Template Wizard. Type **templates** or **template wizard** in the Office Assistant search box and press Enter to see a list of Help topics.

Creating Your Own Workbook Templates

Whenever you have to create the same type of workbook repeatedly, using a template will save you a vast amount of time. Templates provide several simple advantages over merely modifying an existing workbook. Template files typically are stored in one place; you don't have to remember where the original workbook is saved or what you named it. By using a template file, you prevent accidentally saving your new data on top of your original data. Template files create new workbooks, which always prompt you for a file name.

Workbook templates can contain one or more worksheets. The number of worksheets, the specific data and formulas included, and the print settings of the template are duplicated when you create a new workbook based on the template.

There are a few things to remember when you create your own template files:

■ Remove any unused worksheets from the workbook *before* you save it as a template.

▶ **See** "Inserting and Deleting Worksheets," **p. 117**

■ Use the Delete key to remove any data that is used to build the template file. This will keep all formulas and formatting and enable you to avoid having to remove the data when you create a new file from the template.

■ For the template to appear in the New dialog box along with the other template files, you have to save it in the Templates folder, which usually is in the following location on your hard drive:

Program Files\Microsoft Office\Templates

● If you save a template directly in the Template folder, it will appear on the General tab of the New dialog box.

● Save your custom templates in the Spreadsheet Solutions folder to have all built-in and custom templates listed together under the Spreadsheet Solutions tab in the New dialog box. Alternatively, a new folder such as "Custom Books" can be created to store templates you have created, which will keep them separate from the built-in templates. This is particularly advantageous if you plan to customize the built-in templates. You can keep the original built-in template in the Spreadsheet Solutions folder and place all custom templates in a separate folder.

● If you are using a network and need to make a custom template available to others, store the template in a shared area of the network. Create a shortcut to the network location or template and have users place the shortcut in their Templates folder.

■ Template files are saved with an .XLT extension. Excel template file icons appear with a thick yellow band across the top of the icon image.

■ When you create a new file based on a template, a copy of the template appears—not the original template. The name of the template, with a sequential number, appears as a placeholder name, much the same way that new workbooks are named BOOK1, BOOK2, and so on.

Figure 5.4 illustrates a workbook that needs to be created quarterly. It contains a sheet for summarizing monthly expenses and a chart that graphs the expenses.

Part

I

Ch

5

FIG. 5.4

This figure illustrates an example of a workbook that needs to be created periodically—a good candidate for a template file.

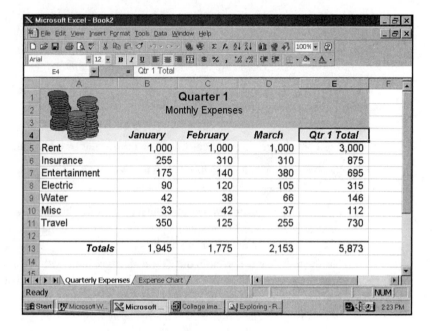

To create your own workbook template, follow these steps:

1. Create a new workbook that contains the sheets, default text (such as titles, column, and row labels), formulas, macros, and other formatting you want to appear in new workbooks that are based on this file.

2. To preview the first page of a template in the New dialog box, choose File, Properties. From the Summary tab, select the Save Preview Picture check box. Choose OK.

3. Choose File, Save As. The Save As dialog box appears (see Figure 5.5). To save the workbook as a template file, it is easiest to begin at the bottom of the dialog box and work your way up.

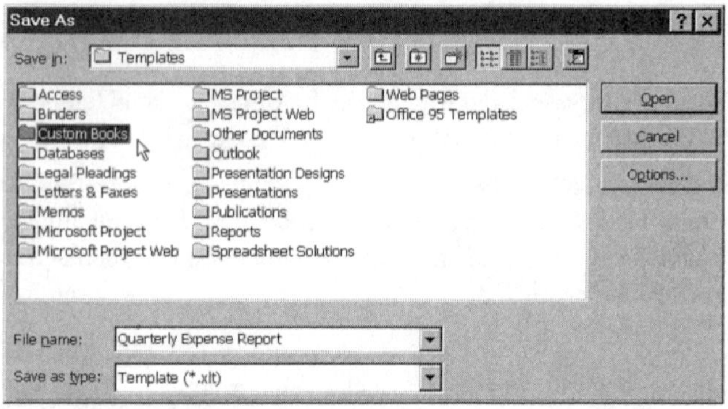

FIG. 5.5

The choices you make in the Save As dialog box affect where your template is saved.

4. In the Save As Type box, choose Template (*.xlt). When you select Template (*.xlt) from the Save As Type box, the Templates folder is displayed automatically in the Save In drop-down list box.

5. In the File Name text box, type the template name. In Figure 5.5, Quarterly Expense Report has been entered as the template name.

6. Double-click the Spreadsheet Solutions folder or create a new folder in which to store your custom template. In Figure 5.5, a folder called Custom Books has been created to store the template file.

  To create a new folder in the Save As dialog box, use the Create New Folder button from the dialog box toolbar.

7. Choose Save.

8. Close the template file.

After a template has been created, you can create new files based on the template or you can open the template to make any adjustments to the template file. See the section "Using Templates," later in this chapter for information on accessing and using your template files.

Creating Your Own Worksheet Templates

In some situations, you may need to insert a single custom worksheet into an existing Excel workbook. To create a worksheet template, follow these steps:

1. Create a new workbook that contains only one worksheet. See "Inserting and Deleting Worksheets" in Chapter 2 to learn more about deleting extra worksheets. Include the text, formatting, and formulas you want to appear on the worksheet.

2. To preview the template in the New dialog box, choose File, Properties. From the Summary tab, select the Save Preview Picture check box. Choose OK.

3. Choose File, Save As. The Save As dialog box appears.

4. In the Save As Type box, choose Template (*.xlt).

5. In the File Name text box, type the template name.

6. For the template to appear in the New dialog box along with the other template files, you have to save it in the Templates folder:

   Program Files\Microsoft Office\Templates

When you select Template (*.xlt) from the Save As Type box in step 4, the display should change to show the Templates folder in the Save In drop-down list box. If it does not, choose the drop-down list box and select the Templates folder by using the path explained above.

Worksheet templates can be stored directly in the Templates folder or in folders inside the Templates folder. The Spreadsheet Solutions folder or a new folder you create inside the Templates folder are ideal for storing your custom templates.

7. Choose Save.

8. Close the template file.

If you use a wide variety of common worksheets in your workbooks, you can create additional custom worksheet templates. Additionally, to change the default worksheet that is inserted with the Insert, Worksheet command, you can create a default worksheet template. The next section, "Creating Autotemplates," provides specific steps for creating a default worksheet template.

After you create a template file, you can create new files based on the new template. If adjustments need to be made to the template, you can open the file to make changes. See the section "Using Templates," later in this chapter, for information on accessing and using your template files.

Creating Autotemplates

 A workbook *autotemplate* is a default template that is used to control the look and content of all new workbooks. Whether you use the File, New command or the New button on the Standard toolbar to create a new file, the workbook autotemplate is used as the basis for the new file.

Autotemplates are most often used to change Excel's default font, formatting, header and footer print options, or other workbook attributes.

Creating a workbook autotemplate is identical to creating an ordinary template, with two exceptions—the autotemplate is saved in the XLStart folder and must be named **Book**.

Although the autotemplate is applied to each new workbook created, any new worksheets added to a workbook will not have any of the formats or content applied to the workbook autotemplate. This can be remedied by creating a worksheet autotemplate. Like the workbook autotemplate, the *worksheet autotemplate* controls the look and content of all new inserted worksheets. The worksheet autotemplate is saved in the XLStart folder and must be named **Sheet**.

To create a workbook or worksheet autotemplate, follow these steps:

1. Begin a new workbook. Apply any formatting or settings you require. For a worksheet template, remove all but one sheet from the workbook.

2. Choose File, Save As. The Save As dialog box appears. To save the workbook as a template file, it is easiest to begin at the bottom of the dialog box and work your way up.

3. Choose Template (*.xlt) in the Save As Type text box. The Templates folder is displayed automatically in the Save In drop-down list box.

4. For a workbook autotemplate, type **Book** in the File Name text box. For a worksheet autotemplate, type **Sheet** in the File Name text box.

5. Select the Save In drop-down list box and change the folder to XLStart, using the following path:

> Program Files\Microsoft Office\Office\XLStart

6. Choose Save.

7. Close the template file.

Using Templates

After you have created and saved a template file, you can create new workbooks based on the template or you can open the template to make any adjustments to the template file.

To create a new workbook based on a template, choose File, New and select a template from one of the tabs in the New dialog box.

N O T E You cannot use the New Workbook button on the Standard toolbar to access your list of template files. This button creates a new workbook based on the default template. See the previous section, "Creating Autotemplates," for information on customizing the default template. ▪

When you create a new file based on a template, a copy of the template appears—not the original template. As a placeholder name for the new file, the template name, with a sequential number, appears in the Title Bar.

To insert a new worksheet based on a worksheet template file, follow these steps:

1. Right-click the worksheet tab where you want to insert the new worksheet. The shortcut menu appears.

2. Choose Insert to display the list of templates.

3. Select the worksheet template you want to insert.

4. Choose OK.

N O T E You cannot use the Insert, Worksheet command to insert a worksheet template. The Insert, Worksheet command inserts a new worksheet based on the default worksheet template. See the previous section, "Creating Autotemplates," for information on customizing the default template. ▪

Modifying a template file is identical to modifying any other file. Choose File, Open to open a template file.

To restore the original settings for new workbooks and worksheets, simply remove the Book.xlt and Sheet.xlt files you added to the XLStart folder.

T I P   To share your template files with other users over a network, see the section "Sharing Your Workbooks with Other Users" in Chapter 18.

Using the Template Wizard with Data Tracking

The Template Wizard with Data Tracking is an add-in feature in Excel. The Template Wizard will link cells in the template to fields in a database. This is particularly useful with templates that are input forms. When the form is filled in, a corresponding record is created in a database. The information in the database then can be manipulated by using the features of the database.

For example, suppose you want to track the hours that employees worked each week on client projects. You would design a work log form on a worksheet and use the Template Wizard to create the template and links to a database. When the employee completes the work-log form, the copy of the form can be saved or printed. The completed work-log data is copied to the corresponding data fields as a new record in the database.

Additionally, you can use this feature with multiple sites that are connected by a network, where the form is linked to a central database. Store the template on a shared network drive to make it available to all users. You will need to create a shortcut to the template and make sure the shortcut is copied to the Templates folder on each user's desktop. The path to the Templates folder is:

Program Files\Microsoft Office\Templates

The database can be a list in Excel or a database in Access, FoxPro, dBASE, or Paradox.

To create a form template that copies worksheet data to a database, follow these steps:

1. Create a new workbook or open an existing workbook that contains the data you want to copy to a database.

2. Make sure each cell of data that you want to appear in the database has a corresponding label. The labels in the form are used as field names in the database. The labels must appear above or to the left of the cell containing the data.

    If you already have saved a form as a workbook template, create a new workbook from the template. Save the file as a workbook, with a new name. Do not save the file as a template.

3. Choose Data, Template Wizard.

N O T E   If the Template Wizard command is not on the Data menu, you need to install the Template Wizard with the Data Tracking add-in. Choose Tools, Add-Ins to access the Excel add-in features.

4. The Template Wizard contains five steps, with explanations to guide you through the wizard (see Figure 5.6). Follow these steps to create the data-tracking links.

FIG. 5.6

The Template Wizard is used to link cells in a worksheet to fields in a database.

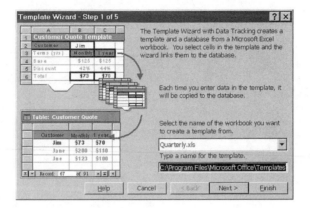

To change the data in the database record, you can reopen and edit the saved copy of the form associated with that record. If you delete the copy of the form, the corresponding record is retained in the database. If the database is not in Excel, you must use the program the database is in to delete the record. You can delete the database record as you would any other record in the database.

Modifying Templates

Periodically, you may want to revise your template files. Editing a template file is identical to the way in which you edit other workbooks. To modify a template, follow these steps:

1. Choose File, Open or click the Open button on the Standard toolbar. The Open dialog box appears.

2. In the Look In list box, find and select the folder that contains the template you want to modify.

3. Double-click the template icon, or select the template and choose Open.

4. Make the necessary modifications.

5. To update the template file, choose File, Save or click the Save button on the Standard toolbar.

The change you make affects only new workbooks or worksheets that you have created; it does not change any existing files based on the template. ●

Part

I

Ch

5

The Visual Impact of Excel

Creating Charts

Charts are visual representations of the data in a worksheet. There are numerous predesigned chart formats available in Excel. You can use these formats as a starting point for your own charts and further customize them for your particular needs.

Charts can be placed next to the spreadsheet data used to create the chart; these are referred to as *embedded charts*. Charts can reside on their own tab in a workbook; these are known as *chart sheets*.

These two methods for creating charts are presented later in this chapter. However, before you create charts in Excel, it is important that you become familiar with chart terminology and the various chart types you can create. ◼

Exploring chart types and terminology

Learn the terms Excel uses to describe the different parts of a chart and the various types of charts available in Excel.

Creating a chart with one keystroke

Use a keyboard shortcut to create a simple chart quickly.

Creating a chart using the Chart Wizard

The Chart Wizard leads you step-by-step through the process of creating charts.

Printing charts

An embedded chart can be printed with or without the worksheet data. Chart sheets are always printed separately from the worksheet data.

Using Charts

Where you place a chart depends on how you intend to use the chart:

■ *Embedded Charts.* These charts are beneficial when you want to see the data and the chart side by side—for example, in a report. Generally, when you want to print or show the data and the chart together, you use an embedded chart. You can, however, print an embedded chart without the worksheet.

■ *Chart Sheets.* Use these charts when you don't want to see the chart next to the data. For example, you may want to have the chart appear in a workbook that resides on a network, so that it is available for all employees to see, but you might not want the worksheet data that generated the chart to be accessible to everyone.

Regardless of whether you create an embedded chart or a chart sheet, the chart is linked to the worksheet data. If the data changes, the chart is updated automatically.

Charts can be created in several ways, using a keyboard shortcut or using a wizard. The quickest is with the keyboard shortcut. This method always produces a chart sheet; the chart is automatically created using the default type. The default type is a 2-D column chart. Changing the default chart type is discussed in Chapter 7, "Modifying Your Charts."

Another method to create a chart is to use Excel's Chart Wizard. Both embedded charts and chart sheets can be created easily with this step-by-step wizard. Using the Chart Wizard enables you to tailor the chart as you build it.

Defining Chart Terms

Each chart in Excel is made up of a series of *chart objects*. Knowing the correct names for these objects makes it easier to create and customize charts. To help identify the chart objects, Excel displays a tip when you point to an object with the mouse. Figure 6.1 illustrates the most common chart objects. Table 6.1 provides descriptions for Excel chart objects.

Table 6.1   Excel Chart Objects

Chart Object	Description
Arrow	A graphic object created with the arrow button on the Drawing Toolbar. An arrow has been added in Figure 6.1 to point from the text box to the 1998 bar for Puerto Rico.
Category Axis	Axis that plots labels from the worksheet. In Figure 6.1, the country names are displayed along the category axis. Typically, the category axis is horizontal. Examples of common category labels include: January, February, …Quarter 1, Quarter 2, …1997, 1998.
Data Label	Usually added to the chart to display the specific value of a data point.

Chart Object	Description
Data Point	A single piece of data within a series, corresponding to a single cell on a worksheet. 1998 sales in the United States is a data point in the 1998 series in Figure 6.1.
Data Series	A row or column of worksheet data. The names of each data series display in the legend. In Figure 6.1, there are two data series, 1997 and 1998.
Data Table	A grid attached to the category axis that displays the specific values being plotted in the chart.
Gridlines	Lines that extend from the tick marks. While gridlines can be added to either axis, they typically are used on the value axis to identify the value of data points.
Plot Area	The rectangular area inside the axes.
Legend	A guide that identifies the different data series. The name of each data series and a colored marker help locate the series in the chart. Although the legend appears by default on the right side of the plot area, it can be moved anywhere in the chart.
Scale	The numeric increments marked on the value axis. The low end of the scale typically is zero. The high end of the scale is higher than the largest number being plotted.
Selection Handles	When you click a chart object, a series of square "dots" appears indicating the object is selected. An object must be selected to modify or move it. In Figure 6.1 the legend is selected.
Text Box	Independent or unattached text you can add to the chart. As with titles, you can move and format independent text. In Figure 6.1, independent text has been added to highlight the change in sales in Puerto Rico.
Tick Marks	Small lines intersecting the category and value axes.
Tip	A form of on-screen help used to identify the chart objects.
Titles	There are 3 titles available in Excel charts: Chart Title, Value Axis Title, and Category Axis Title. The Chart Title typically appears at the top of the chart, outside the plot area, and is used to describe the data being displayed in the chart. In Figure 6.1, the chart title is "Rare Book Republishers Sales." The Value Axis Title describes the type of values being plotted along the value axis. The Category Axis Title is used to describe further the categories displayed on the category axis.
	You can reposition and format titles. To create a new line in a title, press the Enter key.

Part
II

Ch
6

continues

Table 6.1 Continued

Chart Object	Description
Value Axis	The axis that plots data values from the worksheet. In Figure 6.1, the sales figures are displayed along the value axis. Typically, the value axis is vertical. In addition to currency, quantity and temperature can be plotted on the value axis.

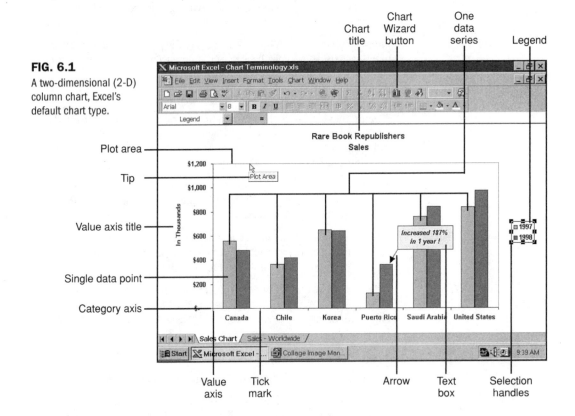

FIG. 6.1

A two-dimensional (2-D) column chart, Excel's default chart type.

The number of rows and columns of data you select dictates how Excel charts the data. If the number of columns is greater or equal to the number of rows, then Excel plots the data in the rows. The column headings are used along the category axis and the row headings become the legend labels. If the number of rows is greater than the number of columns, then Excel plots the data in the columns. The row headings are used along the category axis and the column headings become the legend labels.

As mentioned previously, the chart is linked to the worksheet data. If the data changes, the chart is updated automatically. This link is a formula, called the *series formula*, which indicates the cell references in the worksheet that are being plotted. When you click a series in a chart, the formula bar displays the formula for that series. Charts can be linked to multiple worksheets.

▶ **See** "Linking Worksheets," **p. 78**

After a chart has been created, you can use the Chart menu and Chart toolbar to modify the chart. Customizing charts is discussed in Chapter 7 "Modifying Your Charts."

Understanding Chart Types

There are 14 standard chart types available in Excel. Many of the chart types have variations, or subtypes. Common variations include stacked charts, exploded charts, and 100% charts. *Stacked charts* are used to display cumulative information (totals). *Exploded charts* are used to display one data point separate from the other data points and are common among pie and doughnut charts. *100% charts* are used to display what percentage each data point constitutes all data points in that category.

Some charts types are two-dimensional (2-D) and some are three-dimensional (3-D). The default chart type is a 2-D Column chart (see the left side of Figure 6.2). Three-dimensional variations are available with many chart types.

FIG. 6.2
A 2-D Column chart appears on the left; a 2-D Bar chart appears on the right.

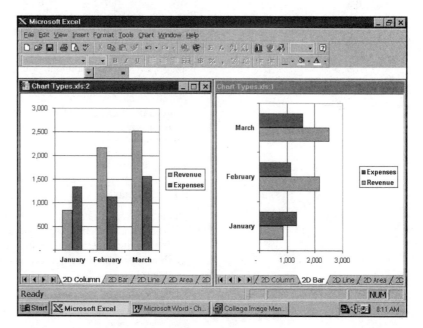

Part
II

Ch
6

The chart types available in Excel are outlined in Table 6.2.

Table 6.2   The Standard Chart Types in Excel

Chart Type	Dimension	Description
Column	2-D, 3-D	Displays vertical bars. The most common chart type and the default chart type in Excel. Variations include: stacked, 100%, 3-D. See the left side of Figure 6.2.
Bar	2-D, 3-D	Displays horizontal bars. Useful when comparing items in a single timeframe or when the category labels are very long. Variations include: stacked, 100%, 3-D. See the right side of Figure 6.2.
Cone, Cylinder, Pyramids	3-D	Attractive 3-D variations of column and bar charts.
Line	2-D, 3-D	Displays data point markers connected by lines. Useful for displaying many data points and trends or changes over time. Variations include: stacked, 100%, 3-D. See the left side of Figure 6.3.
Area	2-D, 3-D	Similar to line charts, with the area underneath the line filled in. Useful for displaying many data points. Variations include: stacked, 100%, 3-D. See the right side of Figure 6.3.
Pie	2-D, 3-D	Displays only one series or category of data. Used to display what percent each data point constitutes of all data points. Variations include: 3-D, exploded, pie of pie, and bar of pie. pie of pie and bar of pie are used to further break out specific components of a wedge of the original pie. The components are displayed as another pie or as a bar. See the left side of Figure 6.4.
Doughnut	2-D	Similar to a pie chart. Displays percentage of the whole, but with multiple series. Displays data in rings. Variations include: exploded. See the right side of Figure 6.4.
XY (Scatter)	2-D	Displays markers for each data point. Used to show clutters of data points. Frequently used to plot scientific data. Variations include: data points only, data points with smooth connecting lines, and data points with straight connecting lines.
Bubble	2-D	A type of scatter chart that displays markers for each data point. The bigger the bubble, the higher the value. Variations include: 3-D.
Stock	2-D	Used primarily for stock prices. Can also be used for weather (high/low/current). Requires data values in a set order. Variations include: high/low/close, open/high/low/close, volume/high/low/close, and volume/open/high/low/close.

Chart Type	Dimension	Description
Surface	3-D	Typically used for topographical maps, such as geographical elevations. Variations include: contour (side view).
Radar	2-D	Value axis radiates from the center. Lines connect all data points in the same series. Variations include: filled.

FIG. 6.3

A 2-D Line chart appears on the left; a 2-D Area chart appears on the right.

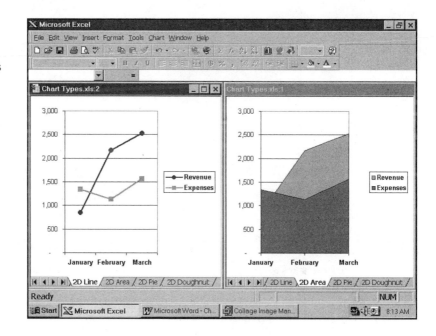

In addition to the 14 standard chart types, there are 20 custom chart types that you can use. You will find special types like *combination charts* and *logarithmic charts* under the custom types. Additionally, some of the standard chart types have been modified to display colorful backgrounds, shading, and other formatting options used to enhance the appearance of the charts.

Part
II

Ch
6

 Excel provides a number of good chart examples through the built-in help screens:

- *Office Assistant.* Type **chart examples** in the Office Assistant search box. Choose **Examples of chart types**.
- *Help Menu.* Choose **H**elp, **C**ontents and Index. On the Index tab, type **examples**. Double-click **charts**.

FIG. 6.4
A 2-D Pie chart appears on the left; a 2-D Doughnut chart appears on the right.

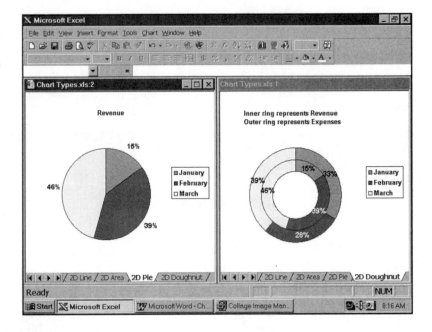

Using a Keyboard Shortcut to Create Charts Quickly

There are two ways to create charts quickly in Excel. The absolute quickest way is to use the keyboard shortcut, F11. The other way is with the Chart Wizard, by accepting all the default settings. Both methods produce a chart that uses the default chart type, a 2-D column chart. The keyboard method creates a chart sheet. The wizard method creates an embedded chart.

Remember—if the number of columns selected is greater than or equal to the number of rows, then Excel plots the data in the rows. The column headings are used along the category axis and the row headings become the legend labels. If the number of rows selected is greater than the number of columns, then Excel plots the data in the columns. The row headings are used along the category axis and the column headings become the legend labels.

After a chart is created, the Chart menu and Chart Toolbar can be used to customize the chart.

▶ **See** "Introducing the Chart Toolbar," **p. 118** "Changing the Chart Type," **p. 119**

▶ **See** "Setting a Default Chart Type," **p. 121**

TIP When selecting cells to build a chart, keep the following tips in mind: Make sure you include the labels in your selection. If your column headings appear in row 4 and your row headings appear in column A, begin your selection in cell A4. This will ensure that all your labels will be included in the chart. If there is a label in cell A4, Excel generally will not include it in the chart.

Make sure there aren't any blank rows or columns in your data. For example, if you have a blank row between your column headings and your data, Excel will ignore it. However, if there is a blank row between the data you want to chart, do not include that row in your selection. Otherwise, Excel includes the blank row in the chart, distorting the chart display. To skip an empty row in your selection, select the first group of cells, then Ctrl and drag to select each additional group of cells. In Figure 6.5, cells A4 to D7 and A10 to D13 are selected.

FIG. 6.5

Use the Ctrl key to select nonadjacent cells to chart.

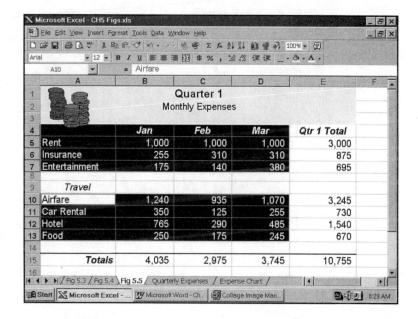

To create a chart sheet, follow these steps:

1. Select the cells containing the data to be charted. Make sure you include the labels in your selection. Do not include blank rows or columns in your selection.

2. Press F11. A 2-D column chart is created automatically as a chart sheet (see Figure 6.6).

3. Modify the chart as needed.

To create an embedded chart, follow these steps:

1. Select the cells containing the data to be charted. Be sure to include the row and column headings if you want them to appear in the chart as category and legend labels.

 2. Click the Chart Wizard button on the Standard toolbar. The Chart Wizard dialog box appears (see Figure 6.7).

3. Choose Finish. A 2-D column chart is created automatically as an embedded chart.

4. Modify the chart as needed.

If you would like to make formatting selections as you are creating the chart, such as choosing the chart type or adding titles, the next section describes how to use the Chart Wizard step-by-step.

Part

II

Ch

6

FIG. 6.6

This figure illustrates a chart sheet created by using the F11 key.

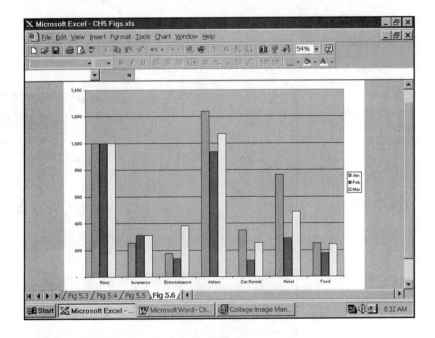

FIG. 6.7

Step 1 of 4 of the Chart Wizard dialog box. Choose Finish to accept all the default settings.

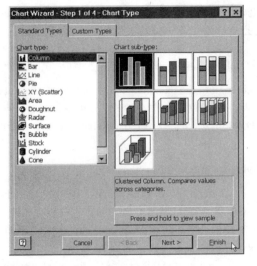

Using the Chart Wizard to Create Charts

The Chart Wizard takes the guesswork out of creating dynamic, professional-looking charts. As you build the chart, the Wizard displays a sample of the chart so that you can see the impact of the choices you make immediately. If you don't like what you see, change it! You can create either embedded charts or chart sheets by using the wizard.

If you need to create a chart from data that is not in adjacent rows or columns, select the first set of rows and columns that include the labels you want to use in the chart. Select additional ranges by holding down the Ctrl key and dragging with the mouse.

If data exists in the worksheet that you do not want to include in a chart, you can hide the rows or columns that contain the data. Select the row or column that you want to hide and use the Format menu to hide the rows or columns.

If the data is formatted in an outline, collapse levels in the outline that you do not want to appear in the chart.

▶ **See** "Outlining Worksheets," **p. 49**

▶ **See** "Creating Charts from Outlined Worksheets," **p. 146**

Using the Chart Wizard is a four-step process:

1. Select the cells containing the data to be charted. Be sure to include the row and column headings if you want them to appear in the chart as category and legend labels. Do not include blank rows in your selection.

 2. Choose the Chart Wizard button on the Standard toolbar. The Chart Wizard dialog box appears.

3. In Step 1 of 4, choose a Chart type. Select from either the Standard Types or Custom Types (see Figure 6.8). If necessary, choose a variation. Preview and choose Next.

FIG. 6.8
Step 1 of the Chart Wizard.

4. In Step 2 of 4, verify the source of the chart data. If you have selected the incorrect cells, use the Collapse Dialog button (see Figure 6.9) to hide the dialog box temporarily so that you can see the worksheet and can select the new data range. Choose to plot the data series by rows or columns.

On the Series tab, you can add or delete plotted series. Verify the sample of your chart and choose Next.

FIG. 6.9

This figure illustrates Step 2 of the Chart Wizard.

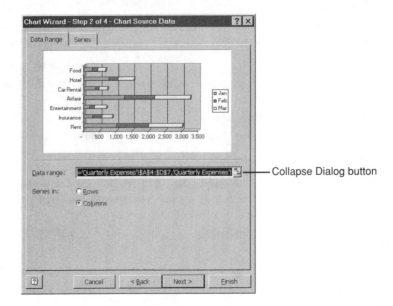

Collapse Dialog button

5. In Step 3 of 4, choose the chart options you would like to apply to the chart. The options include: Titles, Axes, Gridlines, Legend, Data Labels, and Data Table (see Figure 6.10). Refer back to the section "Defining Chart Terms," earlier in this chapter, for more information on these options. Verify the sample of your chart and choose Next.

FIG. 6.10

Step 3 of the Chart Wizard.

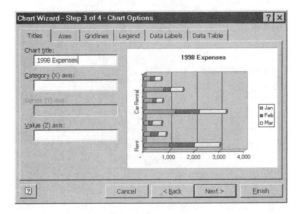

6. In Step 4 of 4, determine where the chart will be placed (see Figure 6.11). Choose As New Sheet to create a chart sheet, or choose As Object in to create an embedded chart. The embedded chart can be placed on any sheet in the active workbook.

The Back button will take you back through the Chart Wizard steps if you want to make other selections.

FIG. 6.11
Step 4 of the Chart Wizard.

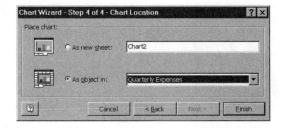

7. Choose Finish to finalize the creation of your chart.

Should you need some additional explanation while working with the Chart Wizard, the Office Assistant button is available during each step of the wizard.

Saving Charts

When you create an embedded chart or a chart sheet in a workbook, the charts are part of the workbook. When the workbook is saved, the charts are saved.

 To save a workbook, select the Save button on the Standard toolbar.

Printing Charts

 The steps you take to print a chart are similar to those that you use to print a worksheet. It is a good idea to preview the chart before you print. To preview a chart, choose the Preview button from the Standard toolbar.

If a chart is embedded in a worksheet, it prints as part of the worksheet by default (see Figure 6.12).

Because the chart is embedded in the worksheet, the Setup options are unchanged. The chart is treated as an object in the worksheet.

▶ **See** "Printing Worksheets," **p. 30**

To print an embedded chart separately from the worksheet, the chart must first be selected. When you preview, only the chart will be displayed in the preview screen. If you plan to print the embedded chart without the worksheet data, or are printing a chart sheet, the Page Setup dialog box is somewhat altered (see Figure 6.13).

In place of the Sheet tab in the Setup dialog box, there is a Chart tab. This provides several choices for printing the chart. You can choose to use the full page, or scale it to fit the page. Use Full Page expands the chart until the margins in all directions are reached. This may distort your chart. Scale to Fit Page expands the chart proportionally.

Part
II

Ch
6

FIG. 6.12

A preview of a worksheet with an embedded chart.

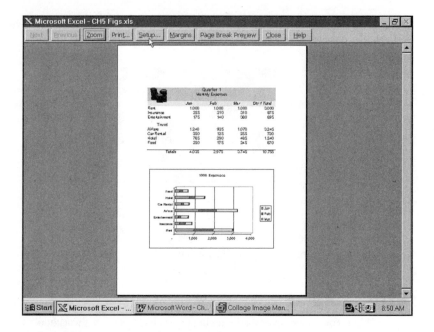

FIG. 6.13

The Page Setup dialog box printing chart sheets or embedded charts without the worksheet data.

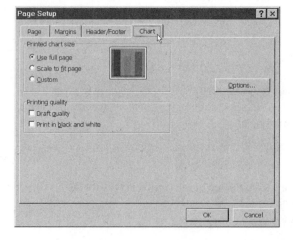

N O T E This chapter covers the basics of charting in Excel. You now are acquainted with chart terminology, chart types, and several methods to create charts. Chapters 7 and 8 provide additional information on Excel charts.

CHAPTER 7

Modifying Your Charts

Chapter 6 discussed charting terms, chart types, and several methods for creating charts. Now it's time to learn how to tailor those charts to fit your needs. You will find that it is just as easy to modify charts as it is to create them because Excel provides a number of convenient tools to help you.

When customizing Excel charts, you can modify the chart objects or add drawn objects to the chart. Objects that are components of a chart are known as *chart objects*. This includes the legend, titles, and trendlines. Objects that are added using the Drawing toolbar are referred to as *drawn objects*. This includes arrows, independent text boxes, shapes, and WordArt. Both types of objects can be added and modified in your charts.

You have the option of either modifying your entire chart or just specific parts of the chart. If you're going to completely redesign the chart, the best procedure is to select the chart and then click the Chart Wizard button. The choices that are available when you create a chart are also available when you modify a chart: you can choose a new chart type, the cells in which the data is to be plotted, the chart options—such as titles, gridlines, and data labels— and the location in which the revised chart will appear. But this only touches the surface of the numerous ways you can customize your charts. ■

Use toolbars to modify charts

The Chart, Drawing, and Formatting toolbars provide quick access to customizing options.

Change chart types

It's important to select the best chart type to display your data. Choose from more than 14 standard and 20 custom chart types. Standard types include column, bar, and pie charts. Excel has added several new types—bubble, cone, cylinder, and pyramid. You can also establish a default chart type.

Format objects

The objects you select to display with your chart can really enhance the chart's appearance. Show the precise numbers that were used to plot the data series by displaying data labels or a data table in your chart. Add text boxes to annotate your chart.

Enhance the appearance of your charts

Really make your charts stand out with the dynamic, eye-catching formatting options available in Excel. Choose from gradient (graduated) fill colors, textures, patterns, and pictures.

Introducing the Chart Toolbar

The Chart toolbar provides a fast way to select and format the chart objects that you want to change. Figure 7.1 shows a worksheet, the embedded chart created from the worksheet data, and the Chart toolbar. Each tool on the Chart toolbar is identified.

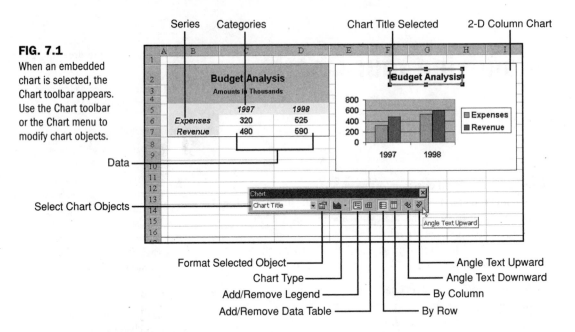

FIG. 7.1

When an embedded chart is selected, the Chart toolbar appears. Use the Chart toolbar or the Chart menu to modify chart objects.

To display the Chart toolbar, follow these steps:

1. Right-click the menu bar or any toolbar. Toolbars currently being displayed will have a check mark in front of the toolbar name.

2. Choose Chart from the list of toolbars. By default, the Chart toolbar displays "floating" on your screen.

3. Double-click the toolbar name in the colored title bar to "dock" the toolbar under the other toolbars already displayed on-screen.

The toolbar remains on-screen until you remove it. Right-click the menu bar or any toolbar and select the name of the toolbar you want to hide. When displayed again, the toolbar will appear in the same position it was before it was hidden.

The By Row and By Column buttons provide a great illustration of how the Chart toolbar can be used to change your chart quickly. Figure 7.2 displays two versions of the same data. In the chart on the left, the data is plotted by rows. In the chart on the right, the data is plotted by columns.

FIG. 7.2
The resulting charts
show the same data in
very different ways.

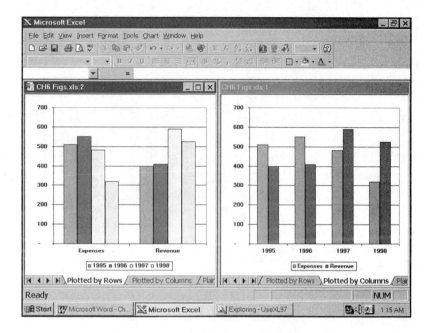

The chart on the left in Figure 7.2 is convenient for comparing the trend in Expenses and the trend in Revenue. The chart on the right shows how the Expenses compare to the Revenue each year.

Changing the Chart Type

Choosing the best chart type is critical to illustrating your worksheet data. The people reading the chart need to be able to decipher rapidly what the chart represents. The column chart, by far, is the easiest chart for people to read, which is why it is the default chart type. However, depending on what you are plotting, another chart type might be more appropriate. In Figure 7.3, the 1996 and 1997 sales figures for 18 states in the western United States have been plotted using a 2-D column chart.

Even a shorter list of categories, such as months, sometimes can be difficult to read on a column or bar chart. This is especially true when several years' worth of data is being plotted.

When you have a large number of items to plot, try a column or bar chart first. If the chart looks overly cluttered, like the one in Figure 7.3, switch to a line or area chart like Figure 7.4. It will be much easier for people to interpret. In Figure 7.4, the same worksheet data is plotted using a 2-D line chart.

Part

II

Ch

7

FIG. 7.3

This 2-D column chart depicts many items on one chart, creating a somewhat cluttered appearance.

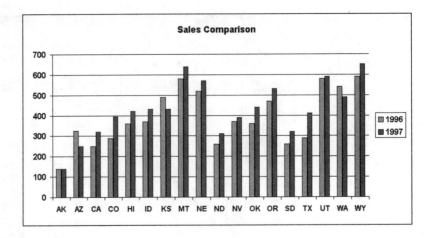

FIG. 7.4

A line or area chart is a good choice when you are plotting more than 6 to 8 categories or series.

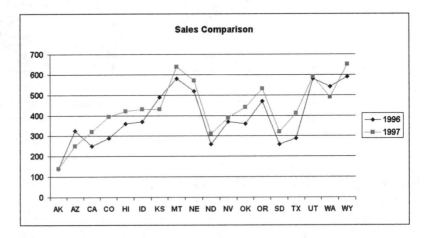

TIP When there are a lot of category labels in a column chart, Excel automatically displays the labels at an angle or skips every other category label. Try using a bar chart instead. You also can try reducing the font size of the category axis labels, or abbreviating the labels in the worksheet.

To change the chart type, follow these steps:

1. If you are changing an embedded chart, click the chart to select it. If you are changing a chart sheet, make it the active sheet.

2. Right-click a blank area of the chart, away from the chart objects. From the shortcut menu, choose Chart Type. The Chart Type dialog box appears.

3. Select either a Standard or Custom chart type. Use the Press and Hold To View Sample button in the Chart Type dialog box to see a preview of your selection.

4. Click OK.

You can also use the Chart Type button on the Chart toolbar to change the chart type; however, the choices there are limited. You will not see most of the chart subtypes or custom chart types that are available in the Chart Type dialog box.

▶ **See** "Understanding Chart Types," **p. 107**

Setting a Default Chart Type

If you find that you are creating a specific type of chart on a regular basis, you can use one of the charts you have already created as the default chart type. This is especially useful if you have specific chart options or formatting that you want to appear by default.

To change the default chart type, follow these steps:

1. Display the chart that you want to use as a sample for the default chart type. If the chart is an embedded chart, click the chart to select it. If the chart is on a chart sheet, make it the active sheet.

2. Right-click a blank area of the chart, away from the chart objects. From the shortcut menu, choose Chart Type. The Chart Type dialog box appears. Select the Custom Types tab, which is located at the top and center of Figure 7.5, next to the Standard Types tab.

3. Click the Set As Default Chart button. A message appears confirming that you want to change the default chart type. Choose Yes. The Add Custom Chart Type dialog box may appear. If it does, enter a name and description for your new default chart. Choose OK to accept the name and description.

4. Choose OK to complete the default chart type change.

FIG. 7.5

Use the Chart Type dialog box to change the default chart type.

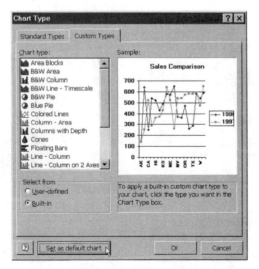

Part

II

Ch

7

The Custom Types tab lists the built-in custom chart types. If you select the User-defined button, the list changes to display the default chart type and any custom chart types you have added. Displaying the User-defined list is not a requirement for changing the default chart type, but you can use it to verify the change.

Adding or Removing Data from Your Charts

There are several methods you can use to add data to an existing chart. The Add Data command is convenient when you want to include another row or column of data from your worksheet. The Source Data command should be used when you need to add and remove data at the same time or when you want to refer to a completely different set of data for the entire chart.

You can use your mouse to drag and drop data from your worksheet into an embedded chart. This method is convenient only if the chart and data are both visible. If you have to scroll or zoom out to see the data and the chart, it is probably easier to use the Add Data command.

The Source Data command is the best way to remove data from a chart.

N O T E If the data you want to add is in another workbook, that workbook must be open to add the data. ■

To use the Add Data command, follow these steps:

1. If you are adding data to an embedded chart, select the chart. If you are adding data to a chart sheet, make it the active sheet. In Figure 7.6, the 1998 data is going to be added to the chart.

FIG. 7.6

The embedded Book Sales chart reflects the figures only for 1996 and 1997, but the 1998 figures are about to be added.

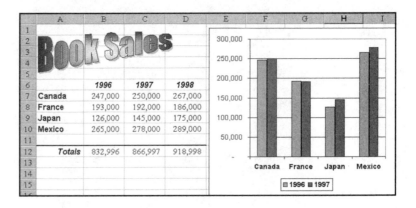

2. Choose Chart, Add Data. The Add Data dialog box appears (see Figure 7.7).

FIG. 7.7

The Collapse Dialog
Box button helps to
shrink the dialog box so
that you can see more
of your worksheet.

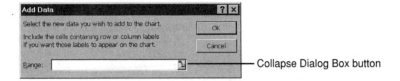

Collapse Dialog Box button

3. The <u>R</u>ange entry box is active. Select the data in the worksheet that you want to add to your chart; make sure you include the corresponding labels. If the data is on another worksheet, activate the worksheet and then select the data. In Figure 7.6, cells B6 to C10 were selected to create the chart. To add the 1998 column of data, cells D6 to D10 will be selected.

 TIP If the Add Data dialog box is covering up the data that you want to select, choose the Collapse Dialog Box button (refer to Figure 7.7). When you use the Collapse Dialog Box button, the dialog box shrinks, enabling you to see more of your worksheet. Click the button again to restore the dialog box. You also can move the dialog box out of your way by dragging the dialog box title bar.

4. After you've selected the additional data, confirm the cell references in the <u>R</u>ange entry box and choose OK. Your chart should be updated, as in Figure 7.8.

FIG. 7.8

The Book Sales chart
now includes the 1998
sales figures.

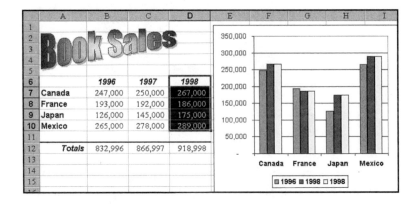

Use the <u>S</u>ource Data command to add or remove data from your chart. Follow these steps to access the <u>S</u>ource Data command:

1. If you are adding data to an embedded chart, select the chart. If you are adding data to a chart sheet, make it the active sheet.

2. Right-click a blank area of the chart, away from the chart objects. From the shortcut menu, choose <u>S</u>ource Data. The Source Data dialog box appears.

There are two methods of adding or removing data using the Source Data dialog box. Using the Data Range tab, you can select an entirely new set of data to plot. Using the Series tab, you can select individual series to add to or remove from your chart.

To select an entirely new set of data, follow these steps:

1. In the Data Range tab, click the Data Range entry box.

2. Select the cells in your worksheet containing the new data to be plotted; make sure that you include the corresponding labels. The worksheet name and cell references appear in the Data Range entry box. In Figure 7.9, ='Book Sales'!$A$6:$D$10 is displayed in the Data Range entry box. The chart will be plotted based on this new set of data.

FIG. 7.9
Use the Collapse Dialog Box button to minimize the Source Data dialog box while you select the cells in your worksheet.

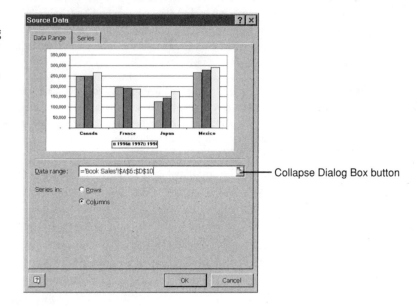

Collapse Dialog Box button

3. The sample chart above the Data Range entry box will revise to reflect the new data you selected.

4. Choose OK to confirm your change.

Figure 7.10 displays the Series tab of the Source Data dialog box. You can use this part of the Source Date dialog box to add or remove individual series of data from your chart.

To add a new series to a chart, follow these steps:

1. In the Series tab of the Source Data dialog box, click the Add button.

2. In the Series text box, a placeholder for the new series entitled Series# will be listed. In Figure 7.10, Series3 is the placeholder.

3. Use the Name and Values boxes, which appear to the right of the Series box in Figure 7.10, to identify the label and data for the new series. Click the Name box and choose the cell in your worksheet that contains the label you want to use for this series. The label will replace the placeholder in the Series text box.

FIG. 7.10

The Series tab in the Source Data dialog box controls the data plotted in your chart.

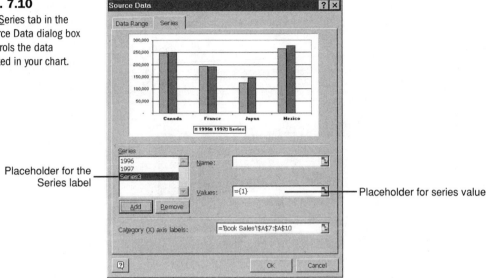

Placeholder for the Series label

Placeholder for series value

4. Use the Tab key to activate the Values box and select any data that appears there. Choose the cells in your worksheet that correspond to the data you want plotted for this series.

CAUTION

If you use the mouse to click the Values box, you will need to select (highlight) the entry in the box. By default, Excel uses a placeholder, typically ={1}, for the series data. If you do not select the placeholder, Excel will attempt to plot this entry along with the data you select in your worksheet. An error will result.

5. The sample chart at the top of the dialog box shows the revised chart.

6. Choose OK to confirm your change.

To remove a series from a chart, activate the Source Data dialog box. From the Series tab, click the name in the Series box that you want to remove and select the Remove button.

Working with the Chart Options

Chart Options are common chart objects that you elect to include or exclude from your chart. The Chart Options include: Titles, Axes, Gridlines, Legend, Data Labels, and Data Table. If you've used the Chart Wizard, the Chart Options are the same options available in the Step 3 of the Chart Wizard. Right-click a blank area of the chart, away from the chart objects. To modify these objects, choose Chart Options from the shortcut menu and you will see the

Part
II

Ch
7

dialog box shown in Figure 7.11. From the Titles tab of the dialog box, you can add a chart or axis title by entering it in the appropriate text box. Chart Title field has already been added in Figure 7.11.

FIG. 7.11

Chart titles and Value axis titles are the most common Chart Options.

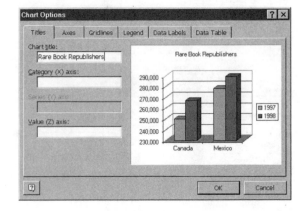

From the Axes tab, shown in Figure 6.12, you can add or remove axes from the display. In Figure 6.12, the value axis has been removed to show a general comparison.

FIG. 7.12

On the Axes tab, the value axis is being removed.

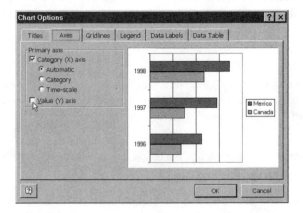

From the Gridlines tab (shown in Figure 6.13), you display or remove chart gridlines. Gridlines are helpful when trying to determine the value of a particular data point. The Value (Y) axis gridlines have been removed in Figure 6.13 because the value axis was removed and the gridlines are no longer required.

From the Legend tab, you can add, remove, or reposition the location of the legend by selecting one of the option buttons shown in Figure 7.14. In this figure, the legend has been moved to the bottom of the chart, providing more area to plot the chart. You can also reposition the legend by selecting and dragging it with your mouse.

FIG. 7.13
Gridlines may be removed via the Chart Options dialog box.

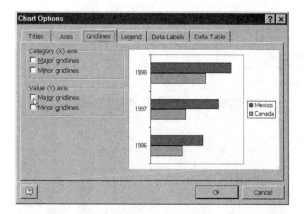

FIG. 7.14
The chart's size changes when the legend is moved to the bottom of the chart.

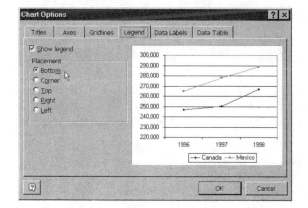

From the Data Labels tab, you can include the data values, percentages, or labels. With pie charts, you can also choose to display *leader lines*—lines that point from the data label to the specific piece of pie. In Figure 7.15, percent data labels have been added to the pie chart.

FIG. 7.15
Pie chart options are different than column, bar, and line type charts. The options vary depending on the chart type.

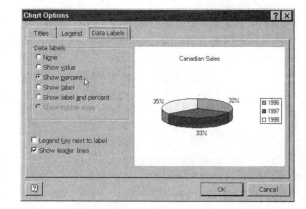

Part

II

Ch

7

From the Data Table tab (shown in Figure 7.16), you can include a table below your chart. The table combines the category axis and the legend to display the precise data being plotted. In Figure 7.16, Show Data Table option has been selected. Because the data table includes the legend information, whenever you add a data table to a chart, remove the legend.

FIG. 7.16

Data tables provide a great way to combine the worksheet data and the chart.

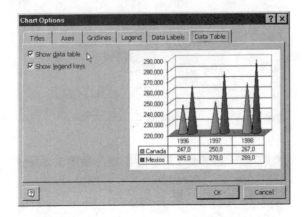

Chart options will vary depending on the chart type you use. Besides the chart options, you can add text and trendlines to your charts. Objects like arrows, ovals, and Word Art can be used to enhance your charts. The next few sections discuss these features.

Using the Drawing Toolbar

The Drawing toolbar contains several buttons to add objects to both charts and worksheets. The toolbar also includes buttons used to enhance the drawn objects. Figure 7.17 displays a few examples of drawn objects and identifies each tool on the Drawing toolbar.

To display the Drawing toolbar, follow these steps:

1. Click the Drawing button on the Standard toolbar. By default, the Drawing toolbar displays "floating" on your screen.

2. Double-click the toolbar name, in the colored title bar, to "dock" the toolbar below the other toolbars already displayed on-screen. If you have previously docked the toolbar, it will appear where you last docked it.

The toolbar remains on-screen until you remove it. Right-click the menu bar or any toolbar and select the name of the toolbar you want to hide. When displayed again, the toolbar will appear in the same position it was, before it was hidden.

The following is a list of drawing basics:

■ To draw an object, select the appropriate tool on the toolbar; the mouse pointer becomes a small thin plus sign. Drag the mouse from the place you want the object to begin and release the mouse where you want the object to end.

FIG. 7.17

The Drawing toolbar buttons can be used to enhance charts and worksheets.

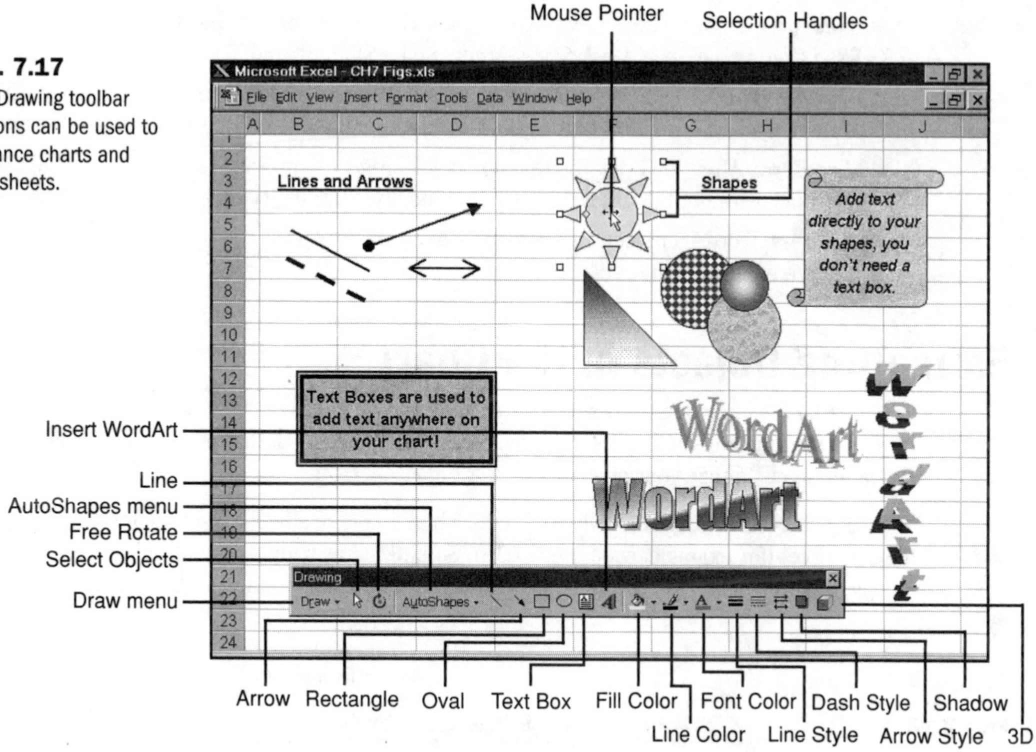

Mouse Pointer

Selection Handles

Lines and Arrows

Shapes

Add text directly to your shapes, you don't need a text box.

Text Boxes are used to add text anywhere on your chart!

Insert WordArt

Line

AutoShapes menu

Free Rotate

Select Objects

Draw menu

Arrow Rectangle Oval Text Box Fill Color Font Color Dash Style Shadow

Line Color Line Style Arrow Style 3D

> **TIP** Use the Shift key with the rectangle to draw a "perfect" square. Ovals become circles and lines are drawn straight when you use the Shift key. Use the Ctrl key to draw an object from the center outward. Shift+Ctrl draws "perfect" objects, from the center outward.

- To move an object, select the object. If the object is a shape, position the mouse pointer in the middle of the object. If the object is a line or arrow, position the mouse pointer on the middle of the line. If the object is a text box or a shape that contains text, position the mouse on the border. A four-headed arrow will be attached to the mouse pointer, as shown in Figure 7.17. Drag to move the object.

- To resize an object, select the object and position your mouse over one of the selection handles. The mouse pointer changes to a two-headed arrow. Drag to resize the object. To keep the object proportional, hold down the Shift key while dragging.

The following are specific points regarding each object:

- *AutoShapes.* A wide range of valuable objects are included in this list: Lines, Connectors, Basic Shapes, Block Arrows, Flowcharts, Stars and Banners, and Callouts. Many of these objects are *filled* objects—objects that have a color inside. You can enhance these objects by using the Fill Color, Line Color, Line Style, Dash Style, Shadow, and 3D buttons.

Part

II

Ch

7

- ■ *Lines and Arrows.* The arrow's head appears at the end of the object. Enhance with the Line Color, Line Style, Dash Style, Arrow Style, Shadow, and 3D buttons.
- ■ *Rectangles and Ovals.* Ovals and rectangles are considered *filled* objects. Enhance with the Fill Color, Line Color, Line Style, Dash Style, Shadow, and 3D buttons.
- ■ *Text Boxes.* After you draw the text box, a flashing prompt waits until you enter the text. Enhance with the Fill Color, Line Color, Line Style, Dash Style, Shadow, and 3D buttons.
- ■ *WordArt.* WordArt objects are best used as chart or worksheet titles. WordArt contains its own enhancements.

Formatting Objects in the Chart

Objects that are components of a chart are known as *chart objects*. Objects that were added by using the Drawing toolbar are referred to as *drawn objects*. Both types of objects can be formatted to customize your charts.

You can achieve some dynamic visual effects when you take advantage of the formatting options in Excel (for example, see Figure 7.18). Something as simple as using Fill Effects to change the area inside the columns completely alters the appearance of the chart.

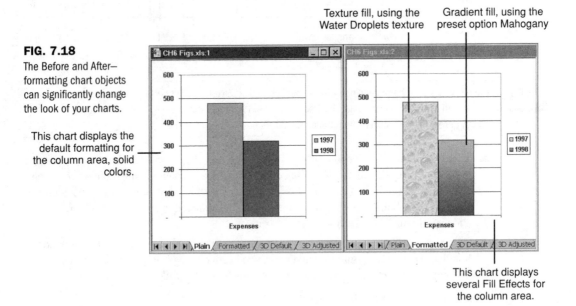

FIG. 7.18
The Before and After—formatting chart objects can significantly change the look of your charts.

This chart displays the default formatting for the column area, solid colors.

Texture fill, using the Water Droplets texture

Gradient fill, using the preset option Mahogany

This chart displays several Fill Effects for the column area.

The formatting options vary from chart object to chart object. Table 7.1 lists some of the most common formatting options.

Table 7.1   Formatting Options for Excel Chart Objects

Format Option	Choices
Pattern	Vary from object to object—includes border or axis color and line style; drop shadow; area fill color and fill effects; tick marks.
Axis	Add a secondary axis. Used primarily with Combination charts.
Y Error Bars	Display plus or minus error bars. Choose the error amount—include fixed values, percentages, standard deviations, standard errors, or custom amounts.
Data Labels	Display values, percentages, or labels next to a series.
Series Order	Rearrange the series order. Particularly useful with 3-D perspective charts when one series is hidden by another.
Options	Miscellaneous options that vary from object to object.
Scale	Used with the Value Axis. Select maximum number, major unit, and number where the category axis crosses the value axis (useful for threshold figures, minimum acceptable values). Includes an option for a logarithmic scale.
Font	Type, style, size, underline, color, background.
Number	Currency, percentages, fractions, and customized (zip codes, phone numbers, social security numbers).
Alignment	Text orientation allows the text to be angled from 90 degrees to –90 degrees, or displayed vertically.
Placement	Used with the Legend. Select an automatic placement for the legend—bottom, corner, top, right, left. You can also move the legend by dragging it with the mouse.

To change the format of a chart object, follow these steps:

1. Select the chart object.
2. Right-click the object to display the shortcut menu.
3. The first choice on the shortcut menu will be Format, followed by the name of the object—for example, Format Data Series.
4. Select the Format command; the Format dialog box appears.
5. Make the format changes you need, then select OK.

If you are having trouble selecting the object you want to modify, there are several buttons on the Chart toolbar that can help. Use the Chart Objects drop-down list button to select the object, and the Format Object button to modify the object.

 If you want to change the font type, size, or styles for all of the text in your chart, select the chart area and then use the buttons on the Formatting toolbar to change the text quickly.

There are several ways to change the appearance of a drawn object. You can right-click the object and choose Format AutoShape, or select the object and choose one of the formatting buttons on the Drawing toolbar.

As with the chart object, the options for formatting drawn objects vary. Table 7.2 lists some of the most common options.

Table 7.2 Formatting Options for Drawn Objects

Format Option	Choices
Colors and Lines	Line color and style; object fill color and fill effect; arrowhead styles.
Size	Height; width; rotation; scale.
Protection	All objects are locked by default. Used in conjunction with worksheet protection to avoid accidental movement or deletion of the object.
Properties	Move and size options as the surrounding worksheet cells are moved and sized.
Font	Type, style, size, underline, color, and background. Available with Text Boxes or shapes that have had text added to them.
Alignment	Horizontal and vertical alignment. Text orientation enables the text to be displayed sideways or vertically. Available with Text Boxes or shapes that have had text added to them.
Margins	Internal margins for text inside shapes or Text Boxes.

 If you want to add text to a shape, you do not have to add a text box on top of a shape. Simply select the shape and begin typing. The text you type will be attached to the shape. When the shape is moved, the text is moved with it. When the shape is resized, the text is adjusted but the font size does not change automatically.

Refer to the earlier section, "Using the Drawing Toolbar," for the steps on drawing and resizing objects.

Changing the Chart Location

Charts can be moved quite easily. Pick from the options below:

- *In the same sheet.* Click and drag to reposition the chart. If necessary, use the Zoom button to see a display of your worksheet.
- *Change to a chart sheet.* Right-click the chart and choose Location from the shortcut menu. Choose the As New Sheet option. You can name the new sheet in the text box, and then click OK.
- *Change to an embedded chart.* Right-click the chart and choose Location from the shortcut menu. Choose the As Object In option. Select the sheet name where you want the embedded chart to appear, and then click OK.
- *Move to a different sheet in a different workbook.* If the chart is an embedded chart, you can use the Edit, Cut and Edit, and Paste commands. If it is a chart sheet, you can drag and drop the sheet into the other book. In both cases, the other workbook must be open. With drag and drop use the Window, Arrange command to display the two workbooks side-by-side.

▶ **See** "Copying and Moving Sheets," **p. 33**

Adding Text

You can add two types of text to your charts. Text can be added in the form of chart and axes titles, or can appear as part of shapes that you draw or in text boxes. To add text to a chart, pick from the following options:

- *Titles.* Right-click the chart and choose Chart Options from the shortcut menu. On the Titles tab, click inside the title box and type the text and then select OK.
- *Drawn Shapes.* Select the shape and then type the text. The text will appear as you type. Press Enter for a new line. Press the Esc key or click away from the shape to accept the text.
- *Text Boxes.* Draw the text box by using the button on the Drawing toolbar. The flashing text cursor appears indicating that you are automatically in the "edit mode." Type the text and press Enter for a new line. Press the Esc key or click away from the text box to accept the text.

Use the buttons on the Formatting toolbar to enhance the text you have added.

Part
II

Ch
7

You also can add a text box without using the Drawing toolbar. First, make sure the chart is selected but that *none* of your titles are selected (otherwise the text you type will replace the title text!). Then just begin typing. The text will appear in the Formula Bar. When you press Enter or click the Enter button (green check), the text will appear in a text box in the middle of your chart. Reposition and format the text as needed.

Adding Trendlines

Trendlines are used to show trends within your series data or forecasts outside the existing series data. A prediction of what a series will do in the future, or what it did in the past, are two ways trendlines can be useful.

Trendlines can be created for specific 2-D charts: area, bar, column, line, stock, xy (scatter), and bubble. You cannot use stacked-type charts with trendlines.

To add trendlines, follow these steps:

1. Select the chart. Choose Chart, Add Trendline; the Add Trendline dialog box appears.

2. On the Type tab, choose one of the trendline types and the series for which the trendline will be drawn. The most commonly used type is Linear.

  To find out more about each type, use the "What's This" help button. Click the button and then click the type. A help screen describes the trend type and displays the equation used to predict the trend.

3. If you want to show a trend using the existing data, choose OK. If you want to forecast into the past or future, select the Options tab. Choose the direction and number of periods that you want the trend to forecast, and then click OK.

   Forecasting into the past is used when the data from previous months or years is unavailable and you want to plot a general trend of what probably happened in the past to reach the point you are at now.

Working with 3-D Charts

Three-dimensional charts are very popular, and with good reason. Generally, they look better than their two-dimensional counterparts. However, you may find it necessary to adjust the elevation, rotation, or perspective of the 3-D charts. To assist you with this, Excel provides the 3-D View command. Right-click on a blank area of the chart, away from the chart objects. From the shortcut menu, choose 3-D View. The 3-D View dialog box appears. In Figure 7.19, the dialog box shows only elevation and rotation options because the chart is a 3-D pie. When working with column or bar charts, the perspective option is available as well. Use the arrow buttons to change the dimensions of your chart. Figure 7.20 shows a pie chart, before and after the dimensional changes.

FIG. 7.19

The 3-D View dialog box provides a sample of your chart as you are adjusting the dimensions.

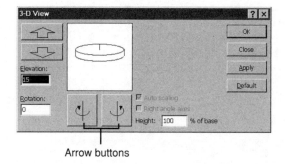

Arrow buttons

FIG. 7.20

Changing the 3-D View settings can really improve your chart's appearance.

3-D pie chart, with the default 3-D settings

3-D pie chart when the elevation and rotation have been adjusted

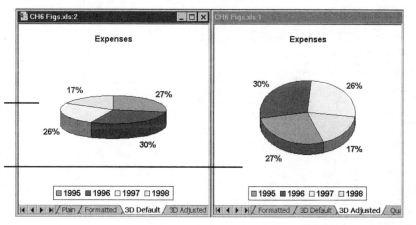

This chapter focuses on modifying your Excel charts. The next chapter, "Creating Complex Charts," takes this one step further to show you some complex chart modifications. You will learn to create combination charts, explode a slice of a pie chart to breakdown the components of that slice, create charts from a worksheet that has been outlined, and create charts that display pictures. ●

CHAPTER 8

Creating Complex Charts

While the chart formatting options discussed in the previous chapter illustrate some terrific ways to enhance your charts, there is so much more you can do with charting in Excel. This chapter focuses on some very specific features. ■

Combination charts

Create charts that can compare more than one type of data.

Handling data series

Learn how Excel uses data series to create powerful combination charts.

Pie charts

Learn to use the Bar in a Pie and Pie in a Pie variations of the pie chart.

Picture charts

Use pictures for data-point markers in Line charts or as the fill inside Bar and Column charts.

Charts from outlines

Create charts from outlined worksheets.

Creating Combination Charts

Combination charts compare more than one type of data, looking for possible interactions between the types of data. These charts can be used to display how close the actual results are to a goal or projection. Combination charts are often used to show (or not show) that a relationship exists between two types of data. For example, do people buy more of your product during the warmer months? If there is a relationship between sales and the weather? Should you increase your production in the warmer months? A combination chart can illustrate whether there is a correlation between these two different kinds of information.

Combination charts typically display the data using different chart types. There are four custom, predesigned combination chart types available for you to choose from, or you can create your own combination chart.

Follow these steps to create a combination chart using one of the predesigned charts:

1. Select the cells containing the data to be charted. Be sure to include the row and column headings if you want them to appear in the chart as category and legend labels. Do not include blank rows in your selection.

2. Choose the Chart Wizard button on the Standard toolbar. The Chart Wizard dialog box appears.

3. In Step 1 of 4 of the Chart Wizard, select the Custom Types tab (see Figure 8.1).

FIG. 8.1

A chart with the Line – Column custom chart type selected.

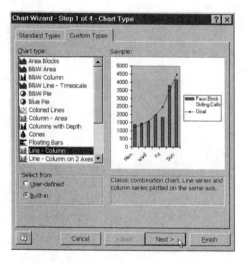

4. Choose one of the four custom combination charts: Column – Area; Line – Column; Line – Column on 2 Axes; or Line on 2 Axes.

5. Proceed through the remaining steps of the Chart Wizard.

▶ **See** "Using the Chart Wizard To Create Charts," **p. 112**

Figure 8.2 shows a simple combination chart. A line represents the goal for the number of telemarketing calls to make each day and a column displays the *actual* number of calls that were made. It is easy to see whether you exceeded, met, or fell short of your goals by using this chart.

FIG. 8.2

A Line – Column combination chart, using one axis.

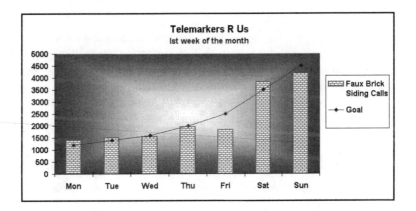

A combination chart depicting the number of car loans approved each month and the average monthly interest rates is shown in Figure 8.3. Because loans and interest rates are different types of data, two value axes are used.

FIG. 8.3

A Line – Column combination chart using two axes.

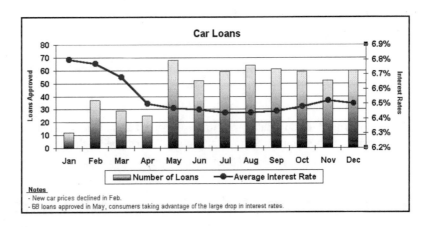

When creating combination charts, keep the following items in mind:

- It is important that you label each value axis to make the chart easier to read (refer to Figure 8.3). You can use the Chart Options command to add titles or create text boxes to label the axis.

- 3D chart types cannot be used in combination charts.

▶ **See** "Working with the Chart Options," **p. 125**

▶ **See** "Adding Text," **p. 133**

Handling Data Series in Combination Charts

When you use one of the predesigned combination chart types, Excel automatically determines which of the data series becomes the first type of chart and which becomes the second type of chart. An even number of data series is handled differently than an odd number of data series.

If there is an even number of data series, the first half of the data series becomes one chart type and the remaining half becomes the other chart type. If there is an odd number of data series, the first half of the data series plus one more of the data series become one chart type, and the remaining data series become the other chart type. Suppose you have five data series and you create a Line – Column chart. The first three series become columns and the remaining two series become lines.

Manually Changing How a Data Series Appears

In the previous example, if you want the fourth data series to also be a column, you have to manually change that data series to a column chart.

Alternatively, you may already have a chart that you want to make into a combination chart. If all the data series appear on the chart already, it is just a matter of changing one or more of the series to the desired chart type.

Changing the chart type used by one of the data series is easy:

1. Right-click the series you want to change and then select Chart Type from the shortcut menu.
2. Pick the type of chart you want to apply to the selected series from the Chart Type dialog box and then choose OK.

▶ **See** "Changing the Chart Type," **p. 119**

If you need to add a data series to use as part of a combination chart, first add the data. Then, using the steps outlined above, change the chart type for the newly added series.

▶ **See** "Adding or Removing Data From Your Charts," **p. 122**

Adding a Second Value Axis to Your Chart

If you create your own combination chart, you might want to add another axis to plot one of your data series. The following are the steps to add a second value axis to a chart:

1. Select the data series you want to appear on the second value axis.
2. Right-click the series and choose Format Data Series from the shortcut menu.
3. From the Axis tab, choose Secondary Axis.

TROUBLESHOOTING

The options on the Axis tab are grayed out. How can I change the data series to plot on the secondary axis? This data series is being used by Excel to plot the data on the primary axis. Select another data series to become the primary axis source. After this is done, you can go back and select the data series to be plotted on the secondary axis.

Creating Effective Pie Charts

Pie charts are designed to display only one series or category of data, usually to show what percentage each item constitutes of the whole pie. Figure 8.4 shows a simple pie chart plotting monthly expenses, showing what percentage each expense is of the total expenses. Because some of the expenses are very large and some are very small, many of the smaller data points are difficult to interpret.

FIG. 8.4

A simple 2-D pie chart.

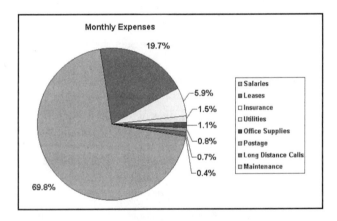

There are two new subtypes of pie charts that can help to make this data easier to read—Bar of a Pie and Pie of a Pie. Figure 8.5 illustrates the *Bar of a Pie* variation. Some of the minor expenses are grouped into one slice, referred to as Other, which collectively represents 4.5 percent of the expenses. This pie slice is linked to a bar, which allows these smaller expenses to be seen more clearly. In Figure 8.5, the Other slice is selected and the ChartTip provides information about the data point.

Another pie chart variation is the *Pie of a Pie* subtype, as shown in Figure 8.6. The Other slice and all the secondary plotted pie slices have been manually exploded to make the chart easier to read.

Either of these two variations can also be used to show a group of related data points. For example, suppose you have a list of expenses for Airfare, Lodging, Food, and Car Rental. If these expenses are small fractions of your total expense, they may be lumped together under an umbrella expense—Travel. With Bar of a Pie or Pie of a Pie, you can show each of the specific travel-related expenses.

FIG. 8.5

A Bar of a Pie, subtype of the pie chart.

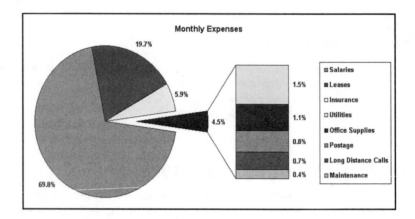

To create either one of the pie chart subtypes shown in Figures 8.5 and 8.6, follow these steps:

1. Select the cells containing the data to be charted. Be sure to include the row and column headings if you want them to appear in the chart as category and legend labels. Do not include blank rows in your selection.

2. Choose the Chart Wizard button on the Standard toolbar. The Chart Wizard dialog box appears.

3. In Step 1 of 4 of the Chart Wizard, select Pie from the Standard Types tab. Choose either the Bar in a Pie or Pie in a Pie subtype (see Figure 8.7).

4. Proceed through the remaining steps of the Chart Wizard.

FIG. 8.6

A Pie of a Pie, subtype of the pie chart.

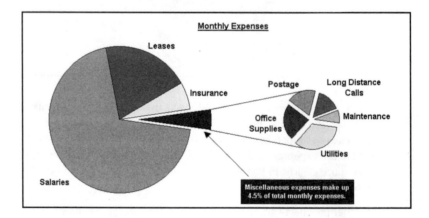

Customizing an Existing Pie Chart

An existing chart can also be changed to one of the new pie chart variations. Use the following steps to accomplish this:

1. Right-click on an empty area of the chart, away from the chart objects.

2. From the shortcut menu, choose Chart Type.

3. Select Pie from the Standard Types tab.

4. Pick a subtype and choose OK.

FIG. 8.7
The six standard subtypes that are available with a Pie chart.

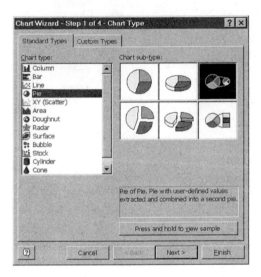

Once created, there are a number of features in these charts that can be customized. Right-click any pie slice, and choose Format Data Series from the shortcut menu. From the Data Labels tab, you can show what percentage each slice constitutes of the whole pie. Alternatively, you can display the value from the worksheet that created the slice or the label from the worksheet that corresponds to the pie slice. It is helpful to people who will view your chart if some type of data label is displayed on the pie charts. Refer back to Figure 8.5 for an example of percentages displayed next to each pie slice. Figure 8.6 displays an example of labels next to each slice, omitting the need for a legend.

 If a particular data label is too long, and you want part of the label to appear on a second line, you can force part of the text to a new line in the label. First click the data labels—this will select all data labels. Then click the label you want to change—this will place a selection border around the selected data label. Click once inside the label to edit the label. To force a particular word to a second line, position the flashing cursor in front of the word, and press Enter. This forces the text to the right of the cursor to move to a second line.

More Ways to Customize Your Pie Charts

The Options tab of the Format Data Series dialog box contains specific choices for customizing the Bar in a Pie or Pie in a Pie charts (see Figure 8.8).

The following list describes each of these options:

■ *Split Series By.* The drop-down list provides four methods that Excel can use to determine which data points appear in the second plot: Position, Value, Percent Value, and Custom.

FIG. 8.8

The Options tab of the Format Data Series dialog box.

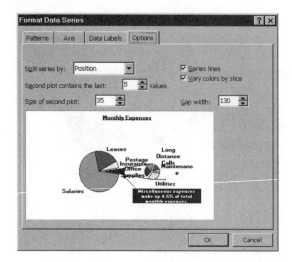

- Position. The last *x* number of data points will be plotted in the second plot. You can indicate the number of data points. With this option, these data points must be listed together at the bottom of the cells selected from the worksheet so that Excel can plot them together.

- Value. The data points less than a specific amount will be listed in the second plot. You can indicate the amount. Regardless of where the data points are located in the worksheet, if they are less than the amount you enter, those data points will be displayed in the second plot.

- Percent Value. Those data points less than a specific percent will be listed in the second plot. You can indicate the percent. Regardless of where the data points are in the worksheet, if they are less than the specified percent, the data point will be displayed in the second plot.

- Custom. You can use the mouse to drag data points between the first plot and the second plot.

■ *Second Plot Contains the Last*. This option varies depending on the selection you make in the Split Series By option.

■ *Size of Second Plot*. The second plot can be larger, the same size, or smaller than the first plot. The range is 200 to 5. Selecting 200 makes the second plot twice the size of the first plot. Choosing 100 makes the second plot equal the size of the first plot. Choosing 5 makes the second plot one-fifth the size (20 percent) of the first plot.

■ *Series Lines*. Display or remove connecting lines between the slice in the first plot to the bar or pie in the second plot. The default displays the lines.

■ *Vary Colors By Slice*. Use different or identical colors for each data point. The default uses different colors.

■ *Gap Width*. Distance between the slice in the first plot and the bar or pie in the second plot. You may decide to widen the gap to provide additional room for data labels.

Creating Charts with Pictures

One way to add pizzazz to your charts is to create picture charts. While pictures can be used with several different chart types, they work best in 2 dimensional line, bubble, column, and bar charts. Use pictures from Excel's clipart library, graphics from another windows program, or create your own picture in the Paint program found under Programs\Accessories\Paint.

An example of using a picture as a marker in a line chart is shown in Figure 8.9. Because the pictures are larger than ordinary markers, a data table is added to the bottom of the chart to provide the precise values for the sales in each country.

FIG. 8.9

A 2-D line chart with pictures marking the data points.

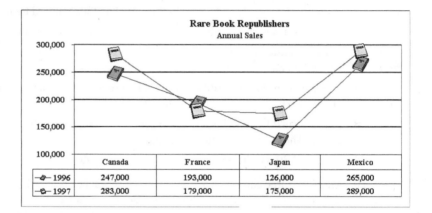

Figure 8.10 illustrates how pictures can be used as a fill for a bar chart. Bar charts created with pictures are often easier to read then column charts created with pictures. The pictures appear side by side rather than stacked on top of one another.

FIG. 8.10

A 2-D bar chart with a repeating picture filling the bars.

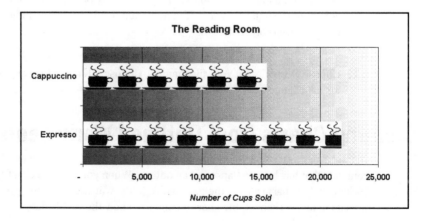

The easiest way to create picture charts is to paste the picture into the data series. Follow these steps:

1. Select an empty area in a worksheet. Insert a picture into the worksheet by using the Insert, Picture command. Clipart is a good place to find pictures.

2. Resize the picture to about half an inch. Make sure you drag one of the corner selection handles to keep the picture proportional while you resize it.

3. Use the Format, Picture command to remove the border surrounding the picture before including it in your chart. Change the Line Color to No Line on the Colors and Lines tab of the Format Picture dialog box. Then select OK.

4. With the picture selected, click the Copy tool on the Standard toolbar.

5. In the chart, select the data series you want to display as a picture.

6. Click the Paste tool on the Standard toolbar. By default, the picture is stretched in the bar or column.

7. To have the picture repeat, as shown in Figure 8.10, right-click the data series and choose Format Data Series from the shortcut menu.

8. In the Format Data Series dialog box, choose the Patterns tab and select the Fill Effects button. The Fill Effects dialog box appears.

9. In the Fill Effects dialog box, choose the Picture tab.

10. There are three choices as to how your picture will be displayed: Stretch, Stack, and Stack and Scale To *x* Units/Picture. Stretch resizes the picture so that it completely fills the area of the data series. Stack displays repeated copies of your picture until the area of your data series is filled, based on the original size of the picture. Stack and Scale To *x* Units/Picture also will display repeated copies of the picture, but at increments you choose.

    For example, in the earlier Figure 8.10, for every 2,500 cups of coffee sold, the picture repeats. When using this option, the picture may be expanded or contracted slightly to adhere to the unit you select. You may want to add a text box indicating the increment each picture represents.

    ▶ **See** "Adding Text," **p. 103**

11. Choose OK to accept your fill changes. Choose OK again to accept your data series format changes.

Creating Charts from Outlined Worksheets

Chapter 2 discusses how to outline an Excel worksheet. It is often useful to create a chart from data that has been collapsed in an outline. When you create a chart from an outlined worksheet, the chart reflects the data visible in the worksheet. When you collapse or expand the data in the worksheet, the chart changes to show the visible data.

Figure 8.11 shows a worksheet that has been outlined. The outline also has been collapsed to display only the regional, quarterly, and grand totals. The details in level 3 have been hidden. The chart in Figure 8.12 was created based on the selected cells shown in Figure 8.11.

▶ **See** "Outlining Worksheets," **p. 49**

FIG. 8.11

An outlined worksheet with the third level collapsed to show just the totals.

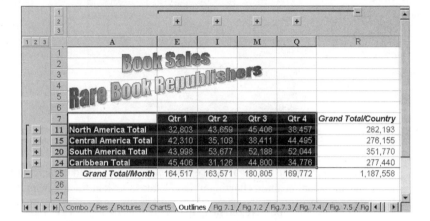

If you want to create a chart based on a worksheet that has been outlined, but do not want the chart to change when the outline is collapsed or expanded, follow these steps:

1. Select the cells in the outlined worksheet to be charted.

2. Choose Edit, Go To, and select the Special button. The Go To Special dialog box appears (see Figure 8.13).

3. Select the Visible Cells Only option. (You can accomplish the same thing by selecting the first cell to be plotted, then using the Ctrl key to select subsequent cells. The method described in these steps, though, is probably *much* faster!)

FIG. 8.12

The chart based on the data selected in Figure 8.11.

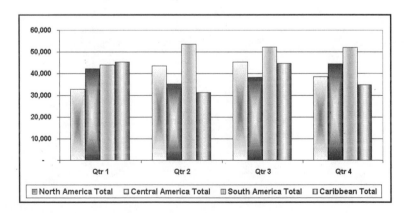

4. Choose OK.

5. Proceed with creating the chart. When the outlined worksheet is collapsed or expanded, the chart will continue to display the worksheet data that was originally plotted.

FIG. 8.13

The Go To Special dialog box.

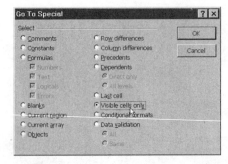

Chapters 6, 7, and 8 in this book are devoted to creating and enhancing Excel charts. For additional information about charting in Excel, take a look at the following resources:

■ The comprehensive online help is a good place to discover more about charts in Excel 97. Type **chart** in the Office Assistant search box and then choose from among the help options listed.

■ If you want to create charts based on filtered data, or data in a pivot table, see Chapter 14, "Using Filtered Data," and Chapter 15, "Unlocking the Power of Pivot Tables."

■ Chapter 17, "Integrating Excel Data into Other Windows Applications," walks you through the procedures to copy and link charts into other Microsoft programs.

■ *Special Edition Using Microsoft Excel 97* by Que provides additional information on creating hierarchical charts, adding error bars to charts, and creating maps based on worksheet data.

PART III

Finding Answers with Excel

CHAPTER 9

Validating and Analyzing Excel Data

Excel provides a number of functions and commands that can be used to validate data entry and explore "what-if" alternatives. This is particularly useful when you are sharing your workbooks with colleagues or other users. Chapter 3, "Formulas and Functions," discusses how to use several of the most popular functions in Excel, including IF. In this chapter, you see how this function can help you check for errors in your worksheets. Additionally, the IF function can be used in combination with other functions to validate data entered into a worksheet.

New in Excel 97 is a tool called Data Validation. You can display a list of valid entries for the user to choose from, insert prompts with notes on data entry, ensure appropriate entries by placing limits on the entries, and have Excel draw circles around invalid entries in the worksheet.

In addition to using functions for validating and analyzing data, Excel provides two commands that you can use to perform "what-if" type analysis on your worksheet data. Goal Seek is a feature where you enter a target goal amount, like actual sales, and Excel calculates what needs to change in your worksheet to reach this goal. Scenarios are useful for saving different sets of values that impact your worksheet. You can display each set of values, or scenarios, to see the impact each scenario makes on your data. A consolidated report can be produced to compare the various scenarios. ■

Using formulas and commands to evaluate and locate data

The IF function is a powerful tool, providing several options for checking calculations and confirming that data is correctly entered into worksheets. The VLOOKUP function is excellent for locating data in lists.

Using the Data Validation tool

Use this new tool to specify the data that can be entered in a cell. You can also create a message to instruct users on the appropriate data to be entered in a cell, or you can display an error message if incorrect data is entered.

Using commands to perform what-if analysis

The Goal Seek command is effective in calculating what needs to change in order to reach a target or goal. Creating scenarios enables you to propose different values and monitor the impact on the results of your worksheets.

Using Formulas to Cross-Check Summary Calculations

Formulas are an effective means of validating the summary calculations in a worksheet. In Figure 9.1, a list of personal computers sold is displayed. The list indicates the quantity and type of computers sold each day. The total number of PCs sold each day appears in row 10. The total number of each PC type sold for the week appears in column G. A grand total of computers sold for the week is calculated in cell G10. In this example, the sum of all daily totals (B10:F10) should equal the sum of all type totals (G4:G8). So, when the grand total is calculated, you can use either sum in cell G10.

By using an IF function, you can create a formula to check that both totals are the same. If they are not the same, you can design the formula to display a warning error message. This type of data-entry verification is known as a *cross-check*. There are several reasons why an error may occur. A constant value might have been typed accidentally over a formula, or a formula may be summing the incorrect cells. These types of errors are common in workbooks that are shared with other users.

▶ **See** "Sharing Your Workbooks with Other Users," **p. 291**

FIG. 9.1
Use formulas to automatically analyze worksheets.

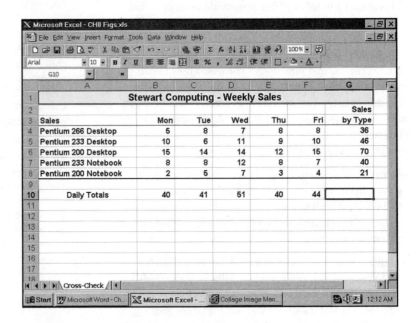

As explained in Chapter 3, the syntax for an IF function is:

=IF(logical_test, value_if_true, value_if_false)

The logical test that will be performed is the cross-check: SUM(B10:F10)=SUM(G4:G8).

If the test is true—meaning that the sums are equal—you simply want to display the results of one of the sums, such as SUM(B10:F10).

If the test is false—meaning that the sums are not equal—you want to be warned that there is an error. This can be accomplished by entering the text you want displayed when the text is false. Text in Excel formulas is surrounded by quotation marks—for example "ERROR".

The IF function in cell G10 will be:

=IF(SUM(B10:F10)=SUM(G4:G8),SUM(B10:F10),"ERROR")

In Figure 9.2, the IF function is entered in cell G10. The warning message ERROR is in the cell to indicate a problem with the worksheet. To illustrate the problem, the totals are calculated below the worksheet: the daily total is 216 and the total by type is 213.

N O T E Whenever there is a cross-check error, the problem exists in one of the individual total calculations. In Figure 9.2, the totals are in row 10 or column G. Chapter 10, "Auditing Excel Files," describes how to identify and correct the problem.

FIG. 9.2
The cross-check formula flags you if there is an error in the worksheet.

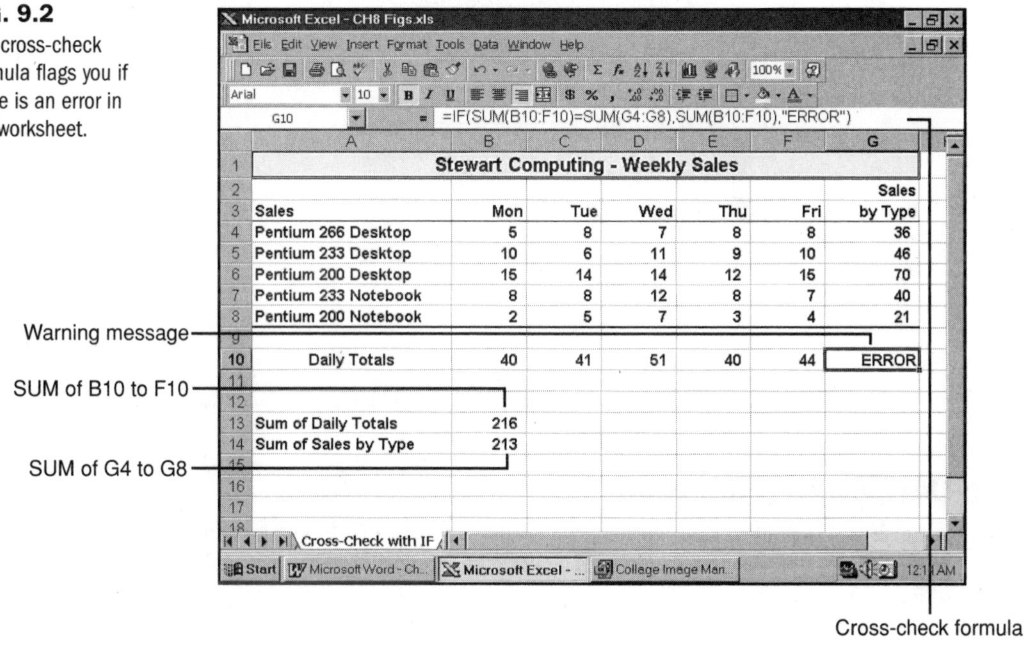

See "Common Worksheet Functions," **p. 61**

See "Using the Go To Special Command," **p. 170**

Using Formulas to Validate Data Entry

IF functions also are used to verify data entry when the data is initially typed into the worksheet. When creating formulas to verify data entry, the formulas frequently include other functions inside the IF function. This is referred to as *nesting functions*, which is discussed in Chapter 3.

Figure 9.3 displays an order form for landscaping plants. Suppose that you want to establish validation checks for the Date Ordered, Type, Item Ordered, and Item Number. Refer to this figure as the DATEVALUE, AND, IF, OR, ISNA, and MATCH functions are discussed in the following sections.

FIG. 9.3

A simple order form. Formulas can be created to check data entry.

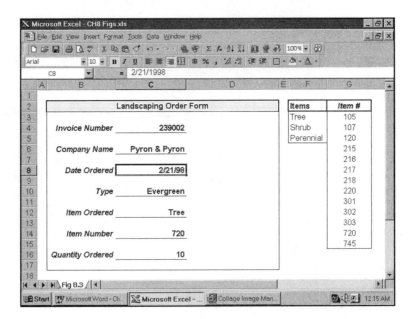

The DATEVALUE Function

For Excel to perform comparisons on dates, the dates need to be converted into serial numbers. The DATEVALUE function is designed to convert dates into serial numbers. The syntax for DATEVALUE is:

=DATEVALUE("date_text")

In the next section, you see the DATEVALUE function used with the AND function.

The AND Function

If the date entered in C8 needs to be in the year 1998, you need to determine if the date is between 1/1/98 and 12/31/98. The simplest way to compare two dates is by using the AND function. The logical test to perform is as follows:

$$\text{AND(C8>=DATEVALUE(“1/1/1998”),C8<=DATEVALUE (“12/31/98”)}$$

If the test is true—meaning that the date entered is in 1998—nothing is displayed. Open and close quotes are used to display a cell with no value.

If the test is false—meaning that the date is either earlier or later than 1998—you want to be alerted that there is an error. The message Invalid Date will be displayed.

The IF function that is used to perform the date validation in cell D8 is the following:

$$\text{=IF(AND(C8>=DATEVALUE(“1/1/1998”),C8<=DATEVALUE(“12/31/98”)),“”,“Invalid Date”)}$$

The OR Function

Similar to the AND function, the OR function can also be used with IF to validate data entry. Continuing with the sample list shown in Figure 9.3, in cell C10, the type of landscaping product ordered can be either Evergreen or Deciduous. An IF function with an OR comparison is a good choice for this validation. The formula is as follows

$$\text{=IF(OR(C10=“Evergreen”,C10=“Deciduous”),“”,“Evergreen or Deciduous”)}$$

If neither Evergreen or Deciduous are entered into the cell, the formula will display Evergreen or Deciduous in the worksheet.

Formulas that contain AND and OR comparisons work well when the data entry is compared against a few alternatives. When the entry needs to be checked against a larger set of alternatives though, listing each alternative in the formula is time consuming and makes the formula unnecessarily complex. Instead, it is simpler to create a formula that compares the entry against a list of valid entries.

The ISNA and MATCH Functions

The ISNA and MATCH functions can be used together to determine whether the entry is in the list of valid entries. You must create somewhere in your workbook a separate list that can be used by these functions to check the entry. When an exact match is not found, the MATCH function returns an error value of #N/A. Because the error message doesn't help you (or others) in correcting the entry, you will probably want to have some helpful message display. By using the ISNA function with the MATCH function, you can display text instead of the error message. You determine the text that is displayed by the ISNA function. The syntax for the MATCH function is:

$$\text{=MATCH(lookup\_value,lookup\_array,match\_type)}$$

The lookup_value is the cell where the entry is typed into the form. The lookup_array is the cells containing the list of valid entries. The match_type is 0, indicating an exact match in the list must be found. For example, to determine whether the Item Ordered is one of the valid items listed in cells F3:F5, the logical test is MATCH(C12,F3:F5,0). If there isn't a match, then the #NA error message displays. To display a text message instead of the error message, add the ISNA function. The ISNA function simply asks if the result is #NA. The formula is then ISNA(MATCH(C12,F3:F5,0)). Combined with an IF function, the message will display indicating the entry is invalid if it is not from the list in F3:F5; otherwise, nothing is displayed.

For the Item Ordered and Item Number used in Figure 9.3, the formulas are as follows:

=IF(ISNA(MATCH(C12,F3:F5,0)),"Invalid Item","")

=IF(ISNA(MATCH(C14,G3:G15,0)),"Invalid Number","")

N O T E   With the MATCH function, the lookup_array does not have to be in the same worksheet. It can be in a different worksheet or workbook. (See the section "Calculations Across Worksheets and Workbooks" in Chapter 4 for more information about referring to cells in other worksheets and workbooks in your formulas.)

Figure 9.4 illustrates the warning messages displayed when invalid entries are typed into the landscaping form for Date Ordered, Type, Item Ordered, and Item Number.

FIG. 9.4

Formulas alert you when invalid entries are made in a worksheet form.

Formula for Date Ordered

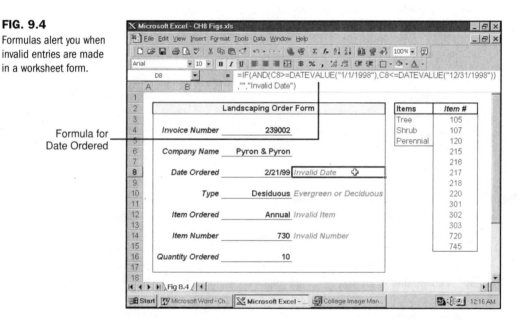

▶ **See** "Nesting Functions," **p. 76**

Using the Data Validation Command to Control Data Entry

The Data Validation command is a new, powerful feature in Excel 97. Through this one command, you have three options to assist the user as data is initially entered into a cell or after the data has been entered. You can specify the data that can be entered in a cell, you can create a message to instruct users on the appropriate data to be entered in a cell, or you can display an error message if incorrect data is entered in a cell. These three options can be used separately or with one another.

A variety of restrictions can be placed on the data entered in a cell. The options displayed in the Data Validation dialog box change depending on what type of restriction you select.

- *Any Value*. This is the default setting; no restrictions are placed on the entries.
- *Custom*. You can enter a formula to determine valid entries. The custom option must be a formula that produces a True or False result.
- *Date*. Allows only date entries. You can specify a range of dates or dates that occur before or after a date you specify.
- *Decimal*. Allows numbers with decimals. You can specify a range of numbers or numbers that are larger or smaller than a number you specify.
- *List*. You can specify a list of valid entries. The list can either be entered into the dialog box (separated by commas), or you can use a range name or cell references for a list. A drop-down arrow appears to display the list of valid entries.
- *Text Length*. You can specify the number of characters for text entries. You can specify a minimum length, a maximum length, or both.
- *Time*. Allows only time entries. You can specify a start time, an end time, or both.
- *Whole Number*. Allows only numbers that are integers. You can specify a range of numbers or numbers that are larger or smaller than a number you specify.

To access the Data Validation dialog box, choose Data, Validation. There are three tabs. The Settings tab, shown in Figure 9.5, is where you select the type of restriction you want on the cell. In Figure 9.5, the Data restriction is selected. By default, the criteria operator is between, and a start date and end date are expected. Select the Data drop-down arrow to see other operators like greater than or greater than or equal to. The Ignore Blank check box allows blank entries in the cell. Clear the Ignore Blank check box to indicate that blank entries are not valid.

Part
III

Ch
9

FIG. 9.5

The options below the Data drop-down will vary depending on what restriction and operator you choose.

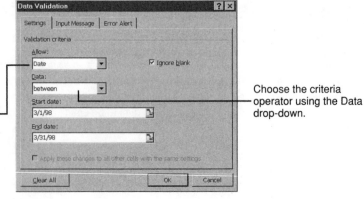

Choose the type of restriction using the Allow drop-down.

Choose the criteria operator using the Data drop-down.

N O T E Specifying the type of data allowed in a cell does not change the cell formatting. You have to apply the appropriate format to the cell. For example, choosing a date restriction does not apply a date format to the cell. Choose Format, Cells to select the desired format. ▨

Another useful restriction is List. If the list of valid entries is short or won't be changing very much, you can type the list of choices directly in the Data Validation dialog box. If the list is long or will change regularly, however, it is best to create the list in a worksheet and assign a range name to the list. The list can be in the active worksheet, in another worksheet in the active workbook, or in another workbook.

▶ **See** "Accessing Range Names," **p. 65**

▶ **See** "Calculations Across Worksheets and Workbooks," **p. 77**

The Input Message tab of the Data Validation dialog box is used to create a message that instructs users on the type of data expected in the cell. The Error Alert tab of the Data Validation dialog box is used to create a message that displays when an invalid entry is typed in.

 In addition to these options in the Data Validation dialog box , you can have Excel draw circles around invalid entries in the worksheet. You must establish Data Validation criteria to use this feature. Choose the Circle Invalid Data button on the Auditing toolbar to draw circles around cells in the worksheet.

Using Formulas to Look Up Information in Lists

Lookup functions are used to search for one value in a list and to return another corresponding value from the list. Lookup functions can be used to find a product name in a price list and return the specific price, or find the tax rate for a particular salary range. Although there are several Lookup functions, VLOOKUP (Vertical Lookup) is most commonly used, as lists tend to be designed in columns rather than rows.

The syntax for VLOOKUP is:

=VLOOKUP(lookup_value,table_array,col_index_num,range_lookup)

As with other functions, arguments that appear in **bold** are required; those not in bold are optional. The specific arguments for the VLOOKUP function must appear in the order just shown.

Figure 9.6 illustrates a spreadsheet in which a Sales Representative earns a bonus based on the sales he makes each month. The Actual Sales number is being looked up in the Bonus Table.

Part III

Ch 9

FIG. 9.6

The arguments for a VLOOKUP function are identified in this figure.

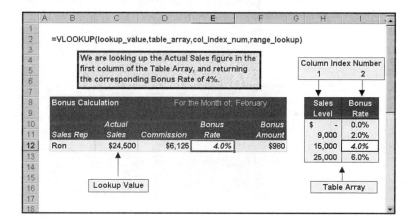

The arguments for VLOOKUP are the following:

- **lookup_value.** The value being searched for in the first column of the table array. The lookup_value can be a number, a cell reference, or text. In Figure 9.6, lookup_value is the Actual Sales figure.

- **table_array.** The list of information in which data is being looked up, commonly referred to as the table. Use a range name or absolute cell reference for the table so the VLOOKUP formula can be copied. Although Figure 9.6 shows the Bonus Table in the same sheet as the commission and bonus calculations, the table often is in another sheet or book. In Figure 9.6, the table shows various Sales Levels. Ron's Actual Sales are $24,500, which is higher than $15,000 but less than $25,000; therefore, he will earn a bonus of 4 percent.

- **col_index_num.** The column index number. If the columns in the table array were numbered, the column index number is the column number from which the matching value will be returned. In Figure 9.6, column 1 is the Sales Level and column 2 is the Bonus Rate. In this example, the column index number is 2.

- *range_lookup.* This argument is optional. If the range_lookup argument is omitted or TRUE, a range (approximate match) lookup is performed. If you enter FALSE for this argument, an exact match lookup is performed. In Figures 9.6 and 9.7, a range lookup is being performed. See Figures 9.8 and 9.9, later in this chapter, for examples of an exact match lookup.

Using VLOOKUP to Find a Range Match in a List

The Bonus Table in Figure 9.7 lists levels of sales rather than each possible sales amount. This is referred to as a *range lookup*.

As you can see in the figure, if the Actual Sales are below $9,000, the Sales Rep does not receive a bonus. If the Actual Sales are $25,000 or more, the Sales Rep receives a 6% bonus.

When using a range lookup, the table should account for the smallest possible value that can be looked up. The first column in the table also must be sorted in ascending order. If you are looking up numbers, ascending is from the smallest to the largest number. If you are looking up text, ascending is alphabetical from A to Z.

Figure 9.7 shows the completed formula for the first Sales Rep, Ron. The formula for looking up the bonus rate is displayed in the Formula Bar.

FIG. 9.7
The VLOOKUP function provides a convenient way to extract a value from a table.

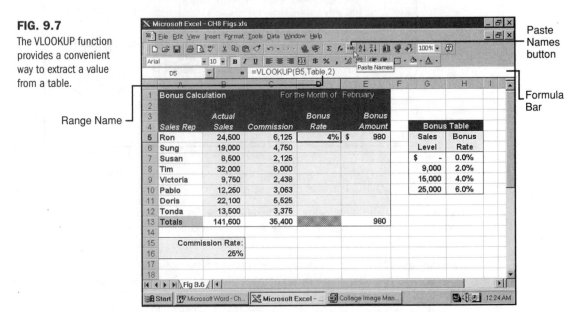

The range name Table is used to identify the table_array. This enables you to copy the formula to the other Sales Reps. To quickly access the list of range names, press F3. From the Paste Names dialog box, select the range name and click OK. As an alternative, the absolute cell references $G$5:$H$8 could have been used for the table_array argument.

▶ **See** "Absolute Cell Referencing," **p. 21**

Using VLOOKUP to Locate an Exact Match in a List

Although the previous example works well for calculating bonuses, it does not work in every situation. Suppose you have a list of products that have been ordered and you want to look up the specific price for each item. If the product does not appear in your price list, you want to be alerted to that fact. This is an *exact match lookup*.

Unlike a range lookup, the table for an exact match lookup does not have to be sorted by the first column; it can be in any order. If an exact match is not found, the error value #N/A is displayed, indicating there is no match.

The syntax for VLOOKUP, using an exact match lookup is:

=VLOOKUP(lookup_value,table_array,col_index_num,range_lookup)

As discussed in the previous section, the range_lookup argument is FALSE when using an exact match lookup.

Figure 9.8 shows a list of landscaping items that have been ordered. The prices for these items must be retrieved from the price list, which is on a separate worksheet in this workbook. Victorian Deco ordered the first item, Item # 218. You need to look up the corresponding price in the Landscaping Price List displayed in Figure 9.9. The Item # is the lookup_value for your VLOOKUP function.

Part

III

Ch

9

FIG. 9.8

This figure shows the list of landscaping orders that will be used in the following table array example.

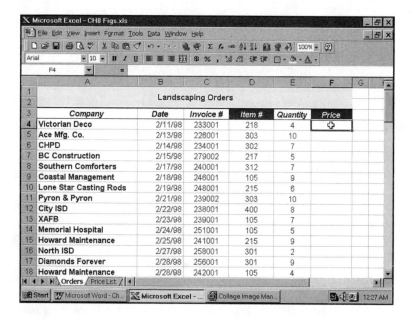

Figure 9.9 shows the Landscaping Price List. Only part of this list will be used in the table_array. The table_array in any VLOOKUP must have the lookup_value in the first column. Because you are looking up the Item # and returning the corresponding price, the table_array in this example is the Item # column through the Price column (C4:F16). In this table_array, the prices are in the fourth column of the array; therefore, the col_index_num is 4.

FIG. 9.9

The price list for all landscaping products.

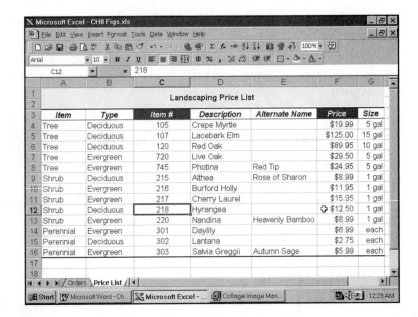

If you intend to copy the VLOOKUP function, either the table_array cell references need to be made absolute or a range name can be used to identify the table.

 TIP To make cell references absolute, use the F4 function key on your keyboard while the cell references are selected.

▶ **See** "Absolute Cell Referencing," **p. 21**

In Figure 9.10, the VLOOKUP function for the first order has been completed and copied to the remaining orders. The Formula Bar shows the formula for Victorian Deco. Because the price list was on another sheet, the name of the sheet (Products) is listed in front of the absolute cell references for the table_array. The Chapter 3 section, "Calculations Across Worksheets and Workbooks," explains how to create (and interpret) calculations made across worksheets and workbooks.

Notice the error message (#N/A) in the orders for Southern Comforters and City ISD. The item numbers for these orders do not exist in the Landscaping Price List (refer to Figure 9.9). Because the VLOOKUP is searching for an exact match, the error message alerts you that there is no match for Item # 312 and Item # 400.

FIG. 9.10

The list of orders with corresponding prices inserted using the VLOOKUP function. When an exact match is unavailable, an error message appears.

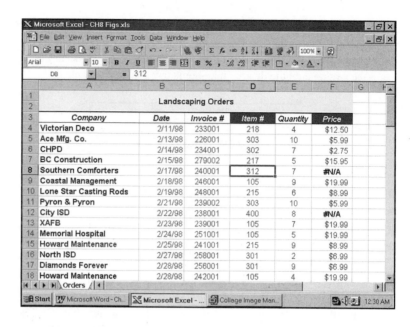

Part

III

Ch

9

TIP The section "Using the ISNA and MATCH functions" earlier in this chapter discusses how to use the ISNA function with an IF to display text rather than the #NA error message. You could use these functions with the VLOOKUP to produce a text message when performing an exact match lookup as well.

N O T E If your table or list is designed horizontally instead of vertically, you can use the HLOOKUP function. ▪

The syntax for HLOOKUP is:

=HLOOKUP(lookup_value,table_array,row_index_num,range_lookup**)**

Conducting a What-If Analysis with the Goal Seek Command

Suppose that you know what you want the result of a formula to be, but not the input value necessary to achieve the result. The Goal Seek command determines the value necessary to reach a particular target or goal.

In Figure 9.11, a formula has been created to calculate current take-home pay. If your goal is $30,000 in take-home pay (gross salary minus taxes, retirement account, and so on), what salary do you require to reach that goal? To determine the salary, Microsoft Excel varies the salary value until the desired take-home pay goal is determined.

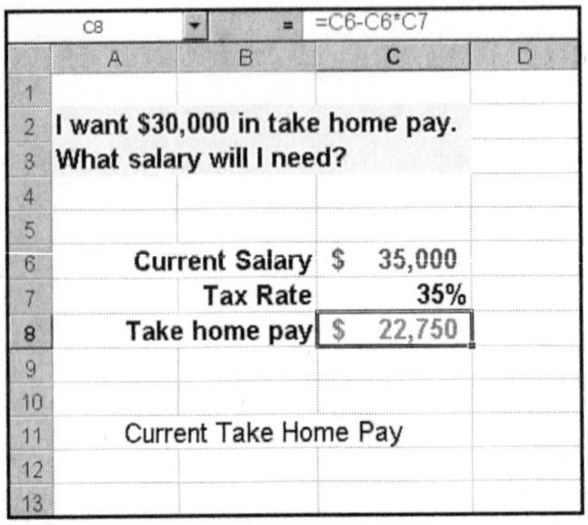

FIG. 9.11

A simple use of the Goal Seek command.

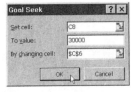

To use the Goal Seek command, choose Tools, Goal Seek. The Goal Seek dialog box appears (see Figure 9.12). The following are the three parts of the Goal Seek command:

- ▨ *Set Cell*. Select the cell that is to show the target or goal. This cell must contain a formula. In the previous figure, Figure 9.11, the cell is C8, the Take Home Pay formula.

- ▨ *To Value*. Enter the target or goal desired. For the example in Figure 9.11, this is $30,000.

- ▨ *By Changing Cell*. Select the cell that is to be adjusted. The Salary, cell C6, is the value that will be changed.

FIG. 9.12

The Goal Seek dialog box requires three entries.

When Excel calculates the value necessary to reach the goal, it displays the Goal Seek Status dialog box (see Figure 9.13) and adjusts the value in the worksheet. If you just want to see the result, but don't want the worksheet changed, select Cancel. To accept the change to the worksheet, choose OK.

FIG. 9.13

The Goal Seek Status dialog box.

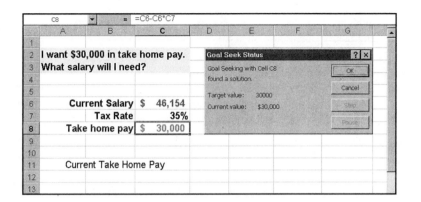

Using a Complex Goal Seek Formula

The previous example demonstrated a simple use of the Goal Seek command. In Figure 9.14, a more complex situation exists. Victoria's sales are $9,750. Based on her Actual Sales, she earns a 25 percent Commission ($2,438) and a 2 percent Bonus Amount ($195), for a Total Compensation of $2,633. Victoria wants to raise her Total Compensation to $5,000. Therefore, she wants to know the total sales required to reach her target compensation.

This example is more complex because the Total Compensation is a formula that adds the Commission (cell D9) and the Bonus Amount (cell F9), as shown in the Formula Bar. The Commission is a formula that takes the Actual Sales for Victoria (cell C9) and multiples it by the Commission Rate (cell D16). The Bonus Amount is a formula that multiplies the Actual Sales (C9) and the Bonus Rate (E9). For Excel to calculate the salary, it has to work through all three formulas, not just the one formula as in the take-home pay example described previously.

FIG. 9.14

A complex Goal Seek calculation works through several formulas to determine the goal.

G9		=D9+F9							
Bonus Calculation		For the Month of: February							
		Actual		Bonus	Bonus	Total			
Sales Rep	Sales	Commission	Rate	Amount	Compensation		Bonus Table		
Ron	24,500	6,125	4%	$980	$7,105		Sales	Bonus	
Sung	19,000	4,750	4%	$760	$5,510		Level	Rate	
Susan	8,500	2,125	0%	$0	$2,125		$ -	0.0%	
Tim	32,000	8,000	6%	$1,920	$9,920		9,000	2.0%	
Victoria	9,750	2,438	2%	$195	$2,633		15,000	4.0%	
Pablo	12,250	3,063	2%	$245	$3,308		25,000	6.0%	
Doris	22,100	5,525	4%	$884	$6,409				
Tonda	13,500	3,375	2%	$270	$3,645				
Totals	141,600	35,400		5,254					
		Commission Rate:							
		25%							

In Figure 9.14, the Set Cell is G9, the Total Compensation for Victoria. The To Value is $5,000 and the By Changing Cell is C9.

> **TIP** Goal Seek is limited to changing one variable. If you need to manipulate multiple variables or want to control the variables, use the Solver, a built-in analysis tool in Excel. To learn more about the Solver, ask the Office Assistant. Type **solving problems** in the Office Assistant search box and press Enter. Select Guidelines For Designing A Model To Find Values With Solver from the list of help topics displayed.

Conducting a What-If Analysis with Scenarios

One of the most practical features in Excel is the capability to create scenarios. A scenario is a proposed or alternative set of worksheet values. You can create and save different scenarios on a worksheet, and then display each set of values to see the impact on the worksheet.

For example, Figure 9.14 showed a Bonus Table listing various Sales Levels and corresponding Bonus Rates. Currently, a total of $5,254 is being paid in bonuses (E13). Suppose there are three alternative bonus rate percentages being discussed. What will be the difference on the total bonuses paid for each of the three proposals?

> **TIP** When creating scenarios, it is wise to save the existing values as your first scenario. Use any name for the first scenario except **Current**. This name is used to indicate which is the active scenario. Good choices for the name of the existing values are **Default** or **Existing**.

To create scenarios, follow these steps:

1. Select the cells containing the values that will change. Do not select the column headings. J7 through J10 are the appropriate cells used earlier in Figure 9.14.

2. Choose Tools, Scenarios. The Scenario Manager dialog box appears (see Figure 9.15).

FIG. 9.15
The Scenario Manager dialog box.

3. Select the Add button. The Add Scenario dialog box Appears. Type in a scenario name for the existing values. The name **Default** has been entered in Figure 9.16. The cells this scenario refers to, as well as who and when the scenario was created, are automatically included in the Add Scenario dialog box.

FIG. 9.16

The Add Scenario dialog box.

4. Select OK. The Scenario Values dialog box appears (see Figure 9.17). Because the first scenario reflects the existing entries, make no changes.

5. To create additional scenarios, select Add. When the Add Scenario dialog box appears, enter the name for the next scenario and click OK. In the Scenario Values dialog box, enter the new values for the scenario.

FIG. 9.17

The Scenario Values dialog box.

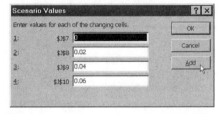

6. Repeat step 5 until all scenarios have been created and click OK. The Scenario Manager dialog box appears listing all the scenarios (see Figure 9.18).

7. To display a scenario in the worksheet, select the name of the scenario and choose Show. To change the values in a scenario, select the name of the scenario and choose Edit. To close the Scenario Manager dialog box, click Close.

When you have a number of scenarios, it is useful to generate a scenario summary report to compare the impact of the scenarios on the worksheet. To create a summary report, choose Tools, Scenarios. In the Scenario Manager dialog box, select Summary. The Scenario Summary dialog box appears (see Figure 9.19). There are two types of reports from which to choose—a Scenario Summary or a Scenario PivotTable. In either case, you will be asked to select the results cell—the cell that you want to compare. In the example we have been discussing, the results cell is F13, the total bonuses paid out (refer to Figure 9.14).

FIG. 9.18

The Scenario Manager dialog box lists four scenarios.

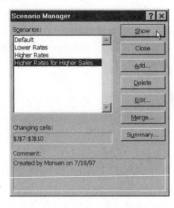

FIG. 9.19

The Scenario Summary dialog box.

A new sheet will be inserted into your workbook displaying the summary report (see Figure 9.20). The Scenario Summary report uses the Excel outline feature.

FIG. 9.20

A Scenario Summary report comparing the four bonus rate scenarios is depicted in this figure.

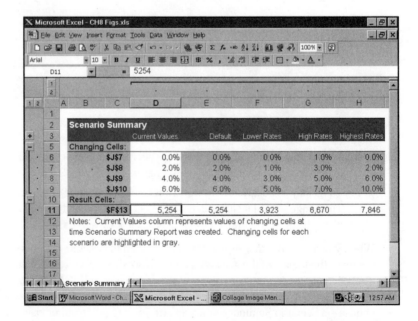

CHAPTER 10

Auditing Excel Files

The key to locating, troubleshooting, and avoiding errors in worksheets is to regularly audit your files. Most auditing consists of verifying that your formulas are making the correct calculations. It also consists of checking the worksheet to make sure a formula hasn't been replaced with other text. Adding comments to worksheet cells can document procedures for filling out a form or explain to anyone who views the worksheet how calculations were derived. ■

Locating special cells in Excel worksheets

Highlight cells that contain constant values or formulas. Uncover formulas that are not using the correct cell references.

Auditing formulas

Use the Range Finder feature to distinguish the cell ranges used in a formula. Display arrows that trace the cells referenced in formulas to locate possible errors.

Error messages

Learn to interpret and correct worksheet error messages. Resolve circular reference errors.

Worksheet annotations

Use cell comments to document procedures to complete formulas and forms. Keep notes or messages that will avoid worksheet errors.

Using the Go To Special Command

Excel worksheets typically consist of data and formulas, which are often linked to other worksheets or workbooks. The Go To Special command provides a beneficial yet simple way to analyze your worksheets. This command helps find cells that meet criteria you specify. For example, you can locate all cells that contain comments, formulas, or errors messages.

A quick way to display the Go To dialog box is to press the F5 key once. Choosing Edit, Go To, or choosing the keyboard shortcut Ctrl+G are the alternative methods of displaying the Go To dialog box. Selecting the Special button displays the Go To Special dialog box (see Figure 10.1).

 T I P   If a single cell is selected when the Go To Special command is used, the entire active workbook is searched. If a range of cells are selected when the command is used, only the cells in the selected range are searched.

FIG. 10.1

Select a criteria for Excel to use in the Go To Special dialog box.

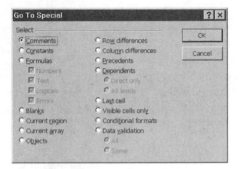

The options in the Go To Special dialog box help locate specific cells in your workbook. The following options are used to analyze your worksheets:

- *Constants.* Identifies all cells that do not contain formulas. By default, all cells that contain constants are selected. However, you can specify only cells with numbers, text, logical values (True or False), errors (cells you have typed #N/A), or any combination of these options. This is useful in identifying cells where there should be constants, not formulas.

- *Formulas.* Identifies all cells that contain formulas. By default, all cells that contain formulas are selected. However, you can specify formulas where the result of the formula are numbers, text, logical values, error messages, or any combination of these options. This option is useful in identifying cells where there should be formulas, not constant values.

- *Row Differences* and *Column Differences.* Compares a formula pattern in one cell to the relative formulas in other cells in the same row or column. This option is useful in identifying errors in formulas.

- *Precedents* and *Dependents*. Selects cells that the active cell refers to (precedents) or selects cells that refer to the active cell (dependents). Cells that are directly or indirectly linked to the active cell can be selected. This option is useful in identifying errors in formulas.

- *Conditional Formats*. Identifies cells that contain formats based on the type of data in the cells. All cells containing conditional formatting or just those that contain the same formatting as the active cell can be selected.

- *Data Validation*. Selects cells that have imbedded data validation.

▶ **See** "Conditional Formatting," **p. 27**

▶ **See** "Using Formulas to Validate Data Entry," **p. 154**

Cross-Checking Summary Calculations

Chapter 9 explains how to use an IF function to cross-check the summary calculations in a worksheet. Figure 10.2 shows the worksheet in which the sum of column G does not equal the sum of row 10. An error is displayed indicating the totals do not match.

 T I P   When there is a cross-check error, the problem is in one of the row or column calculations.

FIG. 10.2
A worksheet in which the sum of column G does not equal the sum of row 10, resulting in an error.

Cross-check formula

| G10 | = | =IF(SUM(B10:F10)=SUM(G4:G8),SUM(B10:F10),"ERROR") |

	A	B	C	D	E	F	G
1		Stewart Computing - Weekly Sales					
2							Sales
3	Sales	Mon	Tue	Wed	Thu	Fri	by Type
4	Pentium 266 Desktop	5	8	7	8	8	36
5	Pentium 233 Desktop	10	6	11	9	10	46
6	Pentium 200 Desktop	15	14	14	12	15	70
7	Pentium 233 Notebook	8	8	12	8	7	40
8	Pentium 200 Notebook	2	5	7	3	4	21
9							
10	Daily Totals	40	41	51	40	44	ERROR
11							
12							
13	Sum of Daily Totals	216					
14	Sum of Sales by Type	213					
15							
16							
17							

There are several reasons why this error may occur. A constant value might have been accidentally typed over a formula, or a formula may be summing the incorrect cells. To check whether a value has been accidentally typed over a formula, use either the Constants or Formulas option in the Go To Special dialog box to highlight those cells in your worksheet. Then look for inconsistencies—constants where there should be formulas. Use both the Row Differences and Column Differences options to make sure the formulas are totaling the correct cells.

In Figure 10.3, the Constants option in the Go To Special dialog box has been selected to identify all cells where there are constant values in the entire worksheet. Those cells that contain constant values (anything but a formula), are highlighted. Notice that cell G7 is selected, indicating that it contains a constant. This cell should be a formula totaling the sales for Pentium 233 Notebooks.

▶ **See** "Using Formulas to Cross-Check Summary Calculations," **p. 152**

FIG. 10.3

Use the Constants option in the Go To Special dialog box to quickly identify cells that are constants but should be formulas

G7 is a constant value, but should — be a formula

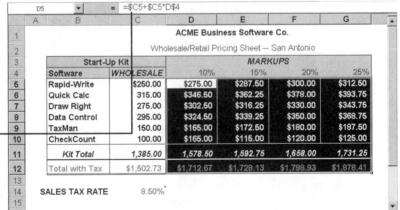

	A	B	C	D	E	F	G
1	Stewart Computing - Weekly Sales						
2							Sales
3	Sales	Mon	Tue	Wed	Thu	Fri	by Type
4	Pentium 266 Desktop	5	8	7	8	8	36
5	Pentium 233 Desktop	10	6	11	9	10	46
6	Pentium 200 Desktop	15	14	14	12	15	70
7	Pentium 233 Notebook	8	8	12	8	7	40
8	Pentium 200 Notebook	2	5	7	3	4	21
9							
10	Daily Totals	40	41	51	40	44	ERROR
11							
12							
13	Sum of Daily Totals	216					
14	Sum of Sales by Type	213					
15							
16							

A1 = Stewart Computing - Weekly Sales

Figure 10.4 shows a worksheet that is calculating markup prices for business software. Since all the markup prices are formulas, it is wise to check for errors in the formulas. Other valuable options in the Go To Special dialog box are Row Differences and Column Differences. In this case, select the cells you want to check before using these options.

FIG. 10.4

When you select a range of cells before using the Go To Special command, only the selected cells will be searched.

Formula for the Rapid-Write software with a 10% markup

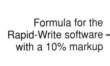

D5 = =$C5+$C5*D$4

	A	B	C	D	E	F	G
1			ACME Business Software Co.				
2			Wholesale/Retail Pricing Sheet -- San Antonio				
3		Start-Up Kit		MARKUPS			
4		Software	WHOLESALE	10%	15%	20%	25%
5		Rapid-Write	$250.00	$275.00	$287.50	$300.00	$312.50
6		Quick Calc	315.00	$346.50	$362.25	$378.00	$393.75
7		Draw Right	275.00	$302.50	$316.25	$330.00	$343.75
8		Data Control	295.00	$324.50	$339.25	$350.00	$368.75
9		TaxMan	150.00	$165.00	$172.50	$180.00	$187.50
10		CheckCount	100.00	$165.00	$115.00	$120.00	$125.00
11		Kit Total	1,385.00	1,578.50	1,592.75	1,658.00	1,731.25
12		Total with Tax	$1,502.73	$1,712.67	$1,729.13	$1,798.93	$1,878.41
13							
14		SALES TAX RATE	8.50%				
15							

Because you want to check not only the markup values, but also the Kit Totals and the Totals with Tax, use the Row Differences option. In each row, the formulas in column D serve as a pattern. All the remaining cells in each row are checked against this pattern, and the cells that do not match the pattern are selected. Figure 10.5 shows the result.

FIG. 10.5

The formulas that do not match the pattern of the first formula in each row are selected

The active cell contains a constant value, not a formula

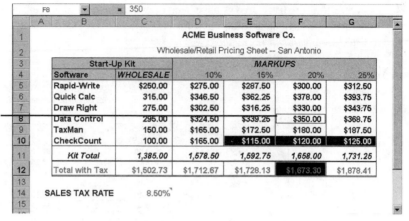

		FB	▼	=	350		

	A	B	C	D	E	F	G
1		ACME Business Software Co.					
2		Wholesale/Retail Pricing Sheet -- San Antonio					
3		Start-Up Kit		MARKUPS			
4		Software	WHOLESALE	10%	15%	20%	25%
5		Rapid-Write	$250.00	$275.00	$287.50	$300.00	$312.50
6		Quick Calc	315.00	$346.50	$362.25	$378.00	$393.75
7		Draw Right	275.00	$302.50	$316.25	$330.00	$343.75
8		Data Control	295.00	$324.50	$339.25	$350.00	$368.75
9		TaxMan	150.00	$165.00	$172.50	$180.00	$187.50
10		CheckCount	100.00	$165.00	$115.00	$120.00	$125.00
11		Kit Total	1,385.00	1,578.50	1,592.75	1,658.00	1,731.25
12		Total with Tax	$1,502.73	$1,712.67	$1,728.13	$1,673.30	$1,878.41
13							
14		SALES TAX RATE	8.50%				
15							

> **TIP** When all but the first cell in a row is selected, as is the case in row 10 of Figure 10.5, the error is probably in the first cell in the row, cell D10.

After a cell is identified as having an error, the next step is finding the cause of the error and resolving it. In the case of cells that contain constant values but should contain formulas, the resolution is straightforward—copy the formula from another cell (usually the cell directly above it) into the cell with the constant value.

In other situations, the problem may be with the cells the formula uses, known as the precedent cells. The next section describes how to locate these cells.

Using the Range Finder to Audit Your Formulas

Errors may occur in your worksheet that will cause incorrect calculations to occur. There are several ways to find the cells that may be causing errors in your formulas. Locating the cells the formula references, the *precedent cells*, is the first step.

A new feature of Excel, the *Range Finder*, helps to quickly identify the cells used by a formula. When you double-click a formula, each cell reference, range of cells, or range name used in the formula is changed to a different color. The borders of the corresponding cells in the worksheet are colored to match the cells in the formula. This makes it easier to find each of the formula's precedent cells.

While the Go To Special dialog box has an option for selecting precedent cells, a more effective method is to use the Trace Precedents command, which draws arrows from the formula to the precedent cells. The Trace Precedents command is accessed through the Tools, Auditing menu.

In the previous Figure 10.5, a cell is identified, D10, which may have an error in the formula. To locate the cells that are used in the formula, invoke the Trace Precedents command. In

Figure 10.6, the trace arrows have been drawn to the precedent cells, showing where the error occurs. The formula is using the wholesale price for the TaxMan software, instead of the CheckCount software.

FIG. 10.6

The trace arrows point to the precedent cells.

The active cell is D10

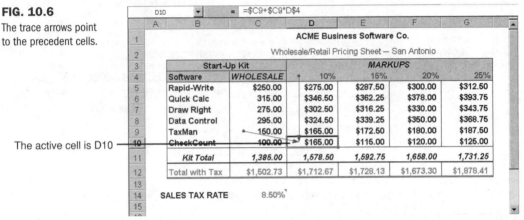

In some cases, the cells containing the error are in cells indirectly linked to the formula. Figure 10.7 shows the precedents traced back several levels from cell D11. To accomplish this, use the Trace Precedents command until all cells have been selected. To remove the trace arrows, use the Remove All Arrow command.

FIG. 10.7

You may need to trace back several levels to locate all cells the formula directly or indirectly uses.

The active cell is D11

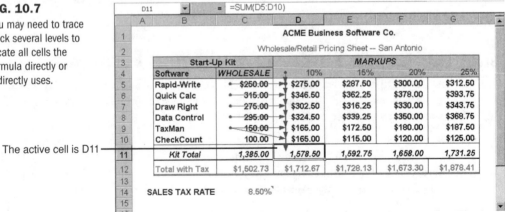

If you intend to perform a great deal of auditing, display the Auditing Toolbar for convenient access to the auditing commands. Choose Tools, Auditing, Show Auditing Toolbar.

N O T E   Trace arrows locate all precedent cells, whether in the active workbook or in other workbooks. If a trace arrow points off the screen or to a worksheet symbol, double-click the trace line to see the precedent cells. ▪

Understanding Excel Error Messages

Error messages display when the result of a formula cannot be calculated. These messages display for several reasons—when the worksheet column is not wide enough to display the result, when a cell used in a formula is blank or contains text, or when cells referenced by a formula are deleted.

The error may be in the formula or in one of the cells to which the formula refers. Table 10.1 describes the Excel error messages.

Table 10.1   Error Messages in Microsoft Excel

Error Displayed	Meaning
#####	The column is not wide enough to display the number in the cell. This error also displays when calculations with dates and time are made incorrectly, specifically when the result of a date or time calculation is negative. Excel cannot display negative date or time results.
#VALUE!	The formula contains an unacceptable argument. For example, when one of the cells in a calculation contains text.
#DIV/0!	The formula or macro is dividing by a cell that is blank or contains a 0 (zero).
#NAME?	The formula includes text, usually a range name or nested function, that Excel cannot recognize. The range name may have been deleted or the function misspelled. A space between the function name and the open parenthesis also results in the error #NAME?.
#N/A	A value is not available to a formula or refers to a cell that contains #N/A. This may occur for several reasons—when an exact match cannot be found using a lookup function, an argument is missing in the formula, or not all the necessary data used by the formula is entered into the worksheet.
#REF!	The formula refers to a cell that is not valid. This usually occurs when cells, or the column or row the cell is in, are deleted.
#NUM!	A number in a formula either is not valid or calculates an invalid result.
#NULL!	Excel expects to find an intersection between two cell ranges and returns the #NULL! error message when it does not find the intersection. This usually occurs when a cell range is entered incorrectly. For example, if a function contains the references (B6:B16D6:D16), the #NULL! will result. A comma is needed to separate B16 and D6 to separate the ranges.

Resolving Circular Reference Errors

A *circular reference* occurs when a formula refers back to its own cell. When a circular reference is made, Excel displays a warning message, as shown in Figure 10.8. You have a choice of resolving the reference by clicking OK or accepting the reference by clicking Cancel.

FIG. 10.8

A warning message displays when a circular cell reference is made in a formula.

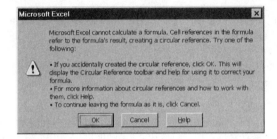

If you click OK, the Circular Reference toolbar is displayed (see Figure 10.9). The toolbar helps to identify each cell in the circular reference.

 TIP The status bar displays the word `Circular` and one of the cell references contained in the circular reference. If there is no cell reference with the word `Circular` in the status bar, the circular reference is not in the active worksheet.

FIG. 10.9

The Circular Reference toolbar automatically appears when a circular reference is created accidentally.

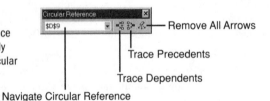

The Circular Reference toolbar provides some very helpful buttons for identifying and resolving circular references. The following list describes each button on the toolbar:

- *Navigate Circular Reference.* A drop-down list box identifying cell references that may be the cause of the circular reference.
- *Trace Dependents.* Displays arrows pointing to cells that refer to the active cell. For example, if the active cell is C12 and a formula in cell C15 refers to cell C12, the arrows point to cell C15. Cell C15 contains the formula and is dependent upon cell C12.
- *Trace Precedents.* Displays arrows pointing to cells to which the active cell refers. For example, if the active cell is C12 and it contains a formula referring to cells C2:C10, the arrows point to cells C2:C10. Cells C2:C10 can contain values or formulas and precede cell C12.
- *Remove All Arrows.* Removes all trace arrows.

Circular References in Scientific and Engineering Functions

Some of Excel's scientific and engineering functions require circular references. To calculate a circular reference formula, Microsoft Excel must calculate each cell involved in the circular reference one time by using the results of the previous iteration. By default, Microsoft Excel calculates either up to 100 iterations or to the point that all values in the circular reference change by less than 0.001 between iterations, whichever comes first.

You may need to change the number of iterations if your formula is one that requires a circular reference. To change the number of iterations, choose Tools, Options. In the Options dialog box, select the Calculation tab. Check the Iteration box, and indicate the maximum number of iterations and degree of change you want Excel to use.

N O T E Most engineering and scientific functions are available in the Analysis ToolPak Add-In. Choose Tools, Add-Ins to install the Analysis ToolPak. ■

Using Comments in Worksheets to Avoid Errors

One way to prevent errors in your worksheets is to attach comments to cells. Comments are especially useful in forms or templates inside which other people will be inputting data. Comments can be attached to any cell. Excel places a red triangle indicator in the upper-right corner of each cell that contains a comment. When you position the mouse pointer in the cell, the comment automatically appears on-screen. Figure 10.10 shows a worksheet with built-in comments.

FIG. 10.10
Use comments to annotate a form or template file.

Comment indicator

Comments display when the mouse pointer is in the cell

Mouse pointer

Selection handle

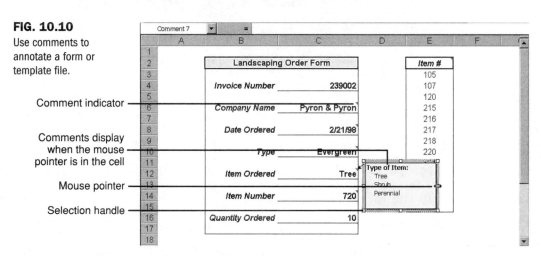

To attach a comment to a cell, right-click the cell and choose Insert Comment from the shortcut menu. A small box appears. The title is the User Name defined in the Options dialog box. Enter the text you want to appear in the comment. Resize the box by positioning the mouse pointer on one of the selection handles and drag to reshape the comment box. Press the Esc key or click in an area away from the box to complete the comment.

After comments have been entered into a worksheet, you can edit, delete, or display the comment through the shortcut menu.

Several of the comment settings are controlled through the Options dialog box. Choose Tools, Options to access the dialog box. On the View tab, you can choose not to display the comment or indicator, to display the indicator only, or to display both comment and indicator. By default, just the indicator appears. In the User Name text box on the General tab, you can enter the text you want to display as the title in the comment box. Any comments created before the change in the User Name text will retain the former title.

 TIP The bold title in the comment is taken from the User Name box in the Options dialog box. You can edit the text directly in the comment in the worksheet, making each title unique to that particular comment.

FIG. 10.11

The Page Setup dialog box must be accessed from the file menu, not through the Print Preview screen, to choose one of the Comment print options.

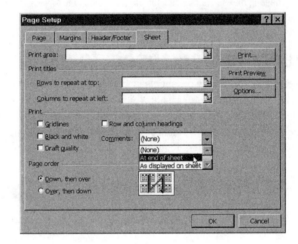

PART IV

Making Your Point with Excel

CHAPTER 11

Designing a List or Database

Worksheets generally fall into two categories: lists and
forms. A *list* is a worksheet designed to contain information about many items. Examples include an employee
roster, a client database, a price list, a list of all orders
received during the year, or even a list of companies and
the total amount each company has in outstanding invoices. A *form* is a worksheet designed to contain information about a particular item, such as a purchase order
form for a single order, an expense report for a specific
month, an invoice statement for one client, or a simple
take-home pay calculation. ■

Defining an Excel list

Almost any information you track
can be used as an Excel list. Excel
provides a number of powerful tools
that you can use to manipulate data
in a list. In order to take advantage
of these tools, the Excel list must be
carefully designed.

Entering data quickly in a list

Discover how the Data Form can
facilitate entering data into lists and
databases. Excel automatically
generates a data form that is based
on your list. Additionally, you can
use the new AutoComplete and Pick
From List features to enter data in
lists.

Creating databases in Excel

Learn how to create an Excel database, which can then be used to
export Excel data into database
programs like Access and FoxPro.
An Excel database is a specific type
of list.

Understanding Lists

A *list* is a contiguous series of related data. Most likely, many of the Excel worksheets you currently use are lists. A list of client information, an employee or student roster, itemized sales figures, or an inventory are all examples of lists. Essentially, any series of worksheet rows that contain information relating to a particular topic is a list.

There are 65,536 rows in each worksheet, an increase from 16,384 rows available in previous versions of Excel. Some very large lists can be maintained in Excel 97.

When creating a list, follow these guidelines:

- *Create one list per worksheet.* Use other worksheets in the same workbook to hold multiple lists. Some of the tools used to manipulate information in lists, such as filtering, can be used on only one list at a time.

- *Enter labels for each column.* Use the first row in the list for column labels. The labels should describe the data contained in each column. If you need to use several words as a label, place the column label in a single cell and format the cell to word-wrap the label. Excel allows only one row of labels in a list. Excel uses the labels to locate and categorize data. Do not leave blank rows between the column labels and the data. If you need to distinguish the labels from the data, either change the height of the labels row, format the cells with a border, or use a different format on the labels to set them apart from the data. In Figure 11.1, the column labels for the list are in row 4. The labels have been formatted to word-wrap.

- *Separate the column labels from the worksheet title.* If you have a title or other headings for the worksheet above the column labels, make sure there is at least one blank row between the title and the column labels. Because Excel accepts only one row of labels, this blank row separates the list from the from the title. Figure 11.1 shows a title in rows 1 and 2. Row 3 is blank to separate the list from the title.

- *Avoid blank rows and columns in the list.* While there can be individual blank cells in a list, there should be no completely blank rows or columns in a list of data. If blank rows or columns have been inserted in the list to space out the data, remove them. Instead, enlarge the row height or column widths. There are several blank cells in Figure 11.1, but no completely blank rows or columns.

- *Column calculations should be separated from the list.* Calculations below your list should be separated from the list by using at least one blank row between the list and the calculations. Calculations to the right of your list do not need to be separated from the list.

- *Separate the list from other worksheet data.* Include blank columns and blank rows between the list and other data on the worksheet. Excel uses these blank columns and rows as the "boundary" of the list.

FIG. 11.1
This worksheet contains lists of information.

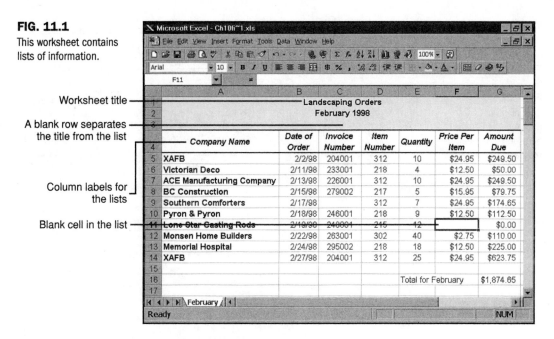

Worksheet title

A blank row separates the title from the list

Column labels for the lists

Blank cell in the list

Entering Data in a List

The column labels are usually the first data entered into a list. To take advantage of Excel's list management tools, the column labels should each be unique; don't use the same label for more than one column. Excel interprets "SALES" and "sales" as identical labels.

There are several new features in Excel 97 that facilitate entering data into a list. As you enter data, the AutoComplete and Pick From List features will help to complete the list more rapidly. Both features are explained in Chapter 1, "Essential Excel—Increasing Your Efficiency." These two features will save you a lot of time typing when the entries in a column are repetitive. For example, when a client's name appears next to multiple orders, you can type in the first few characters of the name and Excel automatically completes the rest of the name for you.

▶ **See** "Using AutoComplete to Enter Data Quickly," **p. 9**

▶ **See** "Pick From List," **p. 9**

Another option for entering information into a list is to use the data form. Excel automatically generates a form you can use to add new rows of information to your list. To access the form, select a single cell in your list and choose Data, Form.

In Figure 11.2, the column headings for a list of landscape orders have been entered. Because specific orders have not yet been entered, a message appears for you to confirm how Excel is to proceed. The labels in row 3 of Figure 11.2 will be used to create the form if OK is selected. If you have not created the appropriate labels, using the guidelines specified in the previous section "Understanding Lists", choose Cancel. The Help button will display a screen about creating column labels for a list.

N O T E   The message shown in Figure 11.2 may also appear if there is a row above your column labels containing data, such as a title, that has been merged to display centered across the top of the list. Insert a blank row between your title and column labels to avoid this problem. ■

FIG. 11.2
If Excel cannot determine the labels to be used in the form, this message is displayed.

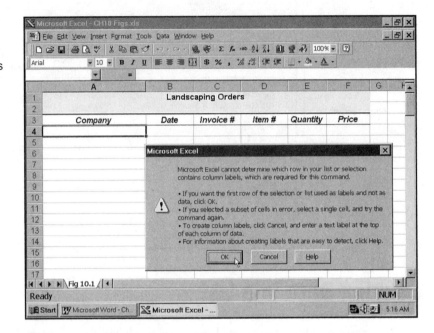

If you have some data in the list, or if you select OK in the message displayed in Figure 11.2, a form based on the column labels in the list appears (see Figure 11.3). The name of the form is taken from the worksheet tab name.

FIG. 11.3
The column labels serve as labels for entering new information into your list.

Form Name

Column labels as fields in the form

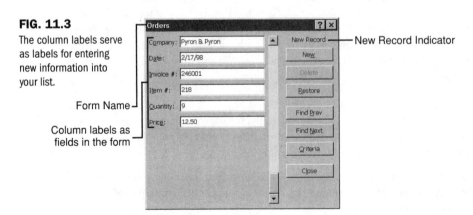

New Record Indicator

In the data form, each row of information in a list is referred to as a *record* and each column in the list is known as a *field*. If you have not entered data into your list, a new record is automatically started for you (refer to Figure 11.3). If some data has been entered in the list, the first record is displayed. To add a new record, select the New button.

To enter a new record into the data form, follow these steps:

1. Type the data in the first field entry box.
2. Use your Tab key or click with the mouse to move to the next field entry box in the form. To move backward in the form, use Shift+Tab or click with the mouse.
3. When you reach the end of the form, press Enter to create a new record. The New button is the active button in the form; therefore, it is not necessary to select it to begin a new record.
4. When you have completed all the entries, choose Close.

Whenever new records are added using the form, Excel places the data in blank rows at the bottom of the list. Excel does not insert rows to add the new data. If there are calculations or other data in the rows below the list and you try to enter a new record using the form, a warning message stating `Cannot extend list or database` will be displayed. You will then have to close the form and insert additional rows, or move the data below the list, before you can enter new records using the form.

Follow these suggestions for entering data:

- To quickly enter the current date or time into a field in your list, use keyboard shortcuts. Ctrl+; (semicolon) is used for the current date and Ctrl+Shift+; (semicolon) is used for the current time.

- When entering data in a list, do not type extra spaces at the beginning of a cell; extra spaces will affect Excel's capability to locate data and sort the list.

▶ **See** "Sorting Lists of Data," **p. 187**
▶ **See** "Using the Data Form to Filter a List," **p. 203**

Using a List as a Database

A *database* is a collection of information related to a particular subject or purpose. Databases are comprised of one or more *tables*, or lists, of information. There are two types of databases: flat file and relational. A *flat file database* is a database in which all the information is placed into one large table. A *relational database* is a database in which the information is divided into several smaller tables. In a relational database, when you need to display data from multiple tables, the tables are related (or linked) together. Excel uses flat file type databases. Access, FoxPro, and dBASE use relational type databases.

In Excel, a database is a specific type of list to which new records routinely are being added. Figure 11.4 illustrates an example of an Excel database.

Databases use a unique set of terminology, some of which is explained in the following list:

FIG. 11.4

This figure illustrates a
database as it appears
while using Excel 97.

DSUM function

Criteria

Database Statistics
using DSUM and
DCOUNTA

Field names

Record

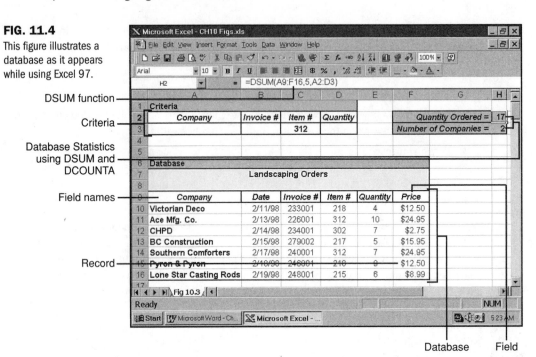

Database   Field

■ *Database.* A database is a range of cells that make up the list. In Figure 11.4, the database extends from A9 to F16. Because Excel uses flat file databases, which are comprised of a single list (or table) of information, sometimes the terms database and table are used interchangeably.

■ *Records.* Each row of information in the list is a record.

■ *Fields.* Each column of information in the list is a field.

■ *Field Names.* The column labels are referred to as field names. In Figure 11.4, the field names are in row 9.

■ *Criteria.* The range of cells listing the specifications of the search. The Criteria includes only those field names from the database that you intend to search.

There are worksheet functions specifically designed to perform calculations on Excel databases. They are listed under the database category in the Paste Function dialog box. In Figure 11.4, the DSUM function is being used to determine the total quantity ordered of Item # 312. The DCOUNTA function is used to determine the number of different orders that were placed for Item # 312.

Chapter 12, "Manipulating Data in Lists," includes a section that explains how to use database functions. Chapter 5, "Working with Templates," includes a section on using the Template Wizard to populate a database.

▶ **See** "Using the Template Wizard with Data Tracking," **p. 87**

▶ **See** "Using Database Functions," **p. 187**

Manipulating Data in Lists

Chapter 11, "Designing a List or Database," discusses how to create lists in Excel. After you create a list, you can increase the usefulness of the list by reorganizing the data. There are four ways to manipulate data is lists: sorting, subtotaling, using database functions, and creating pivot tables. Sorting involves rearranging the list based on criteria you specify. Subtotaling, database functions, and pivot tables are alternatives for summarizing the data in lists. Subtotaling provides calculations for each group or category of data and a grand total at the bottom of the list. Database functions are an alternative to generating subtotals. Similar calculations are performed, but the effect on the worksheet is entirely different. Pivot tables are discussed in Chapter 15 "Unlocking the Power of Pivot Tables."

Sort entire lists of data with a few simple mouse clicks

Excel makes it easy to reorganize the data is your lists. You can sort a list alphabetically, numerically, or using a custom order you define.

Create subtotal calculations effortlessly

Choose from 11 common Excel functions for your subtotal calculations. Multiple subtotals can be calculated in a list at the same time. Excel automatically inserts rows in your list to contain the subtotals.

Use powerful database calculations to summarize the data

Excel includes 12 worksheet functions designed specifically to perform calculations on lists or databases. More complex criteria can be used with the database functions than is available with subtotals.

Sorting Lists of Data

Sorting your data in Excel can be accomplished swiftly and easily. You can sort a list based on one criterion through buttons on the Standard toolbar, or use up to three separate criteria with the <u>D</u>ata, <u>S</u>ort command.

You can sort a list in ascending or descending order. An *ascending sort* lists numbers (1-9), then symbols, followed by uppercase letters (A-Z), and finally lowercase letters (a-z). A *descending sort* lists lowercase letters (z-a), then uppercase letters (Z-A), followed by symbols, and finally numbers (9-1). In Figure 12.1, to sort the list of landscape orders alphabetically by Company, use an ascending sort. To sort the list showing the largest to smallest Amount Due, use a descending sort.

FIG. 12.1

Click the Sort Ascending or Sort Descending buttons to sort a list in ascending or descending order.

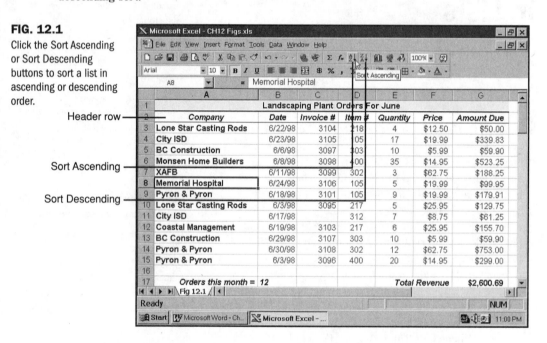

The column in which your active cell is located is used as the basis for the sort. Excel does not sort just the data in that column. The corresponding data in each row moves along with the column in which the sort is performed. For example, in Figure 12.1 the active cell is in the Company column—cell A8, Memorial Hospital. Using an ascending sort, the rows in the list will be rearranged, with the company names appearing in alphabetical order. Rows are sometimes referred to as *records* in an Excel list.

Before sorting a list, however, there are a few things you should keep in mind:

■ *Header row.* When you sort a list, Excel assumes the first row contains column headings and, therefore, does not include the first row in the sort. As discussed in Chapter 11, "Designing a List or Database," the list may contain only one row of column headings.

If other labels are necessary to describe the list, either insert a blank row between the list header row and the other labels, or use the Merge and Center button to center the additional labels. In Figure 12.1, the title of the list, "Landscaping Plant Orders For June," is centered across the list by using the Merge and Center button on the Formatting toolbar. Additionally, Excel uses the column headings as criteria labels when you perform sorts on multiple columns.

- *List selection.* When you select one of the cells in your list, Excel automatically highlights the entire list of data for the sort. Excel automatically sorts the entire contents of a list unless a range of cells is selected.

NOTE If you select more than one cell in the list, Excel sorts only the range of cells you have selected. When you need to sort only a part of the list, make sure you select all the cells containing the corresponding data.

- *Blank cells.* When the column you sort by contains blank cells, Excel places the cells (and their corresponding data) at the bottom of the column. Ascending or descending sorts do not impact this action. In Figure 12.1, the Invoice # column contains a blank in row 11. If the list is sorted by Invoice #, the row (or record) for City ISD moves to the bottom of the list.

- *Blank rows.* Your list should not contain any blank rows. If you select a range of cells that do contain blank rows and then sort the data, the blank rows are moved to the bottom of the range.

- *Calculations.* Always insert a blank row between the list and calculations *below* the list; otherwise, the calculation rows may be sorted with the list. Chapter 1, "Essential Excel—Increasing Your Efficiency," illustrates exactly what happens when you do not insert a blank row between the data in your list and the calculations below the list. Calculations that appear to the right of the list generally should not be separated from the list. Typically, you want these calculations to move with the rows as you sort the list.

▶ **See** "Designing Effective Spreadsheets," **p. 10**
▶ **See** "Understanding Lists," **p. 182**

To perform a simple sort based on one column in your list, follow these steps:

1. Select a cell in the column you want the list to be sorted by. For example, in Figure 12.2 you would select a cell in the Date column if you wanted the list sorted by date.

2. Choose either the Sort Ascending or Sort Descending button on the Standard Toolbar.

3. Excel automatically selects the entire list and performs the sort on the selected cells. The rows are reordered based on the column on which you sorted.

In Figure 12.2, the list has been alphabetically sorted by Company, using the Sort Ascending button on the toolbar.

Suppose that you want to rearrange the information in this list so that you see first the earliest order from those companies who have placed multiple orders. If you select a cell in the Date column and use the Sort Ascending button on the toolbar, the list will be sorted by the date

Part
IV
Ch
12

column. However, the list does not retain the sort by company name. The toolbar buttons sort only by one column in your list. To perform a sort on multiple columns, you need to use the Data, Sort command.

FIG. 12.2

The active cell remains in the same cell (A8) and does not move with the data that is sorted.

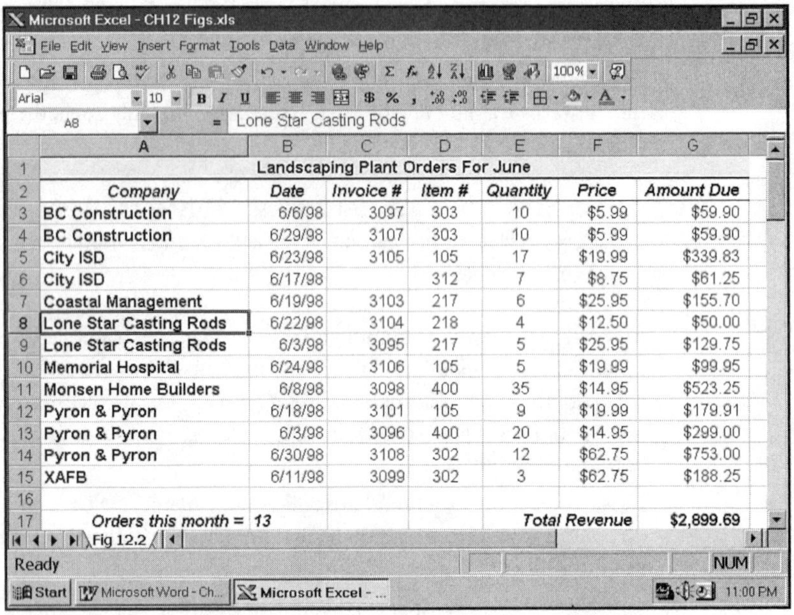

You can select up to three columns for the sort criteria with the Data Sort command. Each column can be sorted in either ascending or descending order.

To perform a multiple column sort, follow these steps:

1. Select any cell in the list.

2. Choose Data, Sort. The Sort dialog box appears (see Figure 12.3).

FIG. 12.3

The heading of the column containing the active cell is listed in the first drop-down box.

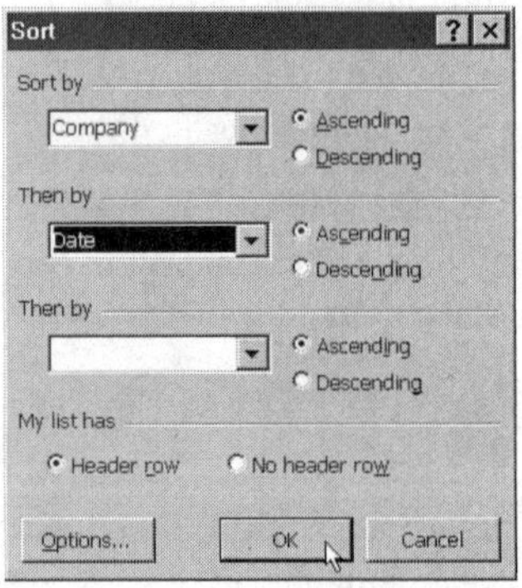

3. From the Sort By list box, choose the column heading by which you want your list first sorted. Select Ascending or Descending for this criteria. In Figure 12.3, the Company column will be sorted in ascending order.

N O T E If your list does not have a header row, or one that Excel can recognize, column letters will display in the drop-down list boxes. ▪

4. From the first Then By list box, choose the column to sort if there are duplicates in the first column. Select Ascending or Descending for this criteria. In Figure 12.3, the Date column will be sorted in ascending order.

5. If you expect duplicates in the second column criteria you selected in Step 4, then use the next Then By list box for your last criteria. Choose the column heading and either Ascending or Descending for this third criterion.

6. By default, Excel assumes that your list has a header row. If the list does not have a header row, Choose No Header Row.

7. Click OK.

Returning a Sort to the Original Order

 Lists can be sorted temporarily to view or print the information in a different order. In these situations, use the Undo button to return the list to the original order. Excel 97 will undo your last 16 actions.

There may be certain lists that you need to sort by different criteria on a routine basis. You need to add a column to your list to act as an index. This ensures the list can be returned to the original order. The index column can be an ascending list of numbers, dates, or letters. Figure 12.4 illustrates a list with a numerical index column. This list can be sorted by the country names or any of the book categories. To return the list to the original sort order, you can sort the list on the index column.

Part
IV

Ch
12

Sorting in a Special Order

Occasionally, you may need to sort a list according to something other than alphabetic or numeric order. You can choose a custom list as the criteria for sorting. Excel provides built-in custom lists for sorting months of the year and days of the week. Additionally, you can create your own custom list.

Figure 12.5 shows a list of expenses sorted by department. Instead of an alphabetical listing of departments, the list is sorted in a custom departmental order.

There are two ways to create a custom list for sorting:

▪ By creating a list from scratch.

▪ By using an existing list in a worksheet. The list cannot contain duplicate entries.

Index	Country	Mysteries	Classics	Computer	Fiction	Non-Fiction	*Total*
1	Canada	6,521	5,478	3,214	9,874	1,254	19,820
2	United States	1,258	1,542	6,547	9,875	2,365	20,329
3	Mexico	2,548	4,563	9,874	6,542	9,658	30,637
4	Belize	2,634	8,523	9,875	4,875	3,698	26,971
5	Costa Rica	1,598	3,215	6,542	3,215	2,587	15,559
6	Panama	4,875	6,548	1,596	6,548	7,412	22,104
7	Ecuador	3,215	1,258	2,587	4,563	6,547	14,955
8	Peru	6,548	2,548	7,412	8,523	9,874	28,357
9	Chile	6,521	5,478	3,214	3,215	1,254	13,161
10	Bolivia	3,215	1,258	2,587	6,548	6,547	16,940
12	Puerto Rico	3,365	1,598	1,126	5,478	6,542	14,744

FIG. 12.4
Each time a new record (row) of information is added to the list, you need to include the incremental index for that record.

Expenses

Department	Employee	Date	Type of Expense	Amount
Administration	Henrietta Lee	6/19/98	Travel	710.92
Administration	Jose Chavez	6/3/98	Travel	475.89
Planning	Yasmine Ali	6/18/98	Software	279.94
Sales	Rick Barretto	6/3/98	Business Lunch	61.50
Sales	Scott Fujimora	6/14/98	Business Lunch	50.64
Sales	Scott Fujimora	6/30/98	Laptop Computer	3,798.27
Communication	Ian Stewart	6/22/98	Printing - Newsletter	159.37
Marketing	Leo Swartz	6/23/98	Business Lunch	38.21
Marketing	Leo Swartz	6/24/98	Employee Recognition	64.90
Marketing	Marc Rodgers	6/8/98	Office Supplies	36.21
Accounting	Anita Salinas	6/6/98	External Auditor	2,390.00
Accounting	Bob Brown	6/29/98	Office Supplies	45.33
Maintenance	David Jacobson	6/17/98	Paint	52.86

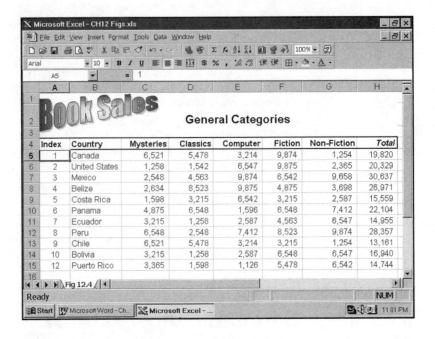

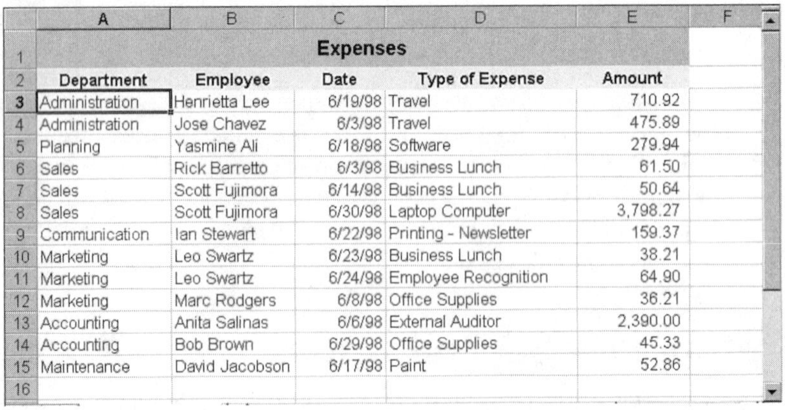

FIG. 12.5
Use a custom sort list when the order you want displayed is not straight alphabetical or numerical.

To create a custom sort list from scratch, follow these steps:

1. Choose Tools, Options. The Options dialog box appears.
2. Select the Custom Lists tab (see Figure 12.6).
3. Choose NEW LIST from the Custom Lists text box.
4. Type the values in the List Entries text box. Press Enter after each entry, or type a comma and a space to separate the entries.
5. Choose Add.
6. Click OK.

FIG. 12.6

Excel provides four custom lists for you to use, or you can create new lists.

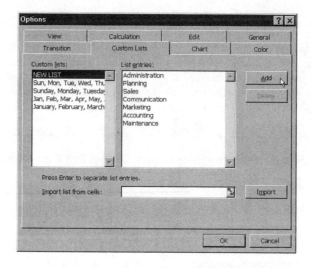

Another way to create a custom list is to import an existing list into the Custom Lists dialog box. The list you import must not contain duplicates. Earlier in Figure 12.5, you could not use the Department column because the department names appear multiple times. When there are duplicates in the column you want to custom sort, create a temporary list somewhere else in your worksheet. Using the data in Figure 12.5 as an example, you would create a temporary list that contains each department name in the order you want the departments sorted. Each department would be listed one time.

To create a custom sort list based on an existing list in a worksheet, follow these steps:

1. Select the cells to use as the custom list order.
2. Choose Tools, Options. The Options dialog box appears.
3. Click the Custom Lists tab.
4. Verify that the Import List From Cells text box (refer to Figure 12.6) is displaying the correct cell references.
5. Choose Import.
6. Click OK.

After you have created the custom sort order, you can sort a list using the custom order by following these steps:

1. Select a cell in the list.
2. The first time you sort a list using a custom order, you must use the Data, Sort command.
3. In the Sort dialog box, choose Sort By list box and select the column you want to sort. A custom sort list can be used only as the first sort criteria.
4. Select Options.
5. From the First Key Sort Order drop-down list, choose a custom order.

Part

IV

Ch

12

6. Click OK to return to the Sort dialog box.

7. Choose a second and third criteria for the list, if necessary, and then click OK.

 TIP Suppose you need to perform custom sorts on two columns in your list, such as department and type of expense. The department is the primary sort and type of expense is the secondary sort. To accomplish this, sort the list only by the type of expense custom order. Then sort the list again, this time only by the department custom order.

The custom lists you create for sorting can also be used with the AutoFill feature in Excel to create labels in your worksheet.

▶ **See** "Using AutoFill," **p. 16**

Automatic Worksheet Subtotals

After a list is sorted, the Subtotal command can quickly calculate subtotals and a grand total for the list. New rows are automatically inserted in your worksheet to display the subtotals and grand total calculations.

N O T E   The Subtotal command uses an outline to organize the list. See the section "Outlining Worksheets" in Chapter 2 if you are not familiar with Excel outline tools. ■

Before using the Subtotal command, you must make the following three decisions:

- ■ When do you want the subtotals to be calculated?
- ■ What type of calculation do you want performed?
- ■ Where do you want the calculation to appear?

When the subtotals are calculated is determined by the order the list is sorted. Sort the list by meaningful groups. In Figure 12.7, the list is sorted by Type of Expense. In this example, the Subtotal command generates subtotals after each different group of expenses. There will be a subtotal after Business Lunch, Employee Recognition, and so forth. If the list were sorted by Department, subtotals would appear between each Department.

What the subtotal calculates is a separate issue. There are 11 functions that can be used as subtotal calculations in Excel, including: SUM; COUNT; AVERAGE; MAX; MIN; PRODUCT; COUNTNUMS; SDTDEV; SDTDEVP; VAR; and VARP. Frequently, subtotals calculate the sum of a column of numerical data, such as the sum of the Amount column in Figure 12.7. You can also calculate averages, the standard deviation, and count items, including text, in the list. The average amount for each type of expense can be calculated. The number of employees in each department submitting expenses can be counted. In the Average example, the list needs to be sorted by the Type of Expense column. In the Count example, the list needs to be sorted by the Department column.

FIG. 12.7

The only column in this figure that would not produce a meaningful list is the Amount column.

	A	B	C	D	E	F
1			**Expenses**			
2	**Department**	**Employee**	**Date**	**Type of Expense**	**Amount**	
3	Sales	Rick Barretto	6/3/98	Business Lunch	61.50	
4	Sales	Scott Fujimora	6/14/98	Business Lunch	50.64	
5	Marketing	Leo Swartz	6/23/98	Business Lunch	38.21	
6	Marketing	Leo Swartz	6/24/98	Employee Recognition	64.90	
7	Accounting	Anita Salinas	6/6/98	External Auditor	2,390.00	
8	Sales	Scott Fujimora	6/30/98	Laptop Computer	3,798.27	
9	Marketing	Marc Rodgers	6/8/98	Office Supplies	36.21	
10	Accounting	Bob Brown	6/29/98	Office Supplies	45.33	
11	Maintenance	David Jacobson	6/17/98	Paint	52.86	
12	Communication	Ian Stewart	6/22/98	Printing - Newsletter	159.37	
13	Planning	Yasmine Ali	6/18/98	Software	279.94	
14	Administration	Henrietta Lee	6/19/98	Travel	710.92	
15	Administration	Jose Chavez	6/3/98	Travel	475.89	
16						

Where the subtotals appear in the worksheet is the final decision you must make. Often, the subtotals are displayed in the last column of the list, but you are not required to put the subtotals there. It would be logical to place the average type of expense subtotals in the Amount column. The number of employees submitting expenses can be placed either in the Department, Employee, Type of Expense, or even the Amount column.

To create subtotals and grand totals, use these steps:

1. Sort the list by the column on which the data will be grouped.

2. Select a single cell in the list and choose <u>D</u>ata, Su<u>b</u>totals. The Subtotal dialog box appears (see Figure 12.8).

FIG. 12.8

Common worksheet functions are used to calculate subtotals in a worksheet.

Selected by default ⎯

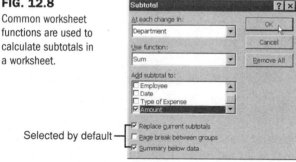

3. From the <u>A</u>t Each Change In drop-down list, select a column by which to group the list. In Figure 12.8, the Department column is selected.

4. Select a function to calculate from the <u>U</u>se Function drop-down list. The SUM function is selected in Figure 12.8.

5. In the A<u>d</u>d Subtotal To list box, choose the column on which the function will perform the calculation. In this case, the Amount column is selected. If there are several columns

you want to subtotal using the same function, you can choose more than one column in the Add Subtotal To list box.

6. Choose OK. The subtotals and a grand total appear in your worksheet.

The worksheet is automatically outlined. You can use the outline symbols or numbers to collapse or expand the outline. Figure 12.9 displays the worksheet collapsed to display the subtotals and grand total.

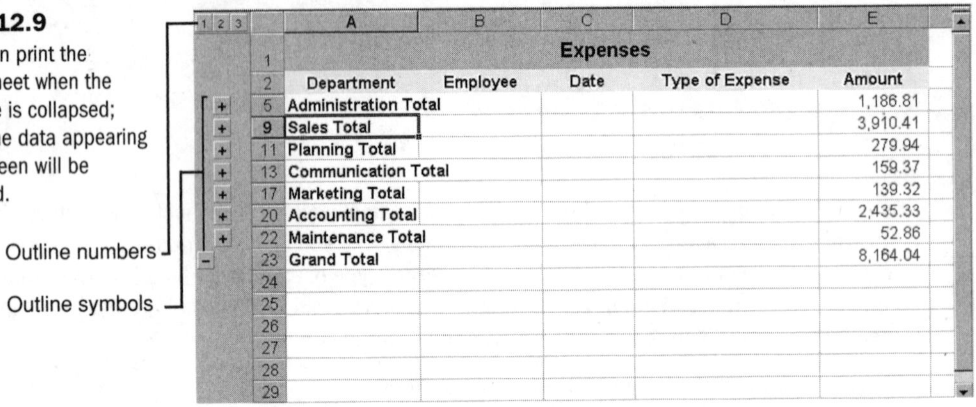

FIG. 12.9

You can print the worksheet when the outline is collapsed; only the data appearing on-screen will be printed.

Outline numbers

Outline symbols

One of the options in the Subtotals dialog box is to Replace Current Subtotals. This is used when you want to remove previous subtotals and replace them with new subtotals.

Another option in the dialog box is to separate the groups by inserting a page break between each group. When the worksheet is printed, each group appears on a separate printed page. This feature is particularly useful with long lists. For example, you might what to provide a list of departmental expenses to each manager.

If you do not want to show a grand total beneath the list, remove the check from the Summary Below Data box.

▶ **See** "Outlining Worksheets," **p. 49**

▶ **See** "Common Worksheet Functions," **p. 61**

You can remove the subtotals, grand totals, and outline symbols from the worksheet through the Subtotals command. Select a cell in your list and choose Data, Subtotals. From the Subtotals dialog box, click the Remove All button.

Calculating Multiple Subtotals in a Worksheet

The Subtotals command enables you to create subtotals using different functions. To accomplish this, remove the check from the Replace Current Subtotals box in the Subtotals dialog box. Only one function at a time can be calculated using the Subtotals command. You have to use the Subtotals command several times, once for each different subtotal to be calculated.

Figure 12.10 illustrates an example of two different subtotals: a count of the employees in each department who have submitted expenses, and a subtotal of the expenses grouped by department.

FIG. 12.10

The first calculation you perform is listed last. Subsequent subtotals are listed above the first one. In this case, the Count was calculated first, then the Total.

Outline numbers ⎯

Outline symbols ⎯

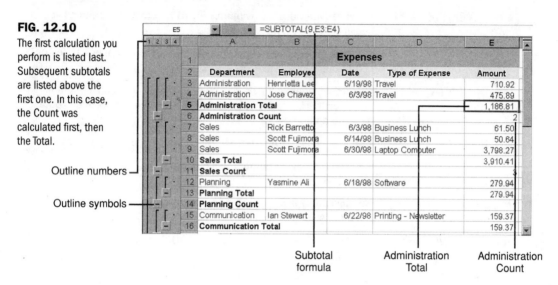

Subtotal
formula

Administration
Total

Administration
Count

Using Database Functions

An alternative to generating subtotals in your list is to use Excel's database functions. While the Subtotals command is an excellent choice when you need to print the subtotals and grand totals, using database functions is a terrific way to display the results on-screen. Unlike the Subtotals command, the list does not have to be sorted to use the database functions. Of even greater importance is the fact that more complex criteria can be used with the database functions than can be used with subtotals.

There are 12 worksheet functions specifically designed to perform calculations on Excel lists or databases. The advantage to using these functions rather than the standard functions is the capability of the database worksheet functions to perform calculations on part (a subset) of the list. You specify criteria that identifies specific rows (records) in the list, and the calculations are performed on those rows (records). Standard functions, however, perform the calculations on the entire list. Table 12.1 describes each of the database functions.

NOTE An Excel database is a special type of list. Refer to "Using a List as a Database" in Chapter 11 to learn about Excel databases and the terminology used with databases. ■

Part
IV

Ch
12

Table 12.1   The 12 Database Functions Available in Microsoft Excel

Function Name	Description
DAVERAGE	Averages the values in a column (field) that match conditions you specify.
DCOUNT	Counts the cells in a column (field) that contain numbers, based on conditions you specify.
DCOUNTA	Counts the nonblank cells in a column (field), based on conditions you specify. This function is useful when the column contains both text and numbers.
DGET	Extracts a single row (record) that matches conditions you specify.
DMAX	Returns the largest number in a column (field) that matches conditions you specify.
DMIN	Returns the smallest number in a column (field) that matches conditions you specify.
DPRODUCT	Multiplies the values in a column (field) that match conditions you specify.
DSTDEV	Estimates the standard deviation based on a sample from the selected list or database entries.
DSTDEVP	Calculates the standard deviation based on the entire population of the selected list or database entries.
SDUM	Adds the numbers in a column (field) in a list or database that match conditions you specify.
DVAR	Estimates the variance based on a sample from the selected list or database entries.
DVARP	Calculates the variance based on the entire population of the selected list or database entries.

Most of the functions are statistical calculations. Each function uses three arguments: database, field, and criteria. You need to be familiar with these arguments before you use the database functions. The following list explains these arguments:

■ *Database*. The range of cells that make up the list. In Figure 12.11, the database extends from A9 to F16. Each row of information in the list is a record.

■ *Field*. The particular column in the database being searched. Each column of information in the list is a field. To search the Item # field in the worksheet displayed in Figure 12.11, **"Item #"** or **4** is entered as the column (field) in the database function. If the column (field) name is entered in the function, it must be enclosed in quotes. If a number is used, the number must correspond to the column in the database range. In this case, 4 indicates that Item # is the fourth column in the database.

■ *Criteria.* The range of cells listing the specifications of the search. Criteria are placed in separate cells in the worksheet, often above the database. The Criteria is a range consisting typically of two rows — of one row of labels that match the column (field) names and one row for the specific criteria being searched. In Figure 12.11, the criteria range is A2 to D3. The Criteria includes only those column (field) names from the database that you intend to search—a listing of all the column names is not necessary.

Figure 12.11 illustrates an example of an Excel list using the database functions. The criteria specifies Item # 312. The DSUM function is being used to determine the total quantity ordered of Item # 312. The DCOUNTA function is used to determine the number of different orders that were placed for Item # 312.

FIG. 12.11

The range names Database and Criteria have been used in the DCOUNTA formula.

DCOUNTA function

Criteria

Database statistics using DSUM and DCOUNTA

Database

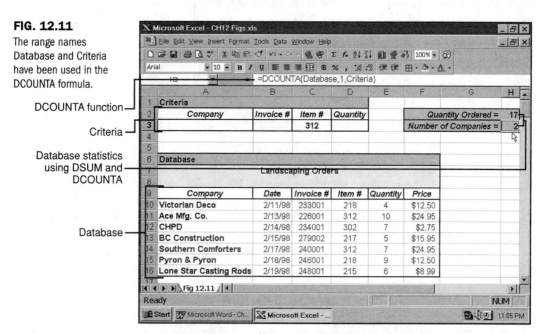

Range names are used frequently in database functions to help identify the database and the criteria. Creating and using range names is discussed in Chapter 2.

▶ **See** "Using Range Names," **p. 53**

The criteria range can be located anywhere on the worksheet. If you add information to your list through the Data, Form command, you should not place the criteria range below your list. Excel attempts to add new information to the first row below the list when you use the Data Form. If the first row below the list is not blank, Excel cannot add the new information to your list.

TIP To see a grand total calculation, leave the criteria blank.

Part
IV

Ch

12

To use the database functions, follow these steps:

1. Create your list and set up the criteria area in your worksheet.

2. Select the cell in which you want the calculated answer to appear.

 3. Click the Paste Function button on the Standard toolbar. The Paste Function dialog box appears (see Figure 12.12).

FIG. 12.12

The Paste Function dialog box assists in using Excel's predefined functions.

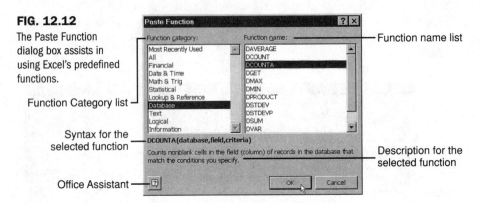

4. Choose the Database categories in the Function Category list box.

5. Choose the function from the names in the Function Name list box. The syntax and description for the selected function appear below the Function Category list box. In Figure 12.12, the DCOUNTA function is selected. A description of the selected function appears toward the bottom of the dialog box.

6. Select OK and the Formula Palette appears, detailing the arguments for the function (see Figure 12.13).

FIG. 12.13

The Formula Palette box leads you through the specific syntax required for the function that you select.

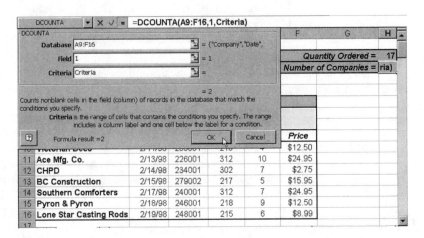

7. The first argument, Database, is selected—note the flashing cursor in the Database box. A description of the function and the selected argument appears near the bottom of the Formula Palette box.

8. Select the cell or cells in your spreadsheet that contain the database. If you have created a range name for the database, press F3. From The Paste Names dialog box, choose the range name from the list and click OK.

9. Select the Field argument by pressing the Tab key or clicking with your mouse. Enter either the column name in quotes or the corresponding column number. For example, if the list begins in column A and extends from column A to column E, the corresponding column number for column D is 4. However, if the list begins in column C and extends to column G, the corresponding column number for column D is 2.

10. Select the Criteria argument by pressing the Tab key or clicking with your mouse. Select the cell or cells in your spreadsheet that contain the criteria. If you have created a range name for the criteria, press F3. From the Paste Names dialog box, choose the range name from the list and select OK.

11. After you enter in these three arguments, choose OK. The result of the function appears in the worksheet and the function appears in the Formula Bar.

If a criteria is specified before the formula is created, the result of the specific criteria appears. If the criteria is not specified, the calculation reflects all the records (rows) in the list. You can change the criteria at any time; the calculations will be updated automatically.

In a large list, you may want to use more complex criteria with the database functions. If two entries are placed in the criteria area, Excel assumes an AND condition exists on the criteria. For example, if you want to sum the quantity of a particular item a company orders, you enter both the company name and the item name or number. Only those records (rows) that match the criteria are summed.

To produce an OR condition between two criteria, you must use a second row in the criteria area. One criteria is placed in one row, the other criteria is placed in another row. For example, to sum the quantity ordered of two different items, one item name or number is entered in the first row of the criteria, and the second item name or number is entered in the second row of the criteria.

Figure 12.14 shows the result of an OR condition in the criteria area.

Part

IV

Ch

12

CAUTION

When using multiple criteria rows, make sure you enter criteria in *both* rows. A blank row in the criteria area results in the calculation of *all* records in the list.

FIG. 12.14

The criteria indicates records (rows) containing Item # 312 OR Item #218 should be included in the calculations.

Criteria area with two rows produces an OR condition

DSUM function

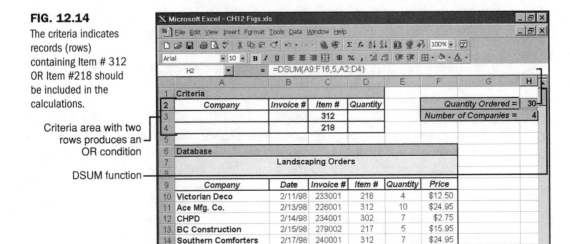

CHAPTER 13

Locating Data with Filters

Chapter 12, "Manipulating Data in Lists," explained how to reorder and perform calculations on groups or categories of data in a list. The sort, subtotal, and database function techniques enable you to manipulate the entire list of data. With very large lists, however, it may be difficult to focus on a specific group within the list. It may be necessary to view only part of the data.

In this chapter, you discover how to display a subset of a list. You accomplish this through filtering, by specifying the information you are seeking, the *criteria*. By identifying this criteria, Excel separates the data and displays only the data you have requested, the *filtered* data. There are three methods in Excel for locating data in lists: the AutoFilter, the Data Form, and the Advanced Filter. The AutoFilter displays only the rows matching your criteria, while the other rows in the list remain temporarily hidden. The Data Form shows rows matching your criteria, one row at a time, providing a convenient way to edit the information. The Advanced Filter enables you to specify complex criteria, including calculations. ■

Understanding criteria

Before using the filtering methods available in Excel, you need to learn how to correctly specify the type of information you are seeking.

Locating data easily

Both the AutoFilter and Data Form are convenient and easy methods to locate data in lists.

Specifying complex criteria

Use Advanced Filters when more complex criteria is needed to locate data in your worksheets.

Understanding Filter Criteria

Before using any of the three methods available for filtering lists, it is important that you understand how to tell Excel what you are seeking. The *criteria* are examples of the data from the list that you want to locate. Excel uses the criteria to search the list and displays only those rows (records) that match the criteria you specify.

Those rows that do not match the criteria will be filtered out and temporarily hidden.

▶ **See** "Understanding Lists," **p. 181**

The specific steps used by the AutoFilter, Data Form, and Advanced Filter to enter criteria are addressed in later sections of this chapter. Regardless of the filtering option you elect to use, however, the manner in which criteria is expressed in these options is virtually identical.

Excel has two types of criteria:

- *Comparison criteria.* Locates data that exactly matches the criteria or that falls within a range specified by the criteria.
- *Computed criteria.* Locates data by using formulas in the criteria.

Comparison criteria are the most widely used and is the focus of this section.

NOTE Criterion refers to one item; *criteria* refers to multiple items. This distinction is important because these terms are used throughout this chapter to distinguish between a search using one item and a search using multiple items.

Comparison criteria can be divided into three categories: exact match, wild card, and comparison operators. When an *exact match* criterion is used, Excel searches the list for an identical match to that criterion. An exact match criterion can be specified for text or numbers, including dates. Figure 13.1 shows a list of consulting work performed in June. The list is not sorted in any particular order. If you enter a company name as the criterion, such as **Pyron & Pyron**, only those rows (records) listing Pyron & Pyron as the company will display. Likewise, suppose you want to know all the work that was performed on June 4, 1998. Entering **6/4/98** as the criterion locates only the consulting work performed on that date. In both examples, you enter the criterion exactly the way it appears in the list.

Excel does not distinguish between uppercase and lowercase letters in criteria.

NOTE Although exact matches can also be used on cells containing formulas, the formula results are searched for, not the formula (or it's components) that is used to generate the result.

Wild cards are symbols you can use when you are not certain of, or aren't concerned about, one or more characters in the criteria. There are two wild cards available in Excel—the question mark (?) and the asterisk (*).

FIG. 13.1

This list of consulting work tracks the date the work occurred, the employee who performed the work, the company account number, a code for the type of work performed, and the hours worked.

	A	B	C	D	E	F
1			Consulting Worklog - June			
2						
3	Company	Date	Employee	Account #	Project Type	Hours
4	Monsen Home Builders	6/3/98	Anita Salinas	3098	217	3.0
5	City ISD	6/3/98	David Jacobson	3105	105	4.0
6	Monsen Home Builders	6/4/98	Anita Salinas	3098	217	8.0
7	Weiss LTD	6/11/98	Rick Barretto	3305	303	10.0
8	Monsen Home Builders	6/5/98	Anita Salinas	3098	217	8.0
9	City ISD	6/4/98	Jose Chavez	3105	105	8.0
10	Pyron & Pyron	6/4/98	Leo Swartz	3095	217	2.5
11	XAFB	6/17/98	Ian Stewart	3097	105	8.0
12	Coastal Management	6/7/98	Yasmine Ali	3099	302	6.0
13	City ISD	6/5/98	Jose Chavez	3105	105	8.0
14	BC Home Construction	6/24/98	Marc Rodgers	3103	400	10.0
15	Coastal Management	6/5/98	Yasmine Ali	3099	302	3.0
16	Northwest ISD	6/6/98	Rick Barretto	3105	400	9.0
17	Northwest ISD	6/7/98	Rick Barretto	3105	400	8.0
18	Pyron & Pyron	6/10/98	Leo Swartz	3095	217	8.0

- The question mark (?) is used as a substitute for one character in the criterion.
- The asterisk (*) is used as a substitute for multiple characters in the criteria.

In Figure 13.1, employee names are listed for each consulting job performed. Because the last name Chavez may have been entered with a *z* or an *s* at the end, Jose Chave? is entered as the criterion to ensure that all of the consulting work done by this employee is returned by the search. The question mark indicates any single character is acceptable as the last character in Jose's name.

The asterisk (*) is another wild card available to use in criteria. In Figure 13.1, there are several companies that build homes. To display the rows (records) for these companies, *home* is entered as the criterion. This example locates all company names that contain the word *home*, regardless of where the word appears in the name. Asterisks can be used before the criteria, after the criteria, or both before and after, as in this example.

 TIP If you need to find the asterisk (*) or question mark (?) symbols in a list, type a tilde (~) before the * or ?. The tilde indicates that you are not using the * or ? as a wild card.

Comparison operators are symbols used to locate data within a specified range. Table 13.1 shows a complete list of the comparison operators.

Table 13.1 The Comparison Operators Available in Filter Criteria

Comparison Symbol	Description
=	Equal
>	Greater than
>=	Greater than or equal to

continues

Table 13.1   Continued

Comparison Symbol	Description
<	Less than
<=	Less than or equal to
<>	Not equal to

Figure 13.2 shows an employee roster of company consultants. The list is ordered by the Specialty column. To display the rows (records) for all employees who earn 40,000 or more, the criterion would be >=40000. To list the employees who have a rating of 1 or 2, the criterion would be <3. Because blank cells are not numbers, those rows (records) with no rating will not be displayed using this criterion.

FIG. 13.2

Use equal (=) comparison operator with nothing following it to find fields that are blank (empty).

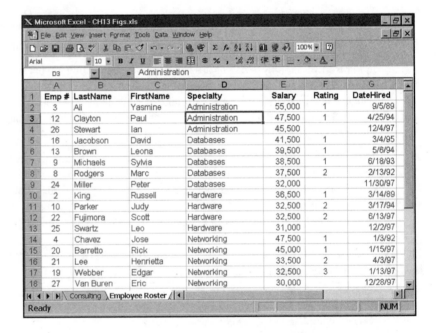

In earlier examples, only single criterion have been shown. To use multiple criteria, there are two logical conditions, AND and OR, with which you need to become familiar:

■ *AND.* Only if a row (record) matches all of the criteria will the row (record) be displayed.

■ *OR.* If a row (record) matches any single criterion, the row (record) will be displayed.

An example of an AND criteria is:

Employees with a Rating of 1 *and* whose Specialty is Networking

An example of an OR criteria is:

Employees whose Specialty is Networking *or* Project Management

Now that you understand how to specify criteria, you must decide which of the three Excel filter methods to use. The following comparisons may help you decide:

- *AutoFilter.* The easiest method for simple filters.
  - Displays multiple rows (records) matching the criteria.
  - Can use single AND and OR conditions.
  - Requires that you use a mouse.
- *Data Form.* The easiest method for editing filtered data or a list that has so many columns that the list headings cannot be viewed on-screen without scrolling.
  - Displays only a single row (record) at a time.
  - Does not allow for OR comparisons.
- *Advanced Filter.* This method is not as easy to use as the other methods, but it is more powerful.
  - Displays multiple rows (records) matching the criteria.
  - Can use multiple AND and OR conditions.
  - Can use computed criteria.
  - Allows you to copy the results of a filter to a separate location.

Specific steps to use the AutoFilter, Data Form, and Advanced Filter to locate data in lists are addressed in the remaining sections of this chapter.

TIP To see additional examples of comparison criteria, use the Office Assistant. Type in **criteria** in the Office Assistant search box and press Enter to see a list of help topics. Select Types Of Comparison Criteria from the list.

Part
IV

Ch
13

Discovering the Power of the AutoFilter

One of the quickest and easiest methods of filtering a list is to use the AutoFilter. As the name implies, the filtering is automatic. To access the AutoFilter, follow these steps:

1. Select a cell in your list.
2. Choose Data, Filter, AutoFilter. Filter arrows appear in the column headings, as shown in Figure 13.3. It is through these filter arrows that you specify the criteria.

There are three filter options that always appear when a filter arrow is selected. Two additional options may appear if your column contains blank cells. In Figure 13.3, the filter arrow for the Rating column has been selected, showing the five filter options (two of which appear because the column contains blank cells). In addition, each unique data occurrence in the column is

FIG. 13.3

Filter options appear
when the Rating column
is selected.

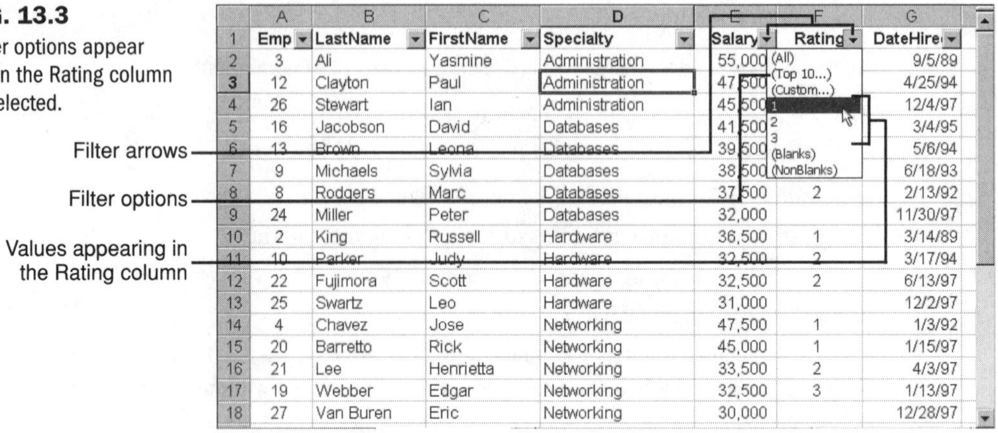

Filter arrows

Filter options

Values appearing in
the Rating column

	A	B	C	D	E	F	G
1	Emp ▾	LastName ▾	FirstName ▾	Specialty ▾	Salary ▾	Rating ▾	DateHire ▾
2	3	Ali	Yasmine	Administration	55,000	(All)	9/5/89
3	12	Clayton	Paul	Administration	47,500	(Top 10...)	4/25/94
4	26	Stewart	Ian	Administration	45,500	(Custom...)	12/4/97
5	16	Jacobson	David	Databases	41,500	1	3/4/95
6	13	Brown	Leona	Databases	39,500	2	5/6/94
7	9	Michaels	Sylvia	Databases	38,500	3 (Blanks)	6/18/93
8	8	Rodgers	Marc	Databases	37,500	2 (NonBlanks)	2/13/92
9	24	Miller	Peter	Databases	32,000		11/30/97
10	2	King	Russell	Hardware	36,500	1	3/14/89
11	10	Parker	Judy	Hardware	32,500	2	3/17/94
12	22	Fujimora	Scott	Hardware	32,500	2	6/13/97
13	25	Swartz	Leo	Hardware	31,000		12/2/97
14	4	Chavez	Jose	Networking	47,500	1	1/3/92
15	20	Barretto	Rick	Networking	45,000	1	1/15/97
16	21	Lee	Henrietta	Networking	33,500	2	4/3/97
17	19	Webber	Edgar	Networking	32,500	3	1/13/97
18	27	Van Buren	Eric	Networking	30,000		12/28/97

listed (in this case, the numbers 1, 2, and 3). Table 13.2 explains each filter option.

The filter arrows remain in the column headings until you turn off the AutoFilter.

Table 13.2   Five Standard Filter Options Available in Each Column When AutoFilter Is Active

Filter Option	Description
All	Used to remove the filter; displays all rows (records) of information.
Top 10	This is a new feature in Excel 97. By default, displays the top 10 most common items in the column. Three viewing alternatives include displaying either the Top or Bottom, any range from 1 to 500, or by either number of items or percent. Can be used on columns that contain only numbers or dates.
Custom	Used to specify custom criteria—*comparison operators*, such as greater than or equal to, *logical conditions* using AND and OR, and wild cards are all accessed through the Custom option.
Blanks	Used to display all rows (records) that contain blanks in the column.
NonBlanks	Used to display all rows (records) that contain data in the column, omitting any blanks.

The Blanks and NonBlanks options are available only if the column you are filtering contains a blank cell.

To specify criteria for an exact match, choose the filter arrow next to the heading in the column you want to filter. Select a value from the list. The list is automatically filtered to display only those rows (records) containing the value you selected. Figure 13.4 shows the exact matches for employees whose specialty is Networking.

FIG. 13.4

Records that match the selected criteria are displayed, while the rows (records) that do not match the criteria are hidden.

Hidden rows

Number of rows (records) that match your criteria

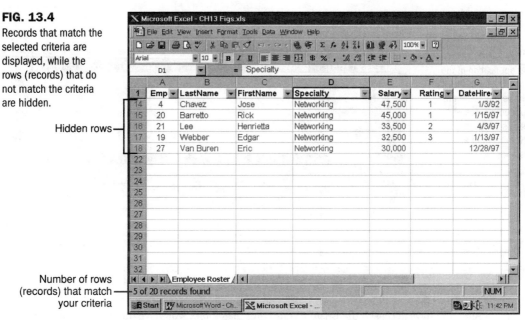

Whenever you filter a list by using the AutoFilter, the filter arrow and row numbers change to blue to alert you that a filter has been applied to the list. The number of rows (records) found appear in the status bar at the bottom-left corner of the screen.

To further refine the filter, you can use other criteria in a different column—for example, to display those employees whose specialty is Networking and who have a rating of 1. An AND condition is assumed when you use criteria in multiple columns with the AutoFilter.

To perform a Top 10 filter, choose the filter arrow next to the heading in the column you want to filter. Choose the Top 10 option and the Top 10 Filter dialog box appears. In Figure 13.5, the filter and the result of the filter on the list are displayed. The criteria in the Top 10 dialog box is the Top 20 Percent. When applied to the Salary column, those employees who earn the top 20 percent of all salaries are displayed, as shown in the rows behind the Top 10 dialog box.

The Top 10 option cannot be applied to columns that contain text.

Part
IV

Ch
13

Using the Custom AutoFilter Dialog Box

The Custom option in the filter arrow list is used when you need to specify multiple criteria, use an OR condition, or include a wild card in your search.

To use the Custom AutoFilter, follow these steps:

1. Select a cell in your list and activate the AutoFilter by choosing Data, Filter, AutoFilter.

2. Select the filter arrow next to the heading in the column that contains the data you want to compare.

3. Choose Custom from the menu; the Custom AutoFilter dialog box appears.

FIG. 13.5

An application of the Top 10 filter to this list shows that there are four employees who earn salaries in the top 20 percent of all salaries.

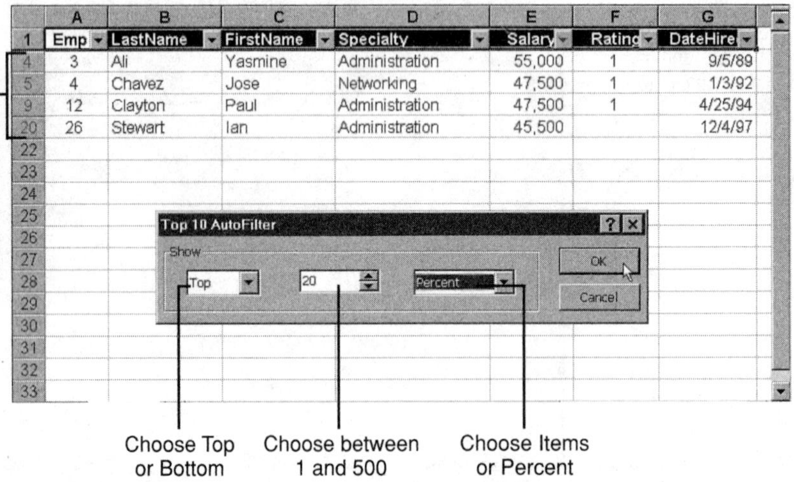

Hidden rows

Choose Top or Bottom   Choose between 1 and 500   Choose Items or Percent

After you have accessed the Custom AutoFilter dialog box, you have three choices for expressing the criteria:

- *To match one criterion.* Select the comparison operator you want to use in the first box under Show Rows Where. Enter the value you want to match in the box immediately to the right of the comparison operator.

- *To match two criteria.* Select the comparison operator and value you want for the first criteria. Then select the And button. Select the comparison operator and value for the second criteria.

- *To match one of two criteria.* Select the comparison operator and value you want for the first criteria. Then select the Or button. Select the comparison operator and value for the second criteria.

N O T E To enter more than two criteria, you must use the Advanced Filter command, discussed later in this chapter.

In Figure 13.6, a Consulting Worklog is displayed. Suppose that you want to locate all rows (records) for consulting performed for the second week in June, June 7 through June 13. Multiple criteria will be required to execute this filter.

To filter a date column by using a range of dates, choose the filter arrow in the Date column. Choose the Custom option and the Custom AutoFilter dialog box appears (see Figure 13.7). Select the comparison operator from the drop-down list in the first box, and then type the date in the corresponding box to the right. In Figure 13.7, the first criteria is used to specify the beginning date in the range. The comparison operator "is greater than or equal to" is used for the date 6/7/98. The second criteria is used to specify the ending date in the range. The comparison operator will be "is less than or equal to" for the date 6/13/98. Because the rows (records) must fall between these two dates, the And logical operator is selected.

FIG. 13.6
The Consulting Worklog, sorted by project type.

	A	B	C	D	E	F
1	Consulting Worklog - June					
2						
3	Company	Date	Employee	Account	Project Typ	Hours
4	City ISD	6/3/98	David Jacobson	3105	105	4.0
5	City ISD	6/9/98	David Jacobson	3105	105	8.5
6	XAFB	6/17/98	Ian Stewart	3097	105	8.0
7	XAFB	6/18/98	Ian Stewart	3097	105	4.0
8	XAFB	6/21/98	Ian Stewart	3097	105	8.5
9	City ISD	6/4/98	Jose Chavez	3105	105	8.0
10	City ISD	6/5/98	Jose Chavez	3105	105	8.0
11	Weiss LTD	6/13/98	Jose Chavez	3305	105	8.0
12	Weiss LTD	6/14/98	Jose Chavez	3305	105	8.0
13	Weiss LTD	6/15/98	Jose Chavez	3305	105	6.0
14	Southwest ISD	6/10/98	Scott Fujimora	3105	105	10.0
15	Monsen Home Builders	6/3/98	Anita Salinas	3098	217	3.0
16	Monsen Home Builders	6/4/98	Anita Salinas	3098	217	8.0

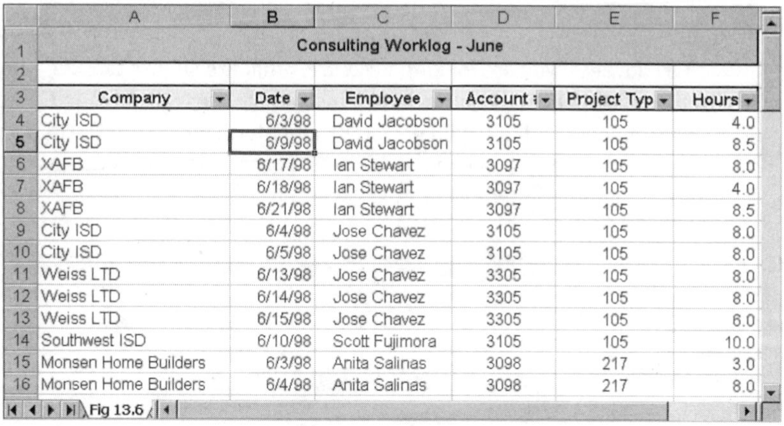

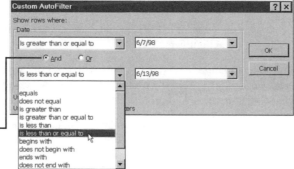

FIG. 13.7
In the Custom AutoFilter dialog box, you can relate only two criteria on the filter for each column.

Select an And or Or condition between the two criteria.

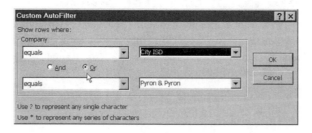

The Custom option is also used to filter a column when searching for several criteria, such as all employees who worked for City ISD or Pyron & Pyron. In this case, an OR condition is used. Figure 13.8 shows the necessary criteria in the Custom AutoFilter dialog box.

FIG. 13.8
Use an OR condition between two criteria to display the rows (records) matching either one of the criteria.

T I P You can use criteria to locate information that matches or does not match the criteria. For example, you could search for all companies except the specified company by using a criterion like "does not equal".

Alternatively, if you are looking for entries that are similar to each other, such as all the Independent School Districts (ISD) for which consulting was provided, you would use a wild card. Unlike an OR condition, you use only one criteria box in the Custom AutoFilter dialog box, but the result may be many company names. Figure 13.9 shows the use of a wild card in criteria in the Custom AutoFilter dialog box.

FIG. 13.9

The asterisk (*) wild card allows multiple characters to appear before *ISD* in this example.

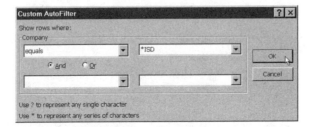

Any number of characters can appear in the same position as the asterisk (*). *ISD will find City ISD, Northwest ISD, and Southwest ISD.

You can even apply filters to more than one column in the list. For example, to see all the rows where Jose Chavez worked on all 105 type projects, the Employee column for Jose Chavez and the Project Type column for 105 are filtered.

After you have applied a filter to a column in your list, the filter remains active until you remove it and restore the column to display all rows (records). To remove a filter from a column in your list, select the filter arrow next to the column heading, and choose All.

Likewise, the AutoFilter remains active until you remove it. To remove the filter arrows from a list, choose Data, Filter, and then select AutoFilter.

▶ **See** "Editing Filtered Data," **p. 217**

Using the Data Form to Filter a List

A Data Form is a form that is created based on the headings and data in the active list. Through the Form, a single row (record) of information from the list is displayed. The Data Form is particularly useful for editing data in a list or when the list has so many columns that the list headings cannot be viewed on the screen without scrolling.

To access the Data Form, follow these steps:

1. Select a cell in your list.
2. Choose Data, Form. A form appears, based on the column headings in your list (see Figure 13.10).

FIG. 13.10

When you access the Data Form, the first row (record) of information is always displayed.

Title of the Data Form comes from the sheet name in your Excel workbook

Column headings

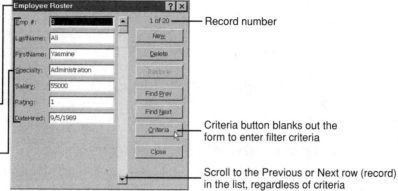

Record number

Criteria button blanks out the form to enter filter criteria

Scroll to the Previous or Next row (record) in the list, regardless of criteria

Excel temporarily assigns each row (record) a number to use when viewing the list information. These numbers do not correspond to the actual row numbers in the worksheet. Rather, these numbers are used by Excel to identify the row (record) of information. This sequential numbering begins at 1 and continues for each row in your list. The numbers appear in the upper-right corner of the Data Form. The record indicator in the upper–right corner of the Data Form dialog box indicates what record you are viewing and how many records are in your list.

To filter the information that appears in the Data Form, follow these steps:

1. Select the Criteria button. The entry boxes next to each field (column heading) are cleared. The Delete button becomes the Clear button and the Criteria button changes to the Form button.

2. Click or use the Tab key to select the entry box in which you want to enter criteria. For example, >=1/1/97 in the DateHired entry box. Refer back to Table 13.1 for a list of the comparison operator symbols you can use in criteria.

3. Use the Find Next button to view each row (record) that matches the criteria you specified.

4. To return to the display of all rows (records) in your list, click the Form button, or press the Enter key.

CAUTION

You must use the Find Next button to view each row (record) that matches the criteria you specified. Any other method of advancing in the list ignores the criteria and displays the next sequential row (record) in the list.

The following list contains a few things of which you need to be aware when working with the Data Form:

Part

IV

Ch

13

■ When you use text criteria in an entry box, a wild card is assumed to be at the end of the text. For example, if *Smith* were entered into the LastName entry box, the rows (records) for *Smith*, as well as *Smithson*, *Smithfield*, and any other employee whose last name starts with *Smith*, will be displayed.

■ Multiple criteria is specified by entering criterion in more than one of the entry boxes. When you enter multiple criteria by using the Data Form, the criteria are always related by the AND condition. You cannot create an OR condition by using the Data Form.

Performing Advanced Filters

The Advanced Filter enables you to search for data that matches complex AND and OR criteria, or calculated criteria. Some of the advantages of using the Advanced Filter instead of the AutoFilter and Data Form are the following:

■ You can enter many combinations of multiple criteria in the criteria range; for example, three or more conditions for a single column or an OR condition between multiple columns.

■ The results of a filter can be copied to a separate location.

■ You can create conditions based on the result of a formula.

Before you can use the Advanced Filter, you must rearrange your worksheet to include a criteria range along with the list. The *criteria range* is a group of cells that contains the column headings in your list, and at least one row below the headings where you can enter criteria. Figure 13.11 shows an example of a worksheet that includes a criteria range and a list.

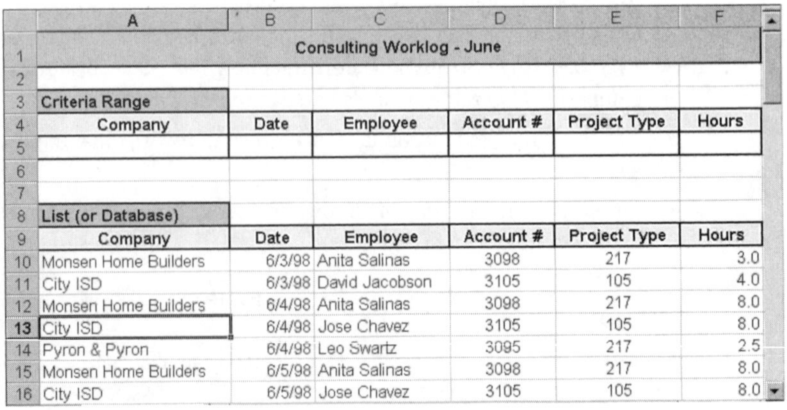

FIG. 13.11

The criteria range in a worksheet is typically located above the list.

	A	B	C	D	E	F
1	Consulting Worklog - June					
2						
3	Criteria Range					
4	Company	Date	Employee	Account #	Project Type	Hours
5						
6						
7						
8	List (or Database)					
9	Company	Date	Employee	Account #	Project Type	Hours
10	Monsen Home Builders	6/3/98	Anita Salinas	3098	217	3.0
11	City ISD	6/3/98	David Jacobson	3105	105	4.0
12	Monsen Home Builders	6/4/98	Anita Salinas	3098	217	8.0
13	City ISD	6/4/98	Jose Chavez	3105	105	8.0
14	Pyron & Pyron	6/4/98	Leo Swartz	3095	217	2.5
15	Monsen Home Builders	6/5/98	Anita Salinas	3098	217	8.0
16	City ISD	6/5/98	Jose Chavez	3105	105	8.0

When creating the criteria range, keep the following items in mind:

■ *First row of the criteria range*. Contains the same headings as the column headings in your list. The headings must be spelled the same, but the Advanced Filter is not case-sensitive. You do not have to enter all the column headings in the criteria range that appear in the list, just the ones you intend to use.

TIP To ensure the column headings in the criteria range match the ones in the list, copy the headings from the list to the first row in the criteria range.

■ *Second and subsequent rows in the criteria range.* Used to enter the specific criteria. If criteria is entered into more than one column in the same row of the criteria range, an AND condition is assumed. If criteria is entered into the same or different columns in different rows of the criteria range, an OR condition is assumed. You can use as many rows as necessary in the criteria range.

To use the Advanced Filter, follow these steps:

1. Create the criteria range as described earlier in this section.

2. Enter the criteria in the second row in the criteria range. If necessary, use additional rows for the criteria.

3. Select a cell in your list.

4. Choose Data, Filter, Advanced Filter. The Advanced Filter dialog box appears (see Figure 13.12).

FIG. 13.12

The Advanced Filter dialog box is navigated by using the Tab key to move down and Shift+Tab to move up.

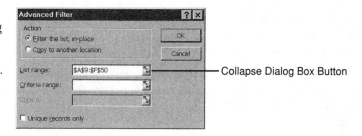
Collapse Dialog Box Button

5. By default, the Filter the List, In-Place option is selected. Like the AutoFilter, the rows matching your criteria will be displayed in the list. Those not matching the criteria will be hidden. To place a copy of the filter results in another location on the active worksheet, choose Copy to Another Location.

6. In the List Range entry box, Excel automatically selects the cells in your list, based on the cell you selected in step 3.

7. Click the Criteria Range entry box. To select the criteria range, you can either type the cell references or use the mouse to select the cells directly in the worksheet. You may need to scroll up in the worksheet to see the criteria range. Use the collapse dialog box button to temporarily hide the dialog box while you select the cells.

8. If you select the Copy to Another Location option in step 5, the third entry box, Copy To, is active. Click the Copy To entry box and type in, or select, the cell in the active worksheet where you want the filtered data to appear.

9. By default, all records that meet the criteria will display. If you know, or suspect, duplicates exist in your list, choose the Unique Records Only check box; only the first row (record) that meets the criteria will display.

Part
IV

Ch
13

10. Choose OK. The data meeting your criteria is displayed.

There are a few things you need to be aware of when working with the Advanced Filter:

- When you use text criteria in an entry box, a wild card is assumed at the end of the text. For example, if *Smith* is entered into the LastName entry box, the rows (records) for *Smith*, as well as *Smithson*, *Smithfield*, and any other employee whose last name starts with *Smith*, will be displayed.

- If a blank row is selected in the criteria range, all records will display.

- If the range name *Database* is used for all or part of your list, Excel assumes the cells the name refers to is the range to be filtered. If the range name *Criteria* is used in the worksheet, Excel assumes the cells to which the name refers is the range where the criteria appears. If the range name *Criteria* does not exist, when you select the criteria range for the first time, Excel will automatically create a range name *Criteria* for the cells.

▶ **See** "Using Range Names," **p. 33**

When you want to enter three or more conditions for a single column, use a new row for each condition.

When you want to enter an OR condition between multiple columns, use a new row for each condition. Figure 13.16 shows an example of a criteria range where the filter will locate all rows (records) that contain either the Weiss LTD company or the employee Rick Barretto.

Figure 13.17 shows an example of a criteria range where multiple conditions in multiple columns and rows have been entered. In this example, the filter will locate all rows (records) that contain either the Weiss LTD company and the project type 105, or the Coastal Management company and the project type 302.

 Computed criteria locates data by using formulas in the criteria. To learn more about computed criteria, use the Office Assistant. Type in **criteria** in the Office Assistant search box and press Enter to see a list of help topics. Select Examples Of Advanced Filter Criteria from the list.

▶ **See** "Sorting Filtered Data," **p. 217**

▶ **See** "Producting Charts from Filtered Data," **p. 217**

CHAPTER 14

Using Filtered Data

Filtering a list is a powerful Excel tool. It enables you to view part of a list of information, based on criteria you specify. Besides merely viewing the filtered data, many of the actions you can perform on the entire list also can be used with a filtered list. The sorting and subtotal features covered in Chapter 12, "Manipulating Data in Lists," can be applied to a filtered list. Filtering can be used to view only those rows in the list that you want to edit. Charts can be created based on the filtered data, and you can copy the visible data to another worksheet, or print the filtered list. ■

Changing filtered data

Use filtering to expedite editing a subset of your list. You can change data in the filtered list and delete rows that are no longer needed.

Organizing a filtered list

Use the sorting feature to change the order of your filtered data. The subtotaling command calculates totals and averages on just the data displayed on-screen.

Displaying the filtered data in charts

Create charts representing the filtered data, which automatically update when you change or remove the filter.

Printing a list of filtered data

The filtered list and charts based on the filtered list can be printed.

Editing Filtered Data

Filtering can be used to help make editing a list of information easier. By producing a subset of your list based on the criteria you specify, you will see only those rows of data that you want to change. For example, in the Landscaping Price List shown in Figure 14.1, the item numbers for all Evergreen-type plants need to be changed to end in zero (0). By filtering the list for just the evergreen plants, the task of editing is completed more quickly.

FIG. 14.1

Whenever a filter is applied to a list, the Status bar indicates that Filter Mode is active.

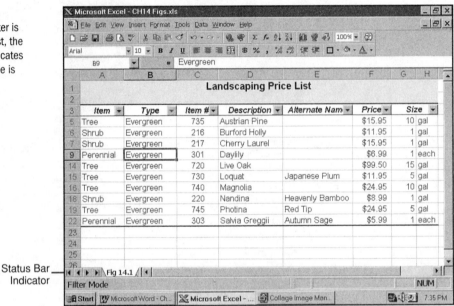

Status Bar — Indicator

In addition to making mass changes easier, other types of editing are expedited by using Excel's data filtering features. For example, you can insert or delete rows (records) in the list. You may need to filter the list to see the existing data before inserting new information. Continuing with Figure 14.1, suppose that you want to offer all evergreen plants in a one-gallon size. By filtering the list, you can see which plants are already available in that size and their corresponding price. New rows (records) can be inserted for those plants not currently offered in that size. The number that appears when you insert a new row is the row number for the new item you add to the list. Filtering also can be used to delete rows (records) that are obsolete, outdated, or otherwise no longer valid entries in your list.

Any cell formatting you apply to a filtered list affects only the data that is currently visible. Suppose that you apply the bold and italic formats to the Evergreen-type plants in Figure 14.1. When the filter is removed, as shown in Figure 14.2, the formatting appears on only those rows (records) visible—the Evergreen-type plants—when the formatting was applied.

▶ **See** "Discovering the Power of the AutoFilter," **p. 203**

FIG. 14.2
The Ready indicator in the Status bar lets you know that you are seeing the entire list and that the filter is no longer active.

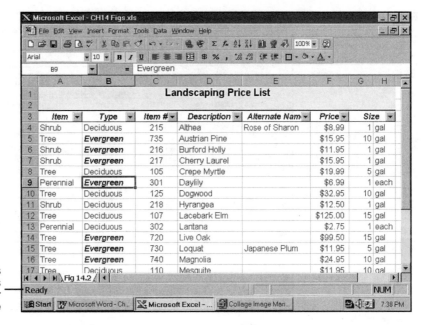

Indicates that filter is no longer active

Sorting Filtered Data

When a filtered list is sorted, only the visible rows (records) reflect the sort. When the filter is removed, the list does not reflect the sort made when the list was filtered. Figure 14.3 shows an employee roster list that has been filtered based upon the employee Rating. The list is sorted in ascending order by Specialty. When the filter is removed in Figure 14.4, the rows (records) that contain a rating of 1 are still listed alphabetically by Specialty, though interspersed among the other rows (records). The rows (records) in the list that have a rating other than 1 are not affected by the sort.

▶ See "Sorting Lists of Data," **p. 187**

Subtotaling Filtered Data

You can use the automatic subtotals feature in Excel on filtered lists. To generate meaningful subtotals, your list must be sorted *before* you apply the filter. (Refer to Chapter 12, "Manipulating Data in Lists," for procedures to sort lists.) Once sorted, apply the filter you require, and then choose Data, Subtotals to create subtotals in the filtered list. In Figure 14.5, the employee roster first was sorted by Specialty, and then the list was filtered to show all employees who have a Rating of 1. Finally, the filtered list was subtotaled by Specialty to count the number of employees in each specialty with a rating of 1. The Grand Count indicates that there are 10 employees with a rating of 1.

Part
IV

Ch
14

FIG. 14.3

Use the Data, Sort command to sort more than one column in your list.

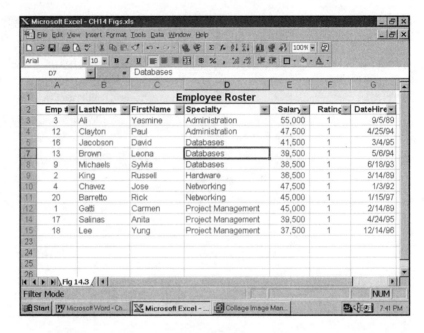

FIG. 14.4

The sort order remains after the filter is removed.

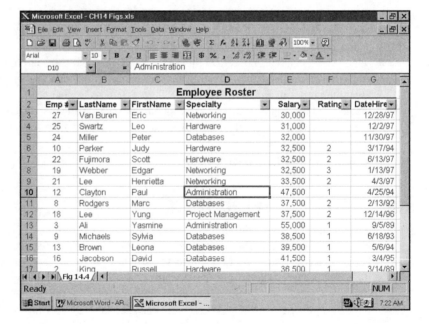

You can generate subtotals using many different functions, including AVERAGE, COUNT, and SUM. The SUBTOTALS function has two arguments: a number representing the function being performed, and the cell references of the data being subtotaled. In Figure 14.5, the number "3" represents the COUNT function.

▶ **See** "Automatic Worksheet Subtotals," **p. 187**

FIG. 14.5
A count of the employees in each department with a rating of 1.

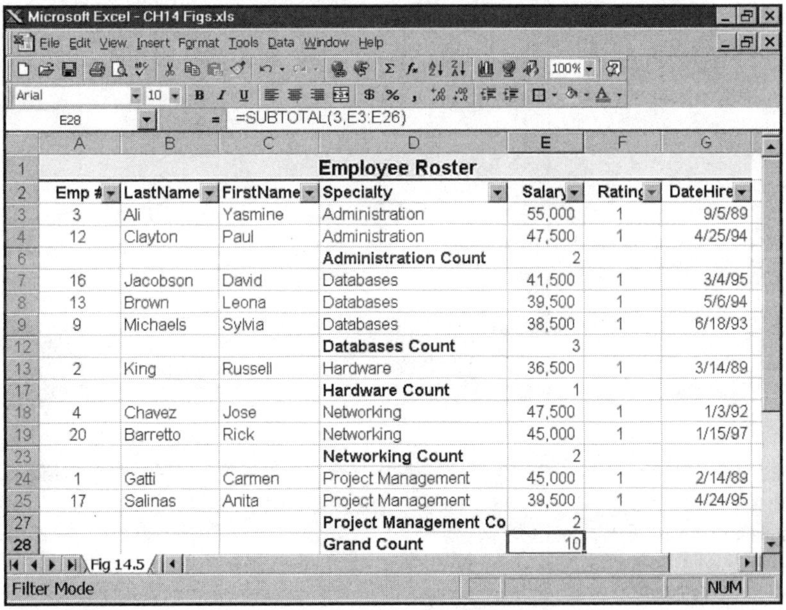

Microsoft Excel - CH14 Figs.xls

E28 =SUBTOTAL(3,E3:E26)

	A	B	C	D	E	F	G
1				Employee Roster			
2	Emp #	LastName	FirstName	Specialty	Salary	Rating	DateHire
3	3	Ali	Yasmine	Administration	55,000	1	9/5/89
4	12	Clayton	Paul	Administration	47,500	1	4/25/94
6				Administration Count	2		
7	16	Jacobson	David	Databases	41,500	1	3/4/95
8	13	Brown	Leona	Databases	39,500	1	5/6/94
9	9	Michaels	Sylvia	Databases	38,500	1	6/18/93
12				Databases Count	3		
13	2	King	Russell	Hardware	36,500	1	3/14/89
17				Hardware Count	1		
18	4	Chavez	Jose	Networking	47,500	1	1/3/92
19	20	Barretto	Rick	Networking	45,000	1	1/15/97
23				Networking Count	2		
24	1	Gatti	Carmen	Project Management	45,000	1	2/14/89
25	17	Salinas	Anita	Project Management	39,500	1	4/24/95
27				Project Management Co	2		
28				Grand Count	10		

Fig 14.5

Filter Mode NUM

If the filter is changed to reflect a different rating, as shown in Figure 14.6, only the Grand Count remains displayed. You have to repeat the Data, Subtotals command to see the subtotals each time the filter is changed. Fortunately, the options you designated originally, with the Subtotals command, remain listed in the Subtotals dialog box. All you have to do is click OK to reapply the subtotals. If the filter is removed, the subtotals for the entire list are displayed.

Normally, when you execute the Subtotals command, an outline is applied to your list automatically. When a list is filtered, however, the outline is not displayed. You can apply an outline to your filtered, subtotaled list by using Data, Group and Outline, Auto Outline. Once applied, you can use the outline symbols to collapse the list. Figure 14.7 shows the list from Figure 14.5, with the outline applied and collapsed to show just the Specialty subtotal counts and Grand Count. Although this display is useful for printing or charting purposes, you must be careful when using it, as explained in the Caution that follows.

FIG. 14.6

The Status bar indicates how many records (rows) Excel found with the active filter.

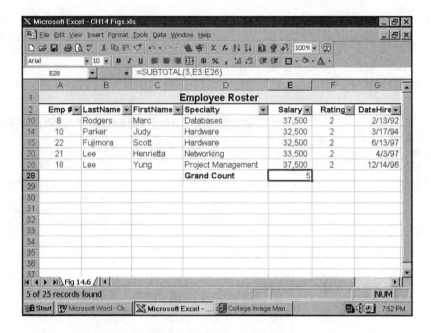

FIG. 14.7

The Rating filter is still applied to the list. The subtotal counts accurately reflect the filter, but the Grand Count does not.

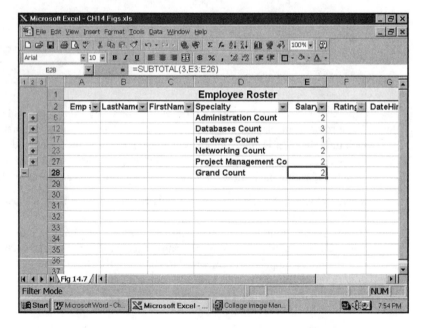

> **CAUTION**
>
> Be careful when applying an outline to a filtered, subtotaled list. When you collapse the list, the Grand Count (or Total) will not be accurate. Note the Grand Count in Figure 14.7. When you expand the outline, it overrides the filter; *all* of the data in your list will be displayed. You will have to reapply the filter and the subtotals to the list. Additionally, you will have to use the Data, Group and Outline, Clear Outline command to remove the lingering outline symbols.

▶ **See** "Outlining Worksheets," **p. 33**

You cannot filter the list on the subtotal rows and get the same list produced with the outline shown in Figure 14.7. Because the subtotals are calculations, when you apply a filter to see just those rows, the values they calculate display zeros.

Producing Charts from Filtered Data

You can graph data from your filtered list, just as you graph any data in Excel. Chapters 6, 7, and 8 discuss creating and modifying charts in-depth. When you create a chart based on filtered data, you should keep the following points in mind:

- *Label Length and Chart Type.* In Figure 14.7, the labels for the subtotals are very long. A bar chart is a good choice when the category labels are long, especially if the chart is to be an embedded object in the worksheet. Another alternative is to locate the chart on its own worksheet, instead of embedding the chart. This gives you greater flexibility in the chart type you select.

- *Changing or Removing the Filter.* By default, when a filter is changed, the chart changes to reflect the new filter. If the filter is removed entirely, the chart will update to represent *all* the data in your list.

Figure 14.8 shows a chart sheet based on the subtotals displayed in Figure 14.7. To make the text more readable, the font size has been increased to 14 and the bold format has been applied to the text.

In Figure 14.9, the list of Commission and Bonus Rates for the Sales Reps have been filtered to show only those Sales Reps whose Bonus Rate was six percent. An embedded chart object has been created to show the Sales Reps and the amount of Actual Sales they made. If the filter is changed to show the Sales Rep who earned a four percent bonus, the chart will change, as shown in Figure 14.10.

Part
IV

Ch
14

FIG. 14.8

A chart sheet is useful when you want to print just the chart, or keep the chart separate from the data.

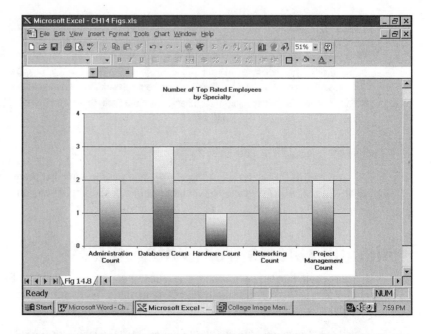

FIG. 14.9

With a pie chart, you can display the actual value that each pie slice represents, as shown here, or you can display the percentage each pie slice constitutes of the total pie.

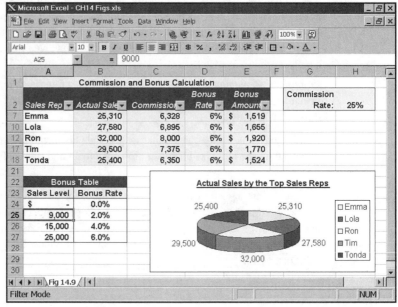

FIG. 14.10

By default, when the filter is changed, the chart changes. In this case, the filter and chart show sales reps whose actual sales are between $15,000 and $24,999, which earns each sales rep a four percent bonus.

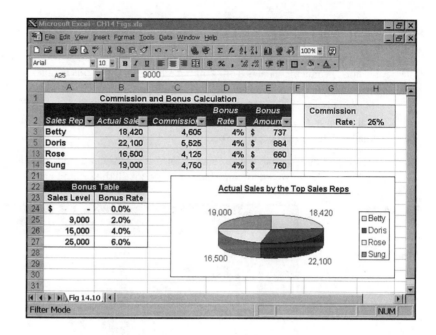

There is a way to fix the cells that are plotted so that, no matter what happens to the filter, the chart always reflects the cells you originally selected to plot. This setting must be made *before* you create the chart.

To create a chart that doesn't change when the filter changes, follow these steps:

1. Apply the filter to the list.
2. Select the cells you want to plot, including any labels you want to appear in the chart.
3. Choose Edit, Go To. From the Go To dialog box, select the Special button.
4. In the Go To Special dialog box, choose Visible Cells Only, then select OK. This option selects the individual cells you have highlighted.
5. Create the chart by using the techniques described in Chapter 6, "Creating Charts."

▶ **See** "Using the Chart Wizard to Create Charts," **p. 103**

TIP If you routinely need to create charts based on filtered data, and ensure the chart always reflects the cells you originally selected to plot, consider adding the Visible Cells Only option as a button on a toolbar. To customize a toolbar, first display the Customize dialog box. Choose Tools, Customize and select the Commands tab in the Customize dialog box. You will find the Select Visible Cells command under the Edit category.

To print a chart based on filtered data, look ahead to "Printing Filtered Data," later in this chapter.

Part
IV

Ch
14

Printing Filtered Data

When you print a list that has been filtered, only the data displayed on-screen will print. In the section "Producing Charts from Filtered Data," earlier in this chapter, you learned to create charts based on the filtered data. If the chart you created is on its own sheet tab, you can print the chart by using the techniques described in Chapter 6, "Creating Charts." However, if the chart is an embedded object in the worksheet, because it is part of a filtered list, it may appear smaller than you expect in the preview screen.

Figure 14.11 shows the preview screen for the worksheet displayed in Figure 14.10. Even with the orientation changed to Landscape, it does not fill the printed page.

FIG. 14.11

Use the Setup button at the top of the Preview screen to change the orientation and scaling.

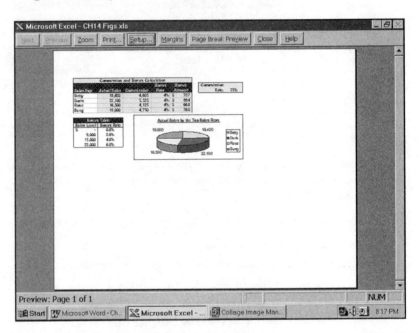

To enlarge the worksheet and chart on the printed page, use the scaling option in the Page Setup dialog box. Follow these steps to enlarge the scale:

1. Display the worksheet containing the filtered list and chart.
2. Choose the Print Preview button on the Standard toolbar to preview the worksheet.
3. Select the Setup Button in the Preview screen (refer to Figure 14.11). The Page Setup dialog box is displayed.
4. On the Page tab, change the orientation to Landscape, if desired.
5. On the Page tab, use the Adjust To entry box to increase the scaling to the percent that best displays the list and the chart. In Figure 14.12, the scaling has been increased to 150 percent.

6. Choose OK to preview the scaling change. If necessary, adjust the scaling percent by repeating step 5.

7. When the filtered list and chart are the size you want, print the worksheet.

▶ **See** "Printing Worksheets," **p. 9**

▶ **See** "Printing Charts," **p. 103**

FIG. 14.12

You can also access the Setup dialog box from the menu bar in Excel. Choose File, Page Setup.

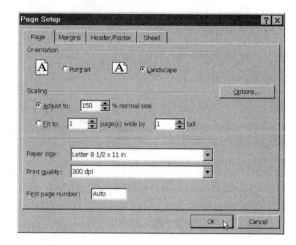

CHAPTER 15

Unlocking the Power of Pivot Tables

Pivot tables, like subtotals and database functions, provide a means of summarizing and consolidating lengthy lists of Excel information. Pivot tables are a powerful and effective tool for arranging and analyzing data. They are called *pivot tables* because you can rotate the rows and columns in a pivot table to see the data summarized differently. Pivot tables can be created from Excel lists or from external sources, such as Microsoft Access, Microsoft FoxPro, and Microsoft Project. ▪

Creating and editing pivot tables

Learn to create pivot tables in Excel by using the PivotTable Wizard. Discover how to format, edit, and update the data in the pivot table.

Using calculations in pivot tables

Choose from among eleven popular Excel functions and eight custom calculations to summarize data in pivot tables.

Filtering and charting data in pivot tables

Explore the use of the Page field as a filter in pivot tables. Plot the pivot table data in Excel charts for a visual representation of the pivot table data.

Creating pivot tables using data from Microsoft Access or Microsoft Project

Use pivot tables to summarize and analyze data from other programs.

Creating a Pivot Table Using an Excel List

Pivot tables can summarize or cross-tabulate large lists of information. Excel provides a wizard to help you create pivot tables. In order to use the pivot table command, the information in your worksheet must be organized in a list, as described in Chapter 11, "Designing a List or Database." Before creating a pivot table based on a list, you should be aware of the following:

- *Column Headings*. Excel uses the data in the first row of the list for the field names in the pivot table. Your list must contain column headings.

- *Range Names*. If you use a range name for the list, it will be easier to refresh and update the pivot table when the list changes.

- *Filters*. If you have applied any filters to your list, Excel ignores them when it creates the pivot table. All data in your list is included automatically in the pivot table. To create a pivot table from filtered data, use the Data, Filter, Advanced Filter command to copy a range of data to another worksheet location, and then base the PivotTable on the copied range.

- *Automatic Subtotals*. Excel automatically creates grand totals and subtotals in the pivot table. You should remove any subtotals (created with the Data, Subtotals command) from the list before you create the pivot table. To remove automatic subtotals, choose Data, Subtotals, and select the Remove All button from the Subtotals dialog box.

▶ **See** "Using Range Names," **p. 53**

▶ **See** "Understanding Lists," **p. 182**

▶ **See** "Automatic Worksheets Subtotals," **p. 194**

▶ **See** "Discovering the Power of the AutoFilter," **p. 207**

The PivotTable Wizard guides you step by step through locating and arranging the data you want to analyze with a pivot table. Figure 15.1 shows a Consulting Worklog for the month of June. The list is sorted by Date. A key element in a pivot table is the information you want to summarize. Generally, only numerical information can be summarized. In the list displayed in Figure 15.1, the numerical column that logically needs to be summarized is the Hours column. In this example, the Account numbers and Project Types are also numbers, but numbers that are being used as labels. You are not going to ask for a total or average of the Account numbers or Project Types, because that would be similar to asking for an average of phone numbers or social security numbers.

Using this list, many different pivot tables can be created; some examples include:

- The total number of Hours worked by Employee
- The total number of Hours worked by Account number
- The total number of Hours worked by Date
- The total number of Hours worked for each Company on each Project Type
- The total number of Hours each Employee worked for each Company
- The total number of Hours each Employee worked on each Project Type

FIG. 15.1
An Excel list must contain only one row of column headings. These headings are used as fields in the Pivot Table.

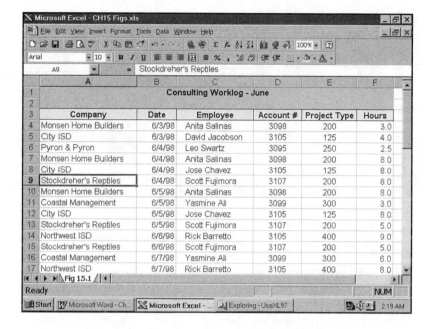

The summaries in the first three examples also can be derived by using either the subtotal command or database functions. They summarize the hours by using one other column from the list. The last three examples can be created only by using pivot tables. These examples summarize the hours by using two other columns from the list, creating the pivot table. A "table" typically has one set of labels for the rows and another set for the columns. The data is summarized for the intersections of each row and column.

Each of the examples in the preceding bulleted list calculates totals, using the SUM function. However, totals are not the only calculation that can be performed in a pivot table. Later in this chapter, the section, "Types Calculations Available In Pivot Tables," provides descriptions and examples of other calculations available in pivot tables.

To create a pivot table, follow these steps:

1. Before starting the PivotTable Wizard, select a cell anywhere in your list. Excel automatically selects the range of cells that comprise the list for you, similar to the way it selects the range of cells in a list when sorting.

2. Choose Data, PivotTable Report. Step 1 of the PivotTable Wizard is displayed, as shown in Figure 15.2.

3. In the first step of the Wizard, identify the source of the data from which the Pivot Table will be created. The default setting is Microsoft Excel List Or Database. Click the Next> button from the PivotTable Wizard.

   Creating Pivot Tables based on external sources and multiple, consolidated ranges is discussed later in this chapter.

FIG. 15.2

Choose the data source for the pivot table. You can use Excel data or data from databases, such as Access or FoxPro.

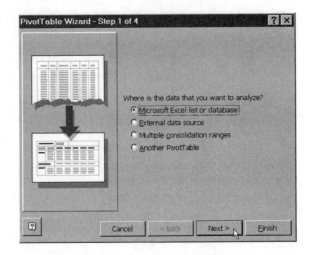

4. In the second step of the PivotTable Wizard, the range of cell references in your list is displayed, as shown in Figure 15.3. Excel automatically highlights the list when you select one of the cells in your list, before starting the PivotTable Wizard. If the incorrect cell range is selected, you can select the range of cells you want. You also can type in a range name, if you created one.

▶ **See** "Using Range Names," **p. 53**

FIG. 15.3

The selected range is displayed automatically as absolute cell references.

5. When the correct cell references or range name appears in the Range entry box, in Step 2 of the PivotTable Wizard, choose the Next> button.

6. In the third step of the PivotTable Wizard (see Figure 15.4), a sample pivot table layout appears.

   The column labels in your list are displayed on the left side of the dialog box. They appear as buttons and are referred to as *fields*. The fields can be placed in four different parts of the pivot table:

   • *Row*. Place the field containing the data you want to become the row labels in the pivot table in the Row area.

   • *Column*. Place the field containing the data you want to become the column labels in the pivot table in the Column area.

FIG. 15.4

The pivot table layout is comprised of four parts. The column headings become *fields* that you can display in any of the four layout areas.

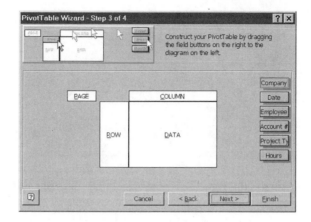

- *Data*. Place the numeric field containing the data you want to summarize in the pivot table in the Data area.

- *Page*. Place the field you want to use as a filter on the pivot table. This area is discussed separately in the section "Using Page Fields in Pivot Tables," later in this chapter.

To place a field in an area of the pivot table layout, drag the field name to the area. In Figure 15.5, the Employee field has been placed in the Row area and the Project Type field in the Column Area. The Hours field has been added to the Data area. In this example, the hours each employee has worked, broken out by project type, will be summarized.

FIG. 15.5

You can display more than one field in the layout areas.

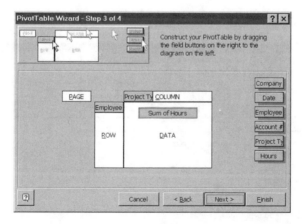

7. When you have completed the layout, click the Next> button. The final step of the PivotTable Wizard displays (see Figure 15.6).

FIG. 15.6

Make sure you place the pivot table in an area where it will not overwrite existing data.

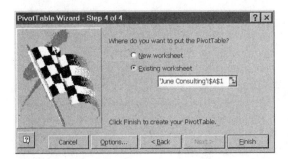

8. In the final step of the PivotTable Wizard, select the location for the pivot table, which can be placed on a new worksheet in the active workbook or in another location.

   - *New Worksheet.* A new worksheet will be added to the active workbook; the pivot table will then be placed on this new worksheet.

   - *Existing Worksheet.* The pivot table can be placed in an existing worksheet in the active workbook or in another workbook. When you select Existing Worksheet, a flashing cursor appears in the entry box next to Existing Worksheet. If the worksheet is in a workbook that is open, use the Window menu to display the workbook and select the worksheet tab and cell where you want the pivot table to begin. If the workbook is not open, you will have to type in the entire path of the workbook, including workbook name, worksheet name, and cell reference.

9. Select PivotTable Wizard Finish to complete the PivotTable Wizard. The pivot table will be displayed, along with the PivotTable toolbar. Figure 15.7 shows an example of a pivot table with the PivotTable toolbar.

FIG. 15.7

The PivotTable toolbar is displayed automatically when you create a pivot table.

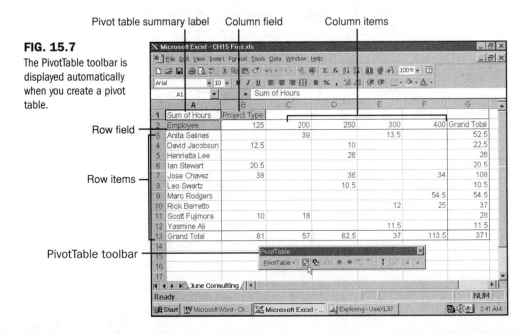

Formatting and Editing a Pivot Table

After a pivot table is created, there are several options you can use to format and edit the results. The pivot table is designed to allow quick selection of various parts of the table. Using Figure 15.7 as an example, Table 15.1 describes what will be selected when you click on the parts of the pivot table.

Table 15.1   Selecting Parts of Table

Clicking this	Selects this
Row field (Employee)	All row labels (employee names)
Row item (IanStewart)	All data, including row Grand Total, for the item in that row
Column field (Project Type)	All column labels (project types)
Column item (200)	All data, including column Grand Total, for the item in that column
Pivot table summary label	Entire table (Sum of Hours)
Grand Total label	Totals in that column or row

The table can be formatted easily to enhance its appearance. The fastest way to format a table is to use the AutoFormat command. Select the entire table by clicking the pivot table summary label, and then choose Format, AutoFormat. From the AutoFormat dialog box, choose one of the many predefined formats to quickly give your pivot table a professional look.

 T I P   You also can use Ctrl+Shift+* to select the entire pivot table.

To format individual parts of the pivot table, select the cells you want to format, and then use either the buttons on the Formatting toolbar or the Format, Cells command.

 To change the number formatting, choose a cell in the data area of the pivot table, and then select the PivotTable Field button on the PivotTable toolbar. The PivotTable Field dialog box is displayed, as shown in Figure 15.8.

Choose the Number button on the right side of the dialog box. The Format Cells dialog box is displayed (see Figure 15.9). Choose a number format for the summary data.

▶ **See** "Using AutoFormat," **p. 27**

There are many components of the pivot table that can be edited. You may decide to replace one field with another, or to reorganize the fields in the pivot table. You also can group row or column items in your pivot table. For example, if your columns display the months in a year, you can group the first three months to create Quarter 1.

FIG. 15.8

Use this dialog box to change both the number formatting and the type of calculation performed on the data.

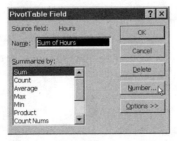

FIG. 15.9

Because the numbers being formatted are *hours*, the number format is selected.

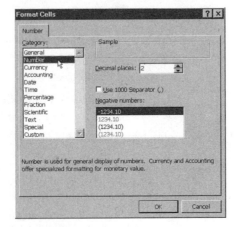

To remove a field and replace it with another field, you first need to select a cell in your pivot table, and then follow these steps:

1. Access the PivotTable Wizard by clicking the PivotTable Wizard button on the Pivot Table toolbar. This displays Step 3 of the Pivot Table Wizard dialog box.

2. Drag the field off of the layout area you no longer need. Next, drag the field into the layout area you now want.

3. Select Finish to revise your pivot table.

To rearrange the fields in the pivot table, access the PivotTable Wizard, and simply drag the fields from one area in the pivot table layout to another area of the layout. Choose finish to display your revised pivot table.

Grouping items in a pivot table enables you to hide or show the items in the group, very similar to the way Excel's outlining feature works. When you hide the items in a group, the pivot table displays the total of the items in the group. Figure 15.10 shows a pivot table that displays monthly sales information, arranged alphabetically by sales representative.

FIG. 15.10

This pivot table has been formatted by using the AutoFormat command.

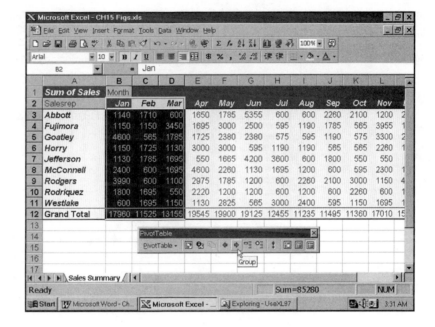

 To group together January, February, and March as Quarter 1, select the items, as shown in Figure 15.10. Next, select the Group button on the Pivot Table toolbar. Above the items, a group name will be inserted, called Group1. Select the label Group1 and type in the name you want to display for the group. Figure 15.11 shows the label **Quarter 1** displayed in the group label. Another field name may appear for the new group. The default field name can be changed. In Figure 15.11, the new field name was changed to **Qtrs**.

 By using the Hide Detail button on the Pivot Table toolbar, you can collapse the detail columns for your first group, and the pivot table will display the summary of the group in the pivot table. The Show Detail button is used to expand the detail columns.

▶ **See** "Outlining Worksheets," **p. 49**

There are several options you have control over in your pivot table. Specifically, you can adjust general pivot table options and field-specific options.

The pivot table options can be selected when you initially create the pivot table or anytime after the pivot table has been created.

- *When creating the pivot table initially.* The pivot table options can be accessed on the final step, Step 4, of the PivotTable Wizard. Refer back to Figure 15.6 for an example that shows Step 4 in the PivotTable Wizard. Choose the Options button in Step 4 to display the PivotTable Options dialog box.

- *After the pivot table is created.* You also can access the PivotTable Options dialog box by selecting Options from the PivotTable menu on the Pivot Table toolbar. Figure 15.12 shows the Options dialog box.

FIG. 15.11

Grouping items can help you further consolidate the display of the data.

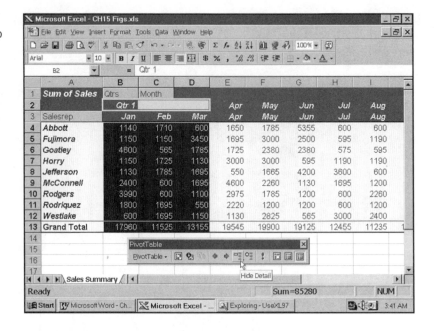

FIG. 15.12

By default, row and column totals are added to pivot tables.

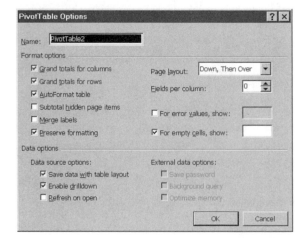

Figure 15.12 shows the default option settings for pivot tables. You can change these settings to modify the pivot table. For example, by default empty cells appear blank in the pivot table. You can specify a value such as 0 (zero) or a dash (—) to be displayed instead.

 TIP To learn more about a pivot table option, click the What's This button (question mark) located in the upper-right corner of the dialog box, and then click an option in the dialog box.

The field-specific options are accessed directly from the pivot table. Double-click the pivot table field to display the field-specific options.

Updating a Pivot Table

When data in your list changes, the pivot table isn't automatically updated to reflect the new data. To update your pivot table, you need to use the Refresh Data command. You can access the Refresh Data command from the PivotTable toolbar, where it appears as an exclamation point (!). If the PivotTable toolbar is not displayed, choose Data, Refresh Data.

When you need to add new rows or columns to your list, adding the rows or columns in the middle of the list ensures the new data is reflected in the pivot table. When you refresh the pivot table, Excel automatically expands the range of cell references used to create the pivot table.

However, if the data form is used to add new rows to your list, or if you add new data at the bottom of the list, Excel continues to use the original range of cell references for the pivot table. The range is not expanded automatically when you refresh the pivot table data. To include new rows or columns added with the data form or added at the end of the list, you have to return to the PivotTable Wizard. When the Wizard appears, by default, it displays Step 3. Use the <Back button to display Step 2 of the PivotTable Wizard. The current range of cell references is listed. To quickly expand the range to include the new rows, use the Shift key and down arrow on your keyboard to select additional rows at the bottom of your list. The worksheet display, behind the Wizard dialog box, changes to show the rows you are selecting. After you have the correct range selected, choose Finish, in Step 2 of the PivotTable Wizard, to update your pivot table.

▶ **See** "Entering Data in a List," **p. 183**

Pivot tables are created from lists of information. Periodically it is necessary to add or remove columns or rows from the list or change the row or column in the list. Whenever the pivot table is refreshed a message will alert you the pivot table was changed as a result of the changes to the list. A sample of this message is displayed in Figure 15.13.

FIG. 15.13
This message alerts you that the pivot table was modified when the data was refreshed.

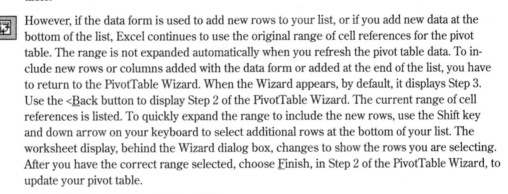

Calculations Available in Pivot Tables

Thus far, data fields in your pivot tables have used default calculations that are based on the SUM function. There are a number of other summary calculations that can be displayed in a pivot table. Additionally, you can create custom calculations, such as Running Total In, which displays the data as a running total for each item, or % of Total, which displays the data as a percentage of the grand total of the pivot table. Table 15.2 lists the excel functions you can use in pivot tables.

Table 15.2 Functions That Can Be Calculated in the Pivot Table Data Field

Function Name	Description of the Calculation
SUM	Adds the numbers in the list by field
AVERAGE	Calculates the average (arithmetic mean) of the numbers in the list
MIN	Locates the smallest number in the list
MAX	Locates the largest number in the list
COUNT	Counts all the items (text or numbers) in your list
COUNT NUMS	Counts only the numbers in a column containing text and numbers
PRODUCT	Multiplies all the numbers in the list to calculate the product
STDDEV	Calculates the standard deviation, based on a sample of numbers in the list
STDDEVP	Calculates the standard deviation, based on all the numbers in the list
VAR	Estimates the variance, based on a sample of numbers in the list
VARP	Estimates the variance, based on all the numbers in the list

You can create custom calculations for the PivotTable data for each item in a field, or for all items in a field. In some of the custom calculations, you must specify a field and value by which all other values are compared. This field and value are referred to as the *base field* and *base value*. Table 15.3 lists the custom calculations you can perform.

Table 15.3 Custom Calculations That Can Be Used in the Pivot Table Data Field

Calculation Name	Description of the Calculation
Difference From	Calculates the difference between the data and a specified base field and base item (value)
% Of	Calculates the percentage a value constitutes of a specified base field and base item (value)
% Difference From	Calculates the difference between the data and a specified base field and base item, but displays the difference as a percentage of the base data
Running Total In	Calculates the data for successive items as a running total

Calculation Name	Description of the Calculation
% of Row	Calculates the data in each row as a percentage of the total for that row
% of Column	Calculates the data in each column as a percentage of the total for that column
% of Total	Calculates the data as a percentage of the grand total of all the data in the pivot table
Index	Calculates each data item as an index, based on the grand totals, using this formula: ((value in cell) × (Grand Total of Grand Totals)) / ((Grand Row Total) × (Grand Column Total))

To change the type of calculation performed on the data, follow these steps:

1. Select the PivotTable Wizard button on the Pivot Table toolbar to activate the Wizard, with Step 3 displayed.

2. Double-click the field in the Data area; the PivotTable Field dialog box, shown in Figure 15.14, is displayed.

FIG. 15.14

The built-in Excel functions are listed in the Summarize By list box.

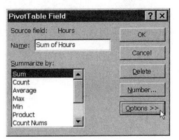

3. Select a function from the Summarize By list of functions, or choose Options to create a custom calculation.

4. If necessary, choose the Number button to change the formatting of the numerical calculations.

5. Select OK. The pivot table will be revised.

Using Page Fields in Pivot Tables

The PivotTable page fields are used to display data for one item separately from the other items in a field. They are used like a filter on the pivot table, and are particularly useful when there is a large amount of data in your list. Figure 15.15 shows Step 3 of the PivotTable Wizard. The Employee field has been placed on the Page field area of the layout. Figure 15.16 shows the resulting pivot table.

FIG. 15.15

Use the Page area to
place a field that you
want to act as a filter
on the pivot table.

The Page area contains
the Employee field

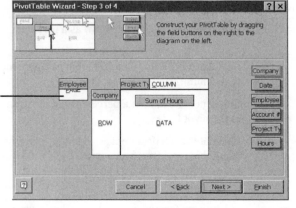

FIG. 15.16

The pivot table with the
Employee field placed
on the Page field area
of the layout.

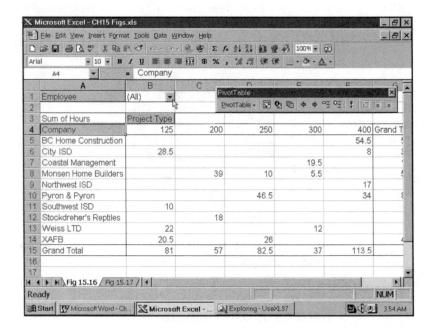

Initially the data for *All* employees is displayed. When the Page field in Figure 15.16 is used to
show just the project information for a selected employee, the pivot table adjusts, as shown in
Figure 15.17. The pivot table filters out all data, except the information for Jose Chavez.

When a pivot table contains a page field, the filtered information that is displayed when a specific item in the page field is selected can be converted to display on separate worksheets. This
feature is useful when you need to print each page as a separate report, or to plot charts based
on each page from the page field. To create separate worksheets from the page field in the
pivot table, follow these steps:

FIG. 15.17
The pivot table displays only the Project Types on which Jose Chavez has worked.

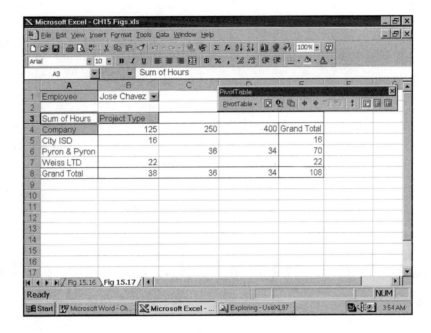

1. Select a cell in the pivot table.

2. Click the Show Pages button on the PivotTable toolbar. The Show Pages dialog box appears.

3. Choose OK. If there is more than one page field, select the desired page field, and then choose OK.

The individual pages are displayed on separate worksheets in front of the original pivot table. The new worksheets are named for the items in the page field. The original pivot table remains intact.

Creating Charts from Pivot Tables

You can create a chart that is based on a pivot table in the same way that you create charts for other Excel data. However, before the chart can be created, a few things need to be done to the pivot table to prepare it for charting.

By default, the pivot table is designed to select entire rows and columns when you click fields or items within a field. This automatic-selection feature must be disabled. From the PivotTable menu of the PivotTable toolbar, choose Select, and then click Enable Selection. This turns off the automatic selection feature.

If there are subtotals in the pivot table, they must be removed or hidden.

Select the data you want to chart, in the main body of the PivotTable, by dragging from the lower-right corner of the data, up to and including the column fields and row fields. Choose the Chart Wizard tool on the standard toolbar. On the second step of the Wizard, you must specify the name of each series and the values for the series. Refer back to Chapter 7, "Modifying Your Charts," for more information.

▶ **See** "Using the Chart Wizard to Create Charts," **p. 112**

▶ **See** "Adding or Removing Data from Your Charts," **p. 122**

When you hide or show details, or rearrange fields in the source PivotTable, the chart created from a PivotTable changes. Only the visible data is plotted on the chart. However, if your PivotTable has page fields, when you display a different page the chart changes and the chart portrayed may not display properly. For example, suppose the page the chart was originally created from contains three columns of data. If the next page you display has five columns of data, only the first three will be plotted.

Creating Pivot Tables Using Data from Other Programs

An important element in creating a pivot table is the data you use. This is called the *source data*. In addition to being able to use data in Excel, you can use an external source for the data. An external data source could be a database, a text file, or sources on the Internet. Some examples of external sources are Microsoft Access, Microsoft FoxPro, dBASE, ORACLE, SQL Server, and Microsoft Project.

Usually, you can specify the external data source when you run the PivotTable Wizard, as described in the first section of this chapter "Creating a Pivot Table Using an Excel List." In order to use data from an external source, you will need to extract the data using a query. With the PivotTable Wizard, you can open query files you have already created or create new queries by using Microsoft Query. When creating queries within the PivotTable Wizard, simply follow the steps to designate the source data.

N O T E Chapter 16, "Retrieving Data from External Sources Using Microsoft Query," discusses how to use Microsoft Query in detail. ▪

In some cases, you may have to retrieve the data before you start the PivotTable Wizard:

▪ Using a template to automatically retrieve (and update) the data

▪ Using a parameter query to retrieve the data

▪ Using a Web query to retrieve data over the Internet

The Excel help screens can provide detailed information on using external sources of data for pivot tables. Type **external source data** in the Office Assistant search box and press Enter to see a list of help topics. Choose About Creating A PivotTable From An External Data Source for specific assistance in using report templates and parameter or Web queries.

Saving Files Containing Pivot Tables

Workbooks containing pivot tables can be unexpectedly large. Excel creates a copy of the source data and stores it as hidden data, with the worksheet that contains the pivot table. If your pivot table references a large amount of data in another file, you are storing the same data twice—once in the original file, and again in the file that contains the pivot table.

You can avoid this duplication by changing a setting in the pivot table Options dialog box. To display this dialog box, choose the PivotTable menu from the PivotTable toolbar, and then select Options. In the Options dialog box, deselect the Save Data with Table Layout check box. When the file containing the pivot table is saved, the hidden copy of the source data is not saved with it. When the pivot table is refreshed, Excel updates it directly from the source data. ●

CHAPTER 16

Retrieving Data from External Sources Using Microsoft Query

An extremely powerful feature of Excel is the capability to retrieve data from external sources so that it can be analyzed and manipulated by the tools in Excel—primarily by using Microsoft Query.

Microsoft Query can be accessed directly from Excel to retrieve specific information from external sources, primarily databases, and to insert the data into your current worksheet. Some examples of the programs you can retrieve data from include Access, FoxPro, dBASE, Paradox, and SQL Server. You also can retrieve information from the Internet by using HTML filters. The data can be filtered, sorted, formatted, or edited in Microsoft Query *before* it is inserted into your worksheet. The data can be retrieved by using either the Query Wizard, an interface in Microsoft Query, or directly from the Microsoft Query window. The Query Wizard walks you through the steps of creating a query, and is very useful when you need to retrieve data from only one table in a database. ∎

Understanding Microsoft Query

How does Microsoft Query work? What is a query? What are ODBC drivers and why do you care about them? Learn the answers to these questions and some of the terminology used with databases and Microsoft Query.

Creating the data source

Designate the location of the data you want to retrieve by creating a data source.

Using the Query Wizard

Learn to use the Query Wizard to retrieve data from one table in an external database.

Using the Microsoft Query window

Use the Microsoft Query window when you need to create a query by using several tables from an external database.

Introducing Microsoft Query

Microsoft Query is an independent application that works with Excel to make it easy to retrieve data from databases, and copy the data into an Excel worksheet. When you insert the data into the worksheet, it becomes a list of information—as if you had typed it in yourself. You can then use any of the tools Excel provides to work with the list. Because lists are an integral part of Excel, there are five chapters in this book devoted to creating and manipulating data in lists:

- Chapter 11, "Designing a List or Database"
- Chapter 12, "Manipulating Data in Lists"
- Chapter 13, "Locating Data with Filters"
- Chapter 14, "Using Filtered Data"
- Chapter 15, "Unlocking the Power of Pivot Tables"

You can use Microsoft Query to bring data into Excel from external databases—to create reports, charts, or to analyze the data. Microsoft Query also can be used to retrieve data from multiple Excel lists, with which you can create a new Excel list.

When you create queries to retrieve data, you have two choices: you can use the Query Wizard or you can use the Microsoft Query window.

- *Query Wizard.* A tool provided with Microsoft Query that helps you create quick and simple query designs to retrieve data. Use the Query Wizard when you want to retrieve data from only one table in a database.
- *Microsoft Query Window.* If you want to retrieve data from multiple tables in a database, the Microsoft Query window enables you to work in more detail to customize and view your data retrieval.

It is important that you understand some of the terminology that Microsoft Query and databases use before you attempt to work with Microsoft Query to retrieve data:

- *Table.* A list of related information, such as a list of orders or client information.
- *Field.* A column of information in a table, including such items as the Name, Mailing Address, and Email Address.
- *Record.* A row of information in a table, such as all the information about one client.
- *Database.* One or more tables of related information. There are two types of databases, flat-file and relational.
- *Flat-File Databases.* Manipulate and query only one table at a time. Filemaker Pro is a flat-file database. An Excel list can also be used as a flat-file database.
- *Relational Database.* Manipulate and query several tables at a time. In a relational database, the different tables are connected (related) by having one or more fields in common. For example, a customer table lists information about each customer, including a field that uniquely identifies the customer, such as an Account Number field. When a

customer places an order, the orders table lists the specifics about the order. Instead of repeating all the customer table information in the customer table, the unique field (Account Number) can be used to relate the customer information with the orders information. Popular relational databases include Access, FoxPro, dBASE, Paradox, and SQL Server.

- *Data Source.* An "address" that Microsoft Query uses to locate the information in the external source. The data source may include information such as the name of the server, directory, and file in which the external data is located. You need to define a data source *before* you query an external source and retrieve information from it. The data source sometimes is referred to as the *query definition.*

- *Joining Tables (or Linking Tables).* The process of relating tables together based on a field that is common to both tables, such as an Account Number field or an Customer ID field.

- *ODBC (Open Database Connectivity) Driver.* A dynamic link library (DLL) file that Microsoft Query and Microsoft Excel use to connect to a particular database. Each database program, such as Access, FoxPro, or SQL Server, requires a *different* driver. Microsoft Query comes with many of the common ODBC drivers.

- *Query.* A question used to retrieve data from a database. Queries often contain specific criteria to retrieve records that match certain conditions or parameters. An example of a query is, "How many of our clients are from Canada?".

- *Returning Data.* Inserting data into an Excel worksheet that has been retrieved from a database.

- *Result Set.* The information, or data, retrieved from the external source.

- *Structured Query Language (SQL).* A programming language that is used to retrieve, update, and manage data. Microsoft Query uses SQL to retrieve data from databases. You don't need to learn SQL, or any other programming or macro language, to use Microsoft Query.

To query an external source, you need to have an ODBC driver installed on your computer. Excel includes many common external source drivers. If the driver is not provided by Excel, you have to install the ODBC driver that you need before you can query the external source. The drivers provided with Excel include: dBase, FoxPro, Access, Paradox, SQL Server, and Text (which includes HTML).

After you retrieve data from an external source, you can rearrange, format, and sort the data. When you are satisfied with the data and its formatting, return the result set (insert the data) into an Excel worksheet.

Starting Microsoft Query

To start Microsoft Query, choose Data, Get External Data, Create New Query. The Choose Data Source dialog box is displayed, as shown in Figure 16.1.

N O T E Microsoft Query is an optional feature in Microsoft Excel and therefore may or may not be installed on your computer, depending on the options you selected when installing Excel 97. If a warning message is displayed when you select Create New Query, then Microsoft Query is installed. If the Office Assistant displays a warning message, it also will display the help option, Install Microsoft Query. Choose this option for step-by-step procedures that guide you through the installation of Microsoft Query. If the Office Assistant is inactive, close the warning message and then activate the Office Assistant. Type **Microsoft Query** in the Office Assistant search box, and then press Enter to see a list of help topics. From the list, choose Install Microsoft Query.

FIG. 16.1

Use this dialog box to create a data source for each database you intend to query.

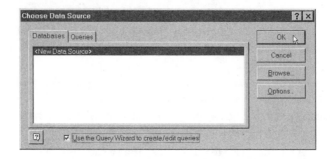

Creating the Data Source

Before you can retrieve external data that you want to use, you must create a data source to identify the data's location. After you create the data source, you can use it to create a query to retrieve the data. To create a data source, follow these steps:

1. In the Choose Data Source dialog box, select <New Data Source>.

2. Click OK. The Create New Data Source dialog box appears (see Figure 16.2).

FIG. 16.2

As you complete each step, the next step in the dialog box becomes active.

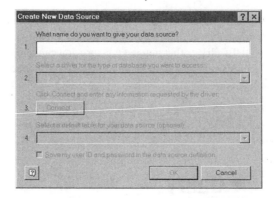

3. In Step 1 of the Create New Data Source dialog box, type a name in the entry box that will help you remember the location (table or file) of the source data you want to retrieve.

Part

IV

Ch

16

4. Step 2 of the dialog box asks you to select a driver for the type of data you want to retrieve. The list of drivers available in Excel appears when you click the drop-down arrow on the far right side of the Step 2 box. The list of drivers are displayed in Figure 16.3.

If the driver you need is not listed, you have to install it.

N O T E Use the Office Assistant to find specific steps for installing ODBC drivers. Type in **install odbc driver** in the Office Assistant search box, and then press Enter to see a list of help topics. From the list, choose Install An ODBC Driver So You Can Access An External Data Source. The step-by-step procedures guide you through the installation. ▪

FIG. 16.3

Choose the built-in driver for the database you want to query.

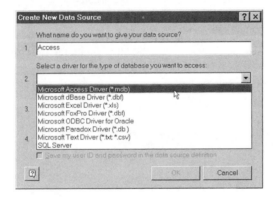

5. After you select the driver, click the Connect button in Step 3. The dialog box that appears will request different information, depending on the driver you selected. Figure 16.4 shows the dialog box for Access 97, and Figure 16.5 shows the dialog box for FoxPro.

FIG. 16.4

In the ODBC Microsoft Access 97 Setup dialog box, click the Select button to designate the location of the Access database.

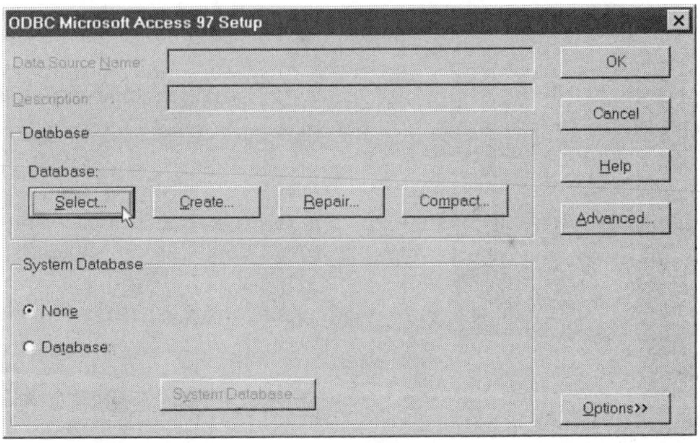

FIG. 16.5

In the ODBC Microsoft FoxPro setup dialog box, remove the check from Use Current Directory, and then click Select Directory.

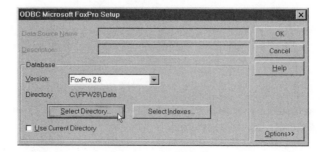

6. When you finish entering the required information in the Connect dialog box, click OK to return to the Create New Data Source dialog box. The path to the source data appears next to the Connect button.

7. Step 4 of the dialog box is optional. If the data you intend to retrieve comes from only one table, use this box to identify it as the default table in a database. If the data you intend to retrieve comes from several tables, leave this box blank. Figure 16.6 shows a completed Create New Data Source dialog box.

FIG. 16.6

A completed New Data Source dialog box for an Access database.

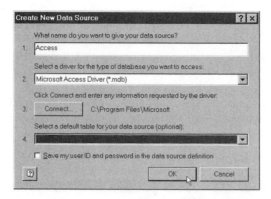

8. After you complete the Create New Data Source dialog box, click OK. The Choose Data Source dialog box is displayed. The data source name you entered in the first step of the Create New Data Source dialog box is listed on the Databases tab of the dialog box.

Now that the data source is created, you are ready to create your query. You have two choices for creating queries:

- *The Query Wizard.* Use this to create a simple query that retrieves data from *one table* in a database.

- *The Microsoft Query Window.* Use this to create a complex query that retrieves data from *multiple tables* in a database.

Regardless of the method you choose to create your query, you can filter your data by specifying criteria, and reordering the data through sorting.

Using the Query Wizard

The quickest and easiest way to create a query in Microsoft Query is to use the Query Wizard. Using the Wizard, you select the columns (fields) of information from one table, and then filter and sort the data before returning it to Excel.

In the Choose Data Source dialog box, choose the data source from the Databases tab, and click OK (see Figure 16.7).

Part

IV

Ch

16

FIG. 16.7

At the bottom of the dialog box, the check box indicates the Query Wizard will be used to create or edit queries.

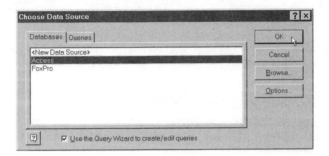

The Query Wizard starts automatically and guides you through the process of creating a query. In Figure 16.7, the Access data source is selected. Figure 16.8 shows the Query Wizard – Choose Columns dialog box, the first step in the Query Wizard. On the left side of the dialog box, a list of tables, and columns in the tables, is displayed. Plus signs (+) next to table names indicate that the columns for that table are hidden. When you click a plus sign, all the columns in a table are displayed (and the sign turns to a minus). Minus signs (–) next to the table names indicate that all the columns in a table are displayed. When you click a minus sign, all the columns in the table are hidden (and the sign turns to a plus).

If you designate a table in the data source, the columns in that table are displayed automatically on the left side of the screen. If you did not designate a specific table, a list of the tables is displayed, as shown in Figure 16.8.

FIG. 16.8

Using the Query Wizard, you can select columns only from the same table.

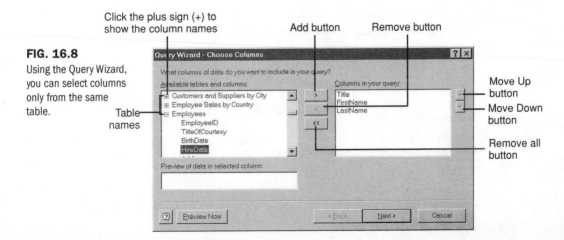

Use these techniques to add or remove columns from the data source:

- To include all the columns in the table, select the table name and click the add button (>). All the column names will be placed in the list on the right.

- To include individual columns, click the plus sign (+) in front of the table name to display the column names. Select the column name in the table listing on the left, and then click the add button (>) for each column you want to add.

- To remove a single column, select the name of the column in the list on the right, and then click the remove button (<). To remove all the column names from the list on the right, click the remove all button (<<).

The order in which you select the columns is the order the columns are displayed when the data is returned to Excel. Use the Move Up and Move Down buttons on the far right side of the dialog box to reorder the columns (refer to Figure 16.8). Select the column you want to move, and then click the appropriate move button.

After you select the columns you want and arrange them in the order you want them to appear in the Excel worksheet, click the Next> button to continue with the Query Wizard.

Filtering Data

After you select the columns of data you want to retrieve, you have the option of filtering the data to retrieve only those records (rows) that meet your specifications. You filter the data by specifying criteria. Establishing filter criteria in the Query Wizard is similar to the way in which you filter data in an Excel list.

▶ **See** "Understanding Filter Criteria," **p. 203**

In the Query Wizard, you can specify a variety of records that contain (or don't contain) one or more specific values, a range of acceptable values, or records that are missing a value (blank field).

Figure 16.9 shows the Query Wizard – Filter Data dialog box. To include all data, skip this step by clicking Next>. To enter filter criteria, follow these steps:

1. Click the column name you want to filter from the list on the left side of the screen. The name of the column appears above the first filter box.

2. From the drop-down list in the first filter box, choose one of the comparison conditions, such as "equals" or "is greater than or equal to," and then enter the sample criteria in the corresponding box on the right side.

3. If necessary, enter another filter criteria. Be sure to select either AND or OR when you use multiple conditions.

4. When you have entered all the conditions, click the Next> button.

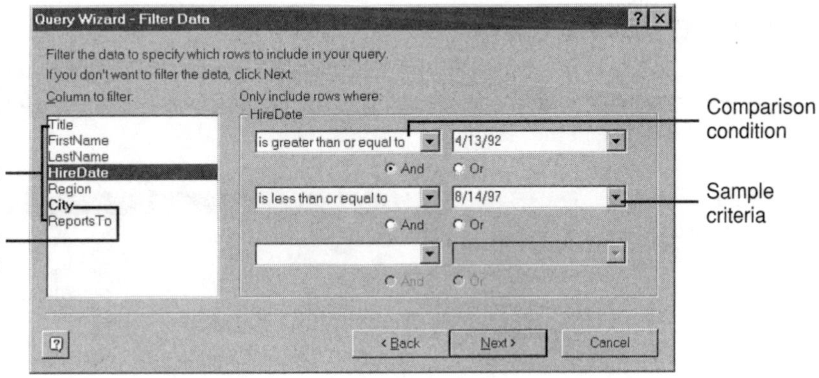

FIG. 16.9
When you specify filters on multiple columns, the column names appear in bold type.

Column names

Filter applied to multiple columns

Comparison condition

Sample criteria

Sorting the Records

The Query Wizard – Sort Order dialog box, shown in Figure 16.10, lets you sort the data before placing it in the Excel worksheet. Sorting in the Query Wizard is virtually identical to sorting a list in an Excel worksheet. You can sort up to three columns of data, using either ascending or descending sorts.

▶ **See** "Sorting Lists of Data," **p. 187**

Like filtering, sorting is optional in the Query Wizard. To skip the sorting option and display the records (rows) in the order they appear in the table, click the Next> button. To specify a sort order for the records, follow these steps:

1. In the Sort by drop-down box, choose the column by which you want the data sorted, and then select either ascending or descending order.

2. If necessary, enter another sort option.

3. When you have entered all the conditions, click the Next> button.

FIG. 16.10
Using the Query Wizard, you can choose three columns by which to sort your data.

Choose the column name to sort on from the drop-down list

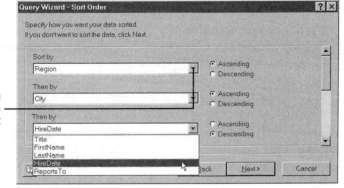

Returning Data to Excel

The last step in the Query Wizard (shown in Figure 16.11) lets you choose to either save your query, return the results immediately to Excel, or display the Microsoft Query window to view the data and edit the results.

FIG. 16.11

It is always a good idea to save your query before clicking Finish.

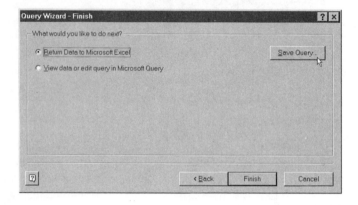

If you intend to (or think you might) use the query again sometime in the future, you should save the query by clicking the Save Query button. This displays the Save As dialog box (see Figure 16.12). By default, the query is saved in a specific folder, which is located in the C:\Program Files\Microsoft Office\Queries folder. Give your query a name that helps you recognize the data it retrieves. After you type the name, click Save, and then the Query Wizard – Finish dialog box is displayed again.

FIG. 16.12

The default name displayed in the Save As dialog box uses the data source name on which the query is based.

To place the data you retrieve into an Excel worksheet, choose Return Data to Microsoft Excel, and then click Finish. When returning the data to Excel, you are asked where to place the data, as shown in Figure 16.13.

FIG. 16.13
The data returned to
Excel may only be
placed in the active
workbook.

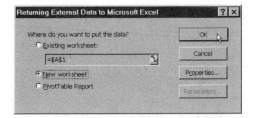

Excel offers the following choices for saving your data, though you must save the data into the
active workbook:

- *The existing worksheet in the active workbook.* You can specify a cell in the existing
  worksheet by marking the upper-left corner of the range where you want the data to
  begin.

- *A new worksheet in the active workbook.* You can place the data in a new worksheet, which
  is inserted in the active workbook.

- *A pivot table report in the active workbook.* You can create a pivot table based on the data.

If you select either Existing Worksheet or New Worksheet, the columns in the worksheet are
adjusted to fit the longest entry, and the column headings are formatted in bold. Figure 16.14
shows an example of the data returned from the query, and the External Data toolbar, which is
automatically displayed.

FIG. 16.14
The External Data
toolbar is automatically
displayed when you
return the data to Excel.

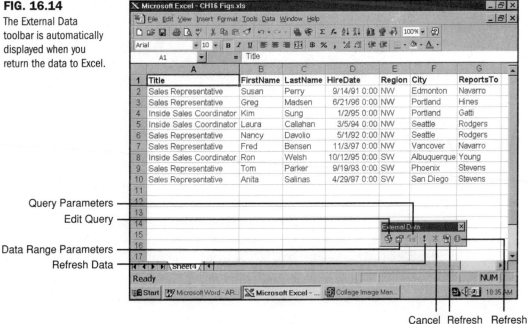

Selecting the PivotTable Report option takes you directly to Step 3 of the PivotTable Wizard.

▶ **See** "Creating a Pivot Table Using an Excel List," **p. 229**

Using the Microsoft Query Window

The Microsoft Query window enables you to view together on one screen all the components of the query (such as tables, fields, and criteria) and the data being retrieved. To display the Microsoft Query window, follow these steps:

1. Start Microsoft Query by choosing Data, Get External Data, Create New Query. The Choose Data Source dialog box is displayed, as shown in Figure 16.15.

FIG. 16.15

The FoxPro data source, created earlier, is selected.

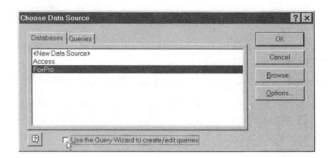

2. From the Databases tab, select the data source you want to use for your query. In Figure 16.15, the FoxPro data source is selected.

N O T E   Before using the Microsoft Query window, make sure you have created the data source that identifies the location of the data that you want to retrieve. See the earlier section, "Creating the Data Source," for the steps to accomplish this. After you create the data source, you can use it to create a query to retrieve the data. ■

3. At the bottom of the dialog box, remove the check from the Use The Query Wizard to Create/Edit Queries check box (refer to Figure 16.15).

4. Click OK to display the Microsoft Query window.

Figure 16.16 illustrates the Microsoft Query window. Like any windows program, Microsoft Query has its own menu bar and toolbar.

The query information is displayed in sections called *panes*. In Figure 16.16, two panes are displayed—the table pane (showing the Customer and Orders tables) and the data pane (which is blank because no table fields have been selected).

If you designated a default table in the source data, the table and the field names are displayed in the table pane at the top of the screen.

If you did not designate a specific table, a list of the tables is displayed in the Add Tables dialog box, as shown in Figure 16.17. Double-click the name of each table you want to add to the query window, then click Close.

Microsoft Query menu bar

Microsoft Query toolbar

Maximize button

FIG. 16.16
To see more data on-screen, maximize the query windows.

Table pane

Pane divider

Query window

Data pane

Status bar

Field names

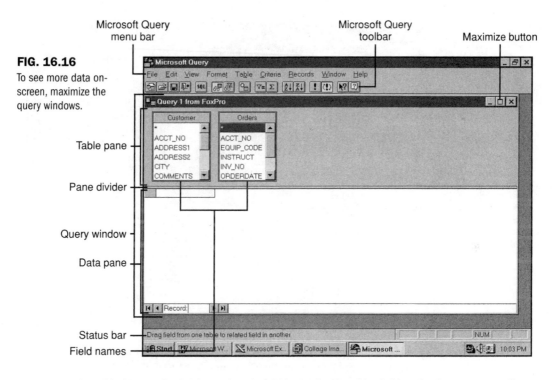

In the table boxes, the fields are listed alphabetically. To add a field to the data pane, scroll through the field names in the table listing, and then double-click the field to add it to the data pane area.

FIG. 16.17
The Add Tables dialog box lists all the tables available in the location specified in the data source.

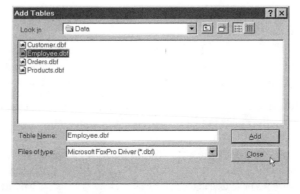

To reorder the fields in the data pane, position your mouse pointer over the name of the field you want to move. The mouse pointer changes to a black, down-pointing arrow; click once to select the field. In Figure 16.18, the ORDERDATE field is selected. Your mouse pointer then changes to a white pointing arrow; hold and drag the mouse pointer to the new location. A thick black line, as shown in Figure 16.18, indicates the location as you drag. Release the mouse when the thick line is at the desired position.

FIG. 16.18

The ORDERDATE field is being repositioned to the left of the EQUIP_CODE field.

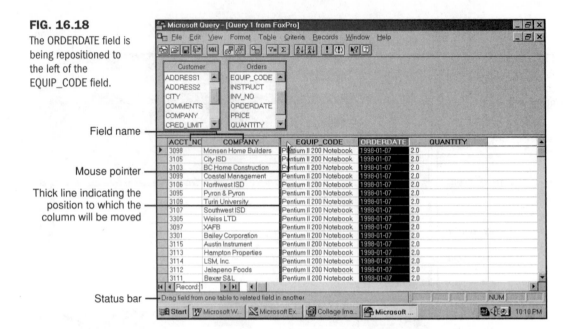

Field name

Mouse pointer

Thick line indicating the position to which the column will be moved

Status bar

In Figure 16.18, the information listed in the data pane is coming from two different tables. ACCT_NO and COMPANY are fields from the Customer table. EQUIP_CODE, ORDERDATE, and QUANTITY are fields from the Orders table. Notice that the data in the EQUIP_CODE, ORDERDATE, and QUANTITY fields list the same information for each record (row). This occurs because the tables are not joined or linked together. The next section describes how to join tables in the Microsoft Query window.

Joining Multiple Tables

When you want to retrieve data from multiple tables, the tables must be joined by a common field. With some databases, such as Access, Microsoft Query joins the tables for you. With other databases, such as FoxPro, you have to manually join the tables.

In Figure 16.19, two tables from a FoxPro database are displayed in the table pane. The common field between the tables is ACCT_NO (Account number).

N O T E One useful feature of Microsoft Query is the status bar. In Figure 16.19, notice the message displaying on the status bar in the lower-left corner. The status bar provides suggestions for the next step to take in the query process. In this instance, it indicates that you need to "Drag Field from One Table to Related Field in Another." ■

To join tables together in the Microsoft Query window, drag the field in the first table to the corresponding field in the second table. A line appears between the tables, as shown in Figure 16.20.

FIG. 16.19

When retrieving data from multiple tables, the tables must be joined.

Table pane

Field names

Data pane

Status bar

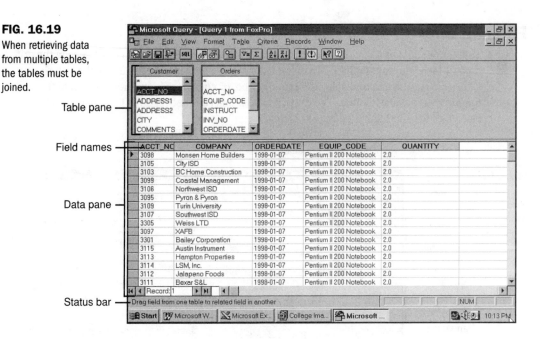

Notice how the fields in the data pane now display information for each order placed by the customers. Additionally, the status bar now displays a new message, recommending that you display the criteria pane to filter the data from the database. The next section provides instructions on how to do this.

FIG. 16.20

After the tables are joined, the information in the data pane is updated.

Join line between tables

Data pane

Status bar

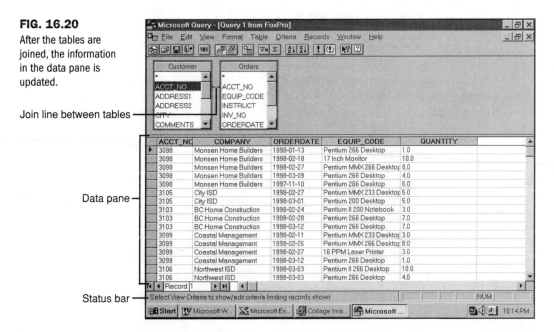

Filtering Data

To filter out data that you don't want to retrieve from the databases, you must specify the criteria by which you want to filter. Microsoft Query uses another pane to display the criteria. Choose View, Criteria to display the criteria pane, or click the Show/Hide Criteria button on the Microsoft Query toolbar. The criteria pane is inserted between the table pane and the data pane, as shown in Figure 16.21.

FIG. 16.21

You can drag the pane dividers to display more of one pane than another.

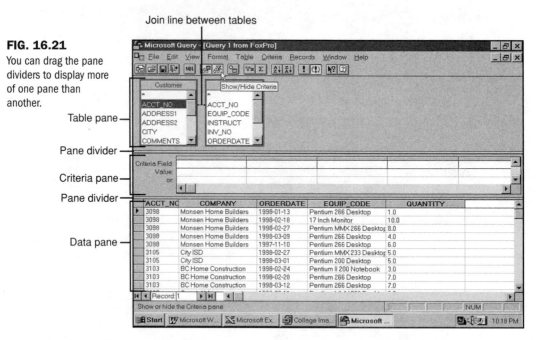

The criteria pane displays the criteria you specify. Although you can use the criteria pane to enter the criteria, it is *significantly* easier to enter the criteria in the Add Criteria dialog box. Choose Criteria, Add Criteria to display this dialog box, as shown in Figure 16.22.

FIG. 16.22

For each new criteria, select a new location in the Criteria pane before accessing the Add Criteria command.

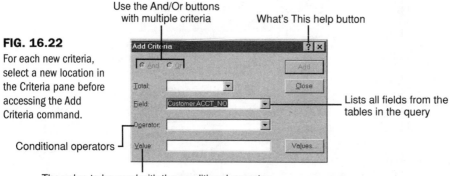

To specify criteria in the Add Criteria dialog box, follow these steps:

1. Click the drop-down arrow in the Field box to display a list of all the fields in the tables selected in the query. The list displays the table name and the field name. You can filter any field.

2. In the Operator entry box, click the drop-down arrow to see a list of possible operators, and then select the operator you want to use.

3. Click the Value entry box. If you want to use a value that exists in this field of the database, click the Values button to select from a list of existing values. If the value you need is not in the list, type the value in the entry box.

4. When you complete the criteria, click Add. After you specify all the criteria, click Close. Figure 16.23 shows an example of the Add Criteria dialog box. The criteria specifies that only those records ordered between 11/1/97 and 12/31/97 are to be retrieved from the database.

FIG. 16.23
The comma between the dates signifies an AND condition. The date the orders were placed must be between 11/1/97 and 12/31/97.

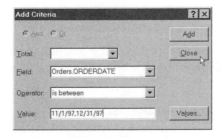

▶ **See** "Understanding Filter Criteria," **p. 203**

The data pane displays the result set, based on the criteria you specified.

The help screens in Microsoft Query provide additional examples of criteria. Use the Office Assistant to search for these help screens. Type in **criteria examples** in the Office Assistant search box. Press Enter to see a list of help topics. Choose *Examples of expressions*. Look through each of the four types of expressions listed in the help screen.

 By default, each time you add a field or specify a criteria, Microsoft Query immediately searches for the records to display in the data pane. If you wait a long time for the screen to update, you can turn off the Auto Query button on the toolbar. After you specify all the fields and criteria, select the Query Now button to retrieve the data.

Sorting Records

 You can sort the list of records before returning them to Excel. Sorting records in Microsoft Query is similar to sorting a list in Excel. Before you sort the records, make sure Auto Query is turned off.

To sort the list of records in the data pane, select the field by which you want to sort by clicking the field name in the data pane. Use the Sort Ascending and Sort Descending buttons on the toolbar to sort the records.

You can sort multiple columns at once by using either an ascending or descending sort on the columns. You cannot sort one column ascending and another column descending in Microsoft Query. However, you can do this after you return the list to Excel.

▶ **See** "Sorting Lists of Data," **p. 187**

To sort multiple columns in Microsoft Query, follow these steps:

1. Arrange the columns from left to right in the data pane in the order by which you want to sort them. For example, if you want to see the orders placed by each company, and the corresponding order dates listed chronologically, the COMPANY field needs to appear first, followed by the ORDERDATE field.

2. After the fields are arranged, select both fields by dragging the mouse pointer across the field headings.

3. Click either the Sort Ascending or Sort Descending button on the toolbar.

Figure 16.24 shows the data result set sorted by Company name, then by Order date. Rearranging the fields after a multi-column sort has been performed does not affect the sort order; the records remain sorted.

FIG. 16.24

After the sort, the ORDERDATE column was moved, but the list is still sorted, first by company name, and then by date ordered.

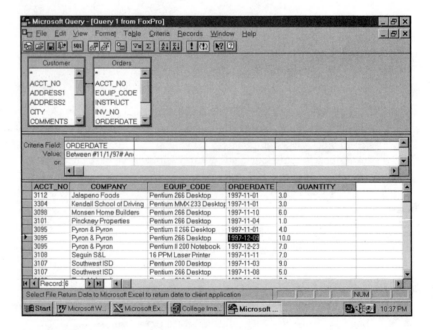

Returning Data to Excel

 To save the query you create, click the Save File button on the Microsoft Query toolbar. The Save As dialog box is displayed. By default, the query is saved in the Queries folder, which is located in the C:\Program Files\Microsoft Office folder. The default name displayed incorporates the source data name upon which the query is based. Provide your query with a name that helps you recognize the data it retrieves. After you type the name, select Save.

 To return the data result set to Excel, click the Return Data button on the Microsoft Query toolbar. The Returning Data to Microsoft Excel dialog box is displayed, as shown in Figure 16.25.

FIG. 16.25

Sheet3 in the current workbook is the destination of the result set.

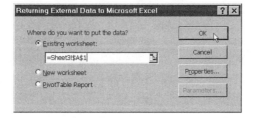

You have several choices for where you want to store the data:

- *The existing worksheet in the active workbook.* You can specify a cell in the existing worksheet, marking the upper-left corner of the range where the data is to begin.

- *A new worksheet in the active workbook.* You can place the data in a new worksheet, which is inserted in the active workbook.

- *A pivot table report in the active workbook.* You can create a pivot table based on the data.

If you select either Existing Worksheet or New Worksheet, the columns in the worksheet are adjusted to fit the longest entry, and the column headings are formatted in bold. Selecting the PivotTable Report option takes you directly to Step 3 of the PivotTable Wizard.

▶ **See** "Creating a Pivot Table Using an Excel List," **p. 229**

Excel and the Outside World

CHAPTER 17

Integrating Excel Data into Other Windows Applications

Moving and copying data

The Clipboard and the Desktop can be used to move or copy data between files. You can use traditional menu commands to share data, or drag and drop data with the mouse. Entire files or "scraps" of files can be shared.

Linking versus embedding

The two primary differences between linking and embedding are where the data is stored and how it is updated after it is placed in the destination (target) file.

Including Excel data in e-mail messages

Attach Excel files to e-mail messages in applications such as Outlook or cc:Mail.

Introducing the Binder application

Use the features of the innovative Binder application to work with files created in different applications, as if they are a single "bound" document. Within one window, you can work with documents created in any Office 97 application.

One of the most practical features of Windows applications is the ease with which data from a file created in one application can be included in a file in another application. For example, a Microsoft Excel worksheet and a PowerPoint slide can be included in a Word document. Windows provides many tools to share data. ■

Alternative Methods for Sharing Data

Data in an Excel worksheet can be shared with another Excel worksheet or with a document in an entirely different application. When sharing data, the original location of the data is known as the *source*. The destination of the data is known as the *target*. The source and target can reside in the same file, in different files in the same application, or in different files in different locations. For example, when sharing an Excel pivot table with a Word document, the source is Excel and the target is Word. The data being shared is sometimes referred to as the *object*.

You can use a variety of methods to share Excel data, including copying, moving, linking, and embedding. Before discussing each alternative, you need to understand the benefits and limitations of each. The following list explains the alternative methods you can use to share Excel information, including a description of each alternative, and reasons *why* you might choose one method over another.

- *Moving.* Moving data removes it from its current location and places it in another location. The data becomes part of the document you move it to. Move data only when you want to permanently relocate it to the target file.

- *Copying.* Copied data remains in its current location and its copy is placed in another location; the original data remains intact. The copy doesn't change when the original changes, unless the original data and the copy are linked. Copy data when you want to share it with another file and still retain the original data; don't copy data if you want the copy to be updated when the original changes.

- *Linking.* Linked data remains stored in the source file, while the target file simply displays a *representation* of the data. The target file actually stores only the location (such as an address) of the source data. The data in the target file mirrors the original source data; when the original data is changed, the representation changes. The target file is automatically updated.

  Linking is useful because the data is stored in only one place the source file. When you copy or embed data, it is stored twice—in the source file and in the target file. The size of a file that contains a link is smaller than files that contain copied or embedded data.

  You can link all or part of an existing file. For example, you can link an Excel chart to a report in a Word document. When the chart in Excel changes, the Word document automatically reflects those changes. With linking, the application and source file have to be available for the data in the linked file to be updated. If the source file is deleted or otherwise becomes unavailable, the target file will display an error.

- *Embedding.* When you embed data, the original data remains in its current location and a copy is placed in another location. The embedded data becomes part of the target file and does not change if the source data is modified. You can embed all or part of an existing file. For example, you might embed a clipart object into an Excel worksheet.

  Embedding is similar to copying, with one very significant difference—when data is embedded, it retains a connection *to the application* in which the data was originally created, *not to the original source data*. You can edit the data while in the target application, and the original data in the source application won't change. Likewise, because embedded data has no links to the source file, it is not updated when the original data changes. When you embed data, the target file requires more disk space than if you link to the information, because the data is stored in the embedded file.

Use embedding when you want to edit the data separately from the source file, or if the source file might be unavailable.

In addition to these four methods, there are other means available to share data. You can share data by including Excel files in e-mail messages, or as part of scheduling tasks, by using Microsoft Outlook or other scheduling and e-mail applications. Use Microsoft Binder to gather documents together from different applications. The documents in a binder are treated as sections in a single file. This enables you to print-preview all the documents together, and to print the files in the binder with consecutive page numbers.

Using the Clipboard and the Desktop

The Clipboard is the traditional method used to move, copy, and link data. If you have used the Cut/Copy and Paste/Paste Special commands, then you already have used the Clipboard. However, a new concept is emerging that enables you to use the Desktop to share data between applications. Both the Clipboard and the Desktop can assist in sharing data:

- *The Clipboard.* The Clipboard is part of Windows, not any one application. It is a temporary place in Windows' memory designed specifically for you to share data between files and applications. The Clipboard can hold one object, such as a group of selected cells, a chart, or a clip art object. The Clipboard is always accessible when you are working on the computer. However, because it uses temporary memory, any data on the Clipboard is lost when the computer is powered off.

- *The Desktop.* The Desktop is also part of Windows, but it is a permanent area designed to store icons. These icons can represent applications such as Excel, unique areas such as the Recycle Bin, folders and files, or objects from within a file. An object that is part of a file is called a *scrap*. The Desktop is accessible only when you can see the Desktop, but because it is a permanent part of Windows, any data stored on the Desktop remains there, even when the computer is powered off. A list of the items on the Desktop is stored in the folder C:\windows\desktop.

Use the Desktop when you want to store data you intend to use over and over again, perhaps in one or more applications.

Both the Clipboard and the Desktop can hold any type of data—text, numbers, graphics—that you may want to use in another file.

When using the Clipboard, data that you move, copy, or link to another application is pasted, if possible, in a format that the application can edit. For example, by default, Excel worksheet data is pasted into Microsoft Word as a Word table; the data is brought in as formatted text. Using the Paste Special command, you have a choice of how the data appears in Word. If you choose to paste the data as unformatted text, the Excel data appears in Word separated by tabs.

If you choose to paste the data as an Excel Worksheet Object, the Excel data appears in Word as an object, similar to clipart.

Excel data that is pasted into a PowerPoint slide appears as an object. The only exception is when you create a PowerPoint chart and paste the Excel data into the charting Datasheet. Excel charts are pasted into Word and PowerPoint as objects.

When using the Desktop, most data is pasted as objects. The section, "Using Scraps of Data," later in this chapter, describes how to use the Desktop to share data.

Moving and Copying Data

You can move and copy Excel data to other parts of the same workbook, to worksheets in other workbooks, or to files in other applications. The Cut/Copy and Paste/Paste Special commands are used to move and copy data in Windows.

> **N O T E** Chapter 1, "Essential Excel—Increasing Your Efficiency," discusses using drag and drop to move or copy data within Excel. This method is useful if the location in which you want to place the data is *visible* on-screen, whether it is a location inside Excel, a location in another application, or on the desktop. See the next section, "Using Drag and Drop to Share Data," for specific instructions on using this technique. ■

▶ **See** "Moving and Copying Data with Ease," **p. 9**

The application and file that contain the data you are moving or copying is referred to as the *source*. The destination application and file in which the data is placed is referred to as the *target*. When you move or copy data, both the source and the target must be open. Although you can arrange the target application and the source application side by side, it is unnecessary because both applications appear on the Taskbar at the bottom of the Windows screen. To move or copy data, follow these steps:

1. Select the cells to be moved or copied in the source document.

2. Choose Edit, Cut (to move) or Edit, Copy (to copy); the data is placed on the Clipboard.

3. Activate the target document and the specific location where you want the data to be placed.

4. Choose Edit, Paste to place the data in the target document.

By default, an attempt is made to paste the data in the target file in a format the target uses. If this isn't possible, the data is pasted as an object instead. Use the Paste Special command to view and select the way in which the data will be pasted. Figure 17.1 shows the Paste Special dialog box. Data from an Excel worksheet is being pasted into a Word document. When you select an alternative from the As list box, the Result description at the bottom of the dialog box explains what the alternative will do with the data.

FIG. 17.1

Use the Paste Special dialog box to pick from a list of alternative formats for the pasted data.

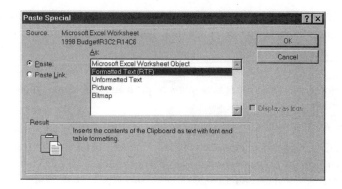

N O T E To copy worksheet data from Excel into Access, you need to use the tools built into Access. Your Excel worksheet must be organized as a list. The first row in the worksheet should contain the field names that you want to use in Access. See Chapter 11, "Designing a List or Database," for more information on creating a list that Access can read.

After you create the list, create or display the table in Access, where the Excel data will be copied. Then, from within Access, choose File, Get External Data, Import. Follow the steps to copy the data from Excel into Access.

If you need to copy the entire screen or a particular window on the screen, such as a dialog box, use the Print Screen key on the keyboard. The Print Screen key is located just to the right of the F12 key on most keyboards. The name on the key may be abbreviated to PrtScrn or PrintScrn. To copy a screen or a window, follow these steps:

1. Display the screen or window exactly as you want it to appear.

2. To copy the entire screen as an object, select the Print Screen key. An image of the screen is placed on the Clipboard.

    To copy the active window on the screen, use Alt+Print Screen. An image of the active window is placed on the Clipboard.

3. Activate the target document and the specific location where you want the image to appear.

4. Choose Edit, Paste to place the image in the target document.

If you want the screen to be its own document instead of an object inside another document, paste it into Paint and save it as a bitmap file. Choose Start, Programs, Accessories to access the Paint program.

Using Drag and Drop to Share Data

There are many different ways to move and copy data, but one of the most convenient methods is *drag and drop*. Using your mouse, you can drag selected cells or Excel charts and drop them into another part of the same worksheet, to a different worksheet, or even to a different application, such as Microsoft Word. You can also drag highlighted data onto the desktop, creating a

Part
V

Ch
17

scrap. To use drag and drop, both the source and target files must be open. In some cases the files must also be visible on-screen, as noted in the following list:

■ If the target destination is another sheet in the same book, another window of the active workbook must be visible to perform the drag and drop. If the target destination is another workbook, this book must be open and visible on-screen to perform the drag and drop.

▶ **See** "Viewing Multiple Worksheets," **p. 33**

■ If the target destination is another application, the target file must be open for you to perform the drag and drop. However, the application doesn't have to be visible on-screen. The names of the open applications appear on the Taskbar at the bottom of the Windows screen.

■ If the target destination is the Desktop, the Desktop must be visible on-screen. Use the Restore button to reduce the size of an application window so that you can see the Desktop.

N O T E   If you want to display the source and target applications side by side on-screen, open both applications. Minimize any other applications you have open but do not want displayed on-screen, and then right-click the Taskbar. Choose either Tile Horizontally or Tile Vertically. The open applications then are displayed together on-screen. ▪

▶ **See** "Moving and Copying Data with Ease," **p. 9**

▶ **See** "Discovering the Power of the AutoFilter," **p. 203**

In Figure 17.2, the Excel data from a filtered list is being copied into a Word document.

If the window for the target (destination) application isn't visible, drag the selection onto the target application button in the Taskbar, keeping the mouse button held down. The application window will appear. Drop the selection where you want it to be inserted in the target application.

Using Scraps of Data

The Desktop is an area in which you can store data from a file. Data that is part of a file is called a *scrap*. The Desktop can hold any type of data, such as text, numbers, and graphics. One advantage of using the Desktop is that the data remains on the Desktop for as long as you need it. There are several advantages to using the Desktop over the Clipboard. Refer to the earlier section, "Using the Clipboard and the Desktop," for a comparison of the Clipboard and Desktop.

Use the Desktop when you intend to paste the same data over and over again, such as a logo or WordArt object.

▶ **See** "Using WordArt to Format Worksheets," **p. 9**

FIG. 17.2

The source and target applications can be arranged (tiled) side by side by right-clicking the Taskbar.

Filtered Excel list table —

Gray insertion point —

Mouse pointer when copying —

Status bar —

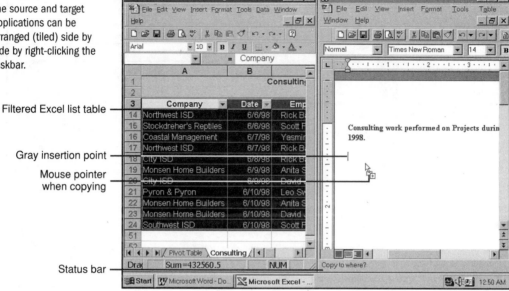

Most data pasted from the Desktop is pasted as an object, similar to clipart. For example, suppose you have stored Excel charts and cells of data on the Desktop. When those scraps are pasted into Word, PowerPoint, or even back into Excel, they are pasted in as objects. Word and PowerPoint scraps are pasted into Excel as objects. A Word text scrap, however, is pasted back into Word as text, not as an object.

To use the Desktop to store or retrieve scraps, it must be visible on-screen. The following steps guide you through creating a scrap on your Desktop:

1. Make sure a part of the Desktop is visible. You can use the Restore button to reduce the size of the Excel window.

2. Select the range of cells or Excel chart from which you want to create the scrap.

3. Right-click the cells or chart, and then choose Copy from the shortcut menu.

4. Right-click a blank area of the Desktop, and then choose Paste from the shortcut menu.

 You also can use the drag-and-drop method if you are copying a range of cells (or text in Word). However, you must use the Copy/Paste commands if you are copying an Excel chart.

In Figure 17.3, the Excel window and the Desktop are visible. There are three scrap icons on the upper-right side of the Desktop. The text that appears under the icon varies, depending on the type of data contained in the scrap. You can edit the text below the scrap icon. Select the icon, and then pause (to be sure you don't double-click), and then click again to edit the text. If you double-click, you open the program that created the scrap.

Part
V
Ch
17

FIG. 17.3

Make scrap icon text descriptive and meaningful.

Excel scrap of worksheet cells

Excel scrap of a chart; the text under the icon is ready to be edited

Word scrap of text

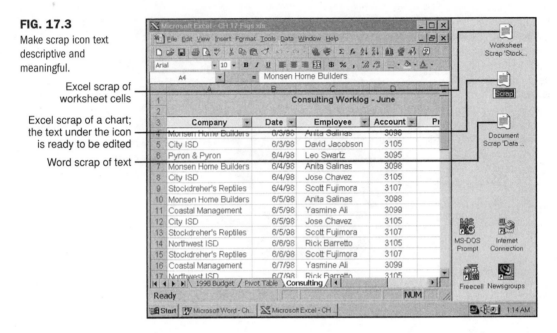

To use the scrap on the Desktop, make sure that the Desktop location of the scrap and the document into which you want to copy the scrap are both visible. Right-click the scrap icon, and then choose Copy from the shortcut menu. In the document that you want the scrap added to, right-click in the location you want the scrap placed and choose Paste from the shortcut menu.

If you plan to use a lot of scraps, consider creating a folder on the Desktop to store all of your scraps. To create a folder on the Desktop, right-click the Desktop, and then choose New, Folder from the shortcut menu. Type a name for the folder and then press Enter.

If you already have scraps on the Desktop, drag and drop them into this folder. Whenever you create a scrap, paste or drag the scrap into this folder. Simply drag and drop or copy and paste scraps from the folder into your document. Figure 17.4 shows an Excel chart scrap being dropped into a Word document.

Linking Data

Perhaps without knowing it, you have already created links between data. When you create formulas to calculate data across worksheets and workbooks, the formulas are links. If the data in the worksheets or workbooks changes, the result of the formula changes. When you create charts in Excel, the chart is linked to the worksheet data. If the data in the worksheet changes, the charts automatically reflect the new data. Pivot tables are another example of linked data; the pivot table is linked to the list of data that the pivot table summarizes.

FIG. 17.4

Scraps can easily be dropped into other applications.

Folder containing the scraps

Contents of scrap folder

Excel scrap of a chart

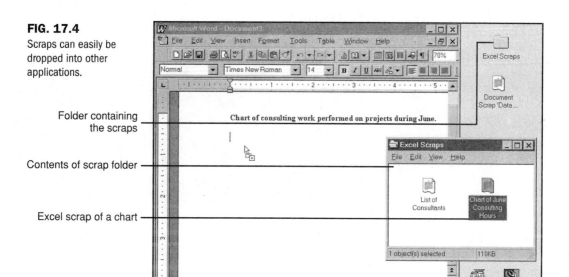

▶ **See** "Linking Worksheets," **p. 75**

▶ **See** "Linking Workbooks," **p. 75**

▶ **See** "Creating a Pivot Table Using an Excel List," **p. 229**

In this section, you learn to link data across the Microsoft Office applications. Linking can be accomplished by using the Edit, Copy and the Edit, Paste Special commands, or the Insert, Object command. The command you choose depends on what you are attempting to link. To link parts of a file, such as a range of cells or an Excel chart, use the Copy and Paste Special commands. To link an entire file, use the Object command. The basic steps for creating a link to part of a file are as follows:

1. Make sure the source document and target document are open. They don't both have to be displayed on-screen.

2. Select the data to be copied in the source document.

3. Choose Edit, Copy. The data is placed on the Clipboard.

4. Activate the target document and the specific location where you want the data to be placed.

5. Choose Edit, Paste Special. When linking from one application to another, the Paste Special dialog box appears, as shown in Figure 17.5.

6. Select the Paste Link option on the left side of the dialog box. In the As list box, choose the option you want to use to create the link. The selected option in the list is the default (and most common) option.

7. Choose OK.

Part

V

Ch

17

FIG. 17.5

When you select an option in the As list box, the Result description, at the bottom of the dialog box, explains what happens when the data is pasted into the target file.

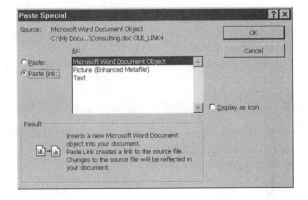

N O T E If the Paste Link option is not available in the target (destination), you either did not copy the data, or the application into which you are copying does not support links. ▪

When linking from one Excel worksheet to another Excel worksheet, the Paste Special dialog box appears, as shown in Figure 17.6. Choose the Paste Link button in the lower-right corner of the dialog box. The data is pasted to the new worksheet.

FIG. 17.6

The Paste Special dialog box, used when pasting within Excel, differs from the dialog box used when pasting between applications.

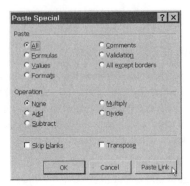

Figure 17.7 shows an Excel chart linked into a Word document. The chart will be displayed fairly large. Position your mouse on a corner selection handle, and then drag to shrink the image. If you do not enlarge from a corner, the object may appear distorted. Using a corner ensures that the object shrinks proportionally.

Figure 17.8 shows an Excel chart linked into a PowerPoint slide. Figure 17.9 shows data from an Excel worksheet being linked into a PowerPoint slide. When the Excel object is pasted, it is displayed fairly small. Position your mouse on a corner selection handle and drag to enlarge. If you do not enlarge from a corner, the object may appear distorted. Using a corner ensures the object enlarges proportionally.

FIG. 17.7
You can link an Excel chart to a Word document. When the chart in Excel is updated, the chart in Word reflects those changes.

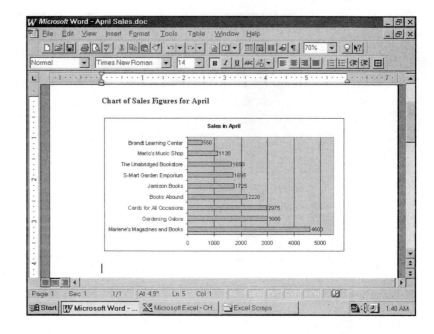

FIG. 17.8
The PowerPoint slide title has been moved up, and the Excel chart enlarged, by using a corner selection handle.

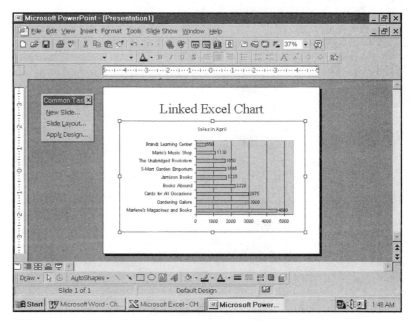

Part
V

Ch
17

FIG. 17.9

Make sure you resize objects from a corner selection handle to keep the object proportional.

Selection handle

Mouse pointer

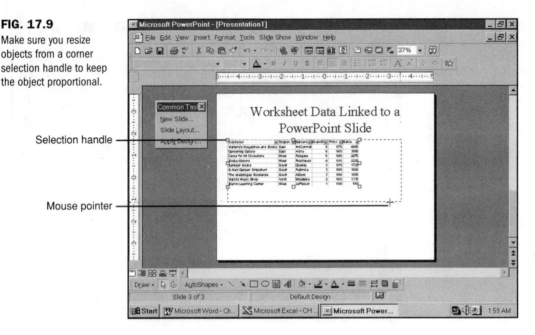

Figure 17.10 shows data from an Excel worksheet being linked into the PowerPoint datasheet, to create a PowerPoint chart from the Excel data. When you paste the Excel data into the datasheet, a warning message appears indicating that any existing data in the datasheet may be written over by the data you are pasting in.

FIG. 17.10

Select the first cell before pasting the linked data.

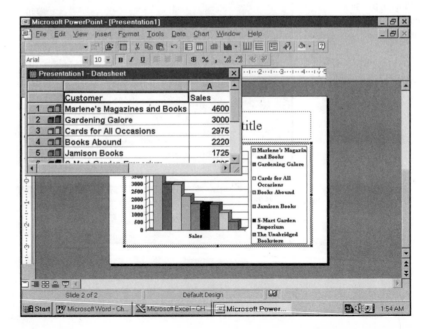

N O T E   To link worksheet data from Excel into Access, you need to use the tools built into Access.
Create or display the table in Access where the Excel data will be linked. Then, from within
Access, choose File, Get External Data, Link Tables. Follow the steps provided to link the data from
Excel to Access. ■

To link an entire file into an Excel worksheet, follow these steps:

1. Choose Insert, Object, and then select the Create From File tab to display the Object
   dialog box (see Figure 17.11).

FIG. 17.11

Use the Create From
File option to insert an
existing file into an
Excel worksheet.

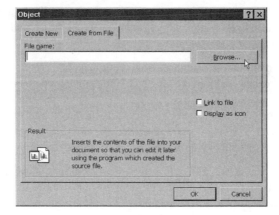

2. Choose the Browse button to open the Browse dialog box.
3. Use the Look In list box to change to the drive and folder that contains the file you want
   to link and choose Insert.
4. Back in the Object dialog box, select the Link to File option.
5. You have the option of linking the object as an icon rather than displaying the actual
   object. This is useful with large files, or when you only want to open the file periodically,
   not every time the workbook opens. Double-click the icon to open the linked file.
6. Choose OK. The object will be inserted and linked in your worksheet.

If you move or rename the source file and the target file is open, the links are updated to point
to the new location or name of the source file. If the target file is not open when the source file
is renamed or moved, however, the target file may not be able to find its source. When this
occurs, follow these steps to reconnect to the source file:

1. Display the Target file.
2. Choose Edit menu, Links.
3. Select the source link you want to reconnect from the Links list box. To select multiple
   links to the same source file, hold down the Ctrl key and click each link.
4. Choose Change Source; the Change Source dialog box appears.

Part
V

Ch
17

5. In the Change Source dialog box (which is virtually identical to the Open dialog box), locate the source file for the selected links, and then select Open.

6. In the Links dialog box, choose Update Now to refresh the data.

7. Choose Close.

Embedding Objects

An object can be an entire file or part of a file, such as a chart or selected range of cells. You can embed existing objects from one file into another file, or use the tools of another application to create new objects that will be embedded into the active file. In the first instance, an original object exists and you embed a copy of the object. In the second instance, you are creating the object; therefore it is the original object.

When you embed an object from another file, the original object remains in that source file and a copy of the object is inserted into the target file. The embedded object becomes part of the target file. It retains a link to the source application, but not to the source file or original object. You can edit the embedded object while remaining in the target application; the original object in the source application will not change. Likewise, because the embedded object doesn't have links to the source file, it won't be updated when you change the original object.

When you insert a chart or WordArt into a worksheet, you have, in fact, *embedded* the object. You can edit the chart or WordArt objects by using the applications that created the object. Because the object was not copied from another file, you are editing the original object.

When you double-click to edit the embedded object, the application that originally created the object will start. You then can edit the embedded object with the commands and tools of the source application. However, if the application used to create the object is not available—for example, you give the document to someone who doesn't have the source application—Windows tries to substitute a different application to manipulate the object so that you can edit it.

The advantages and disadvantages of embedding versus linking are listed as follows:

- *Advantages.* The object resides in the target file. With a link, if the source file is renamed or moved, Excel may be unable to find and update the linked object. The embedded object is edited within Excel, and you choose when to update it.

- *Disadvantages.* Because the entire embedded object is saved inside the Excel document, the file size of the Excel document will be larger. If you update an embedded object by using an application other than the original source application, the object may have lower resolution or may lose some of the original formats. You must update each embedded object individually, which is quite cumbersome when a file has objects that need to be updated frequently. A file containing multiple links can update all the links at one time.

The following list presents some situations in which you should choose to embed an object rather than link it:

■ When you want to keep the worksheet and object together

■ When you have only one source object to embed

■ When you want to control the updates manually from within Excel

The following list presents some situations in which you should choose to link an object rather than embed it:

■ When you have one source file to link to several target files, or one target file which contains many objects that need to be updated

■ When you want to update many links at one time when the source file changes

The method you select to embed an object depends on what you are embedding. Use the Edit, Copy and Edit, Paste Special commands when you want to embed part of a file. Use the Insert, Object command to embed an entire file or an object you will create. To insert a new object (created from scratch) into an Excel worksheet, follow these steps:

1. Choose Insert, Object, and then select the Create New tab. The Object dialog appears (see Figure 17.12).

Part

V

Ch

17

FIG. 17.12
Scroll in the list to see the types of files you can create and embed in Excel.

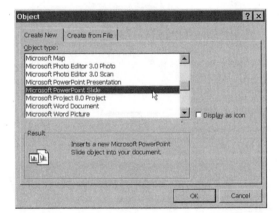

2. From the Object Type list box, choose the source application you want to use to create the embedded object.

3. Choose OK. The selected application will either replace the menu bar commands and toolbars with its own (Office 97 applications will do this), or the application will open in a separate window on top of your Excel worksheet.

4. Create the object you want to embed.

5. When you have created the object, if the application opened on top of your Excel worksheet, choose File from the menu bar. A command to Update, Return, or Exit should be displayed in the File menu; the command varies from application to application. Select the command, and then respond to any prompts that appear, asking you to confirm that you want to update the Excel document by choosing Yes. The object will be embedded in your worksheet.

If the application simply replaced Excel's menu bar and toolbars, click outside the object to embed it in the worksheet.

N O T E   OLE (object linking and embedding) has been updated in Office 97. Now when you create or edit an embedded object, the source application replaces many components in the Excel window with the components it needs from the source application, such as toolbars and menu-bar commands. The title bar displays something like `Microsoft Excel - Document in Excel filename`. This new version of OLE provides a seamless, or transparent transition between Microsoft Office applications. ■

Figure 17.13 shows a PowerPoint slide being created to embed in an Excel worksheet.

FIG. 17.13
Embedding Office 97 objects enables you to create objects "in place," instead of having to leave Excel.

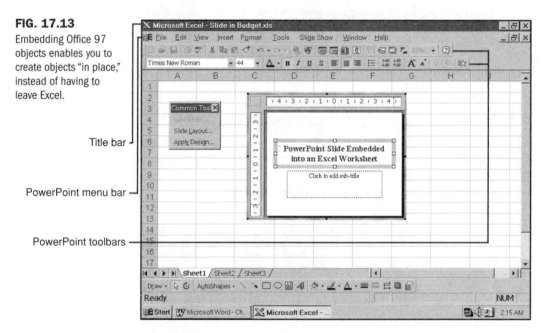

To embed an existing file into an Excel worksheet, follow these steps:

1. Choose Insert, Object, and then select the Create From File tab to display the Object dialog box shown in Figure 17.14.

2. Choose the Browse button to open the Browse dialog box.

3. Use the Look In list box to change to the drive and folder that contains the file you want to embed, and then choose Insert.

4. You have the option of embedding the object as an icon rather than displaying the actual object. This is useful particularly with large files, or files such as sound bites or video clips that you want to play at your discretion. Figure 17.14 shows a file containing a sound bite selected to be embedded into a file.

FIG. 17.14

An Explode.wav sound file has been selected to be displayed as an icon.

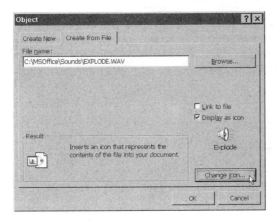

5. Choose OK. The file will be embedded in your worksheet.

If you embed an object as an icon, double-click the icon to open the embedded file. If the object is a sound or video file, right-click the icon, and then choose Object, Play from the shortcut menu. To embed only part of a file, use the Edit, Copy and Edit, Paste Special commands.

Editing Linked and Embedded Data

The advantage to linking or embedding an object into an Excel worksheet is that you can edit the object or linked data by using the commands and tools of the application in which the data was created.

The editing of a linked object takes place in the source application. The quickest way to open the source application is to do the following:

1. Choose Edit, Links. The Links dialog box is displayed.

2. From the Source File list, choose the link you want to edit.

3. Select Open Source; the application and source object will open in a separate window.

4. Edit the object, then Save and Close the file. The edited object appears in the target file.

If the linked object is not updated, choose Edit, Links. From the Source File list, choose the link you want to update, and then choose Update Now. To edit an embedded object, follow these steps:

1. Double-click the object.

2. The selected application will either temporarily replace Excel's menu bar commands and toolbars with its own, allowing you to edit the embedded object in place, or open in a separate window on top of your Excel worksheet.

3. Edit the object as necessary.

Part

V

Ch

17

4. After you modify the object, if the application opens on top of your Excel worksheet, choose File from the menu bar. A command to Update, Return, or Exit should be displayed in the File menu; the command varies from application to application. Select the command shown and then respond to any prompts that appear, asking you to confirm that you want to update the Excel document by choosing Yes. The modified object is displayed in your worksheet.

Grouping Documents with the Binder

The Microsoft Binder enables you to bind together documents from different Microsoft applications into a single "bound" document. Within one window, you can create and edit documents from any Office 97 application. As you switch between documents, the menu bars and toolbars change to reflect the application that created the document you are viewing. You can print an entire binder at one time, and it will use a single header and footer, and print with consecutive page numbers. The binder file can be stored or sent via e-mail as a single file.

You can start a new binder to group documents together from any Microsoft Office-compatible application, such as Word and Excel. To create a new binder, click the Start menu and choose Programs, Microsoft Binder. The Microsoft Binder window opens with a blank binder file, as shown in Figure 17.15. The steps for adding new or existing files to a binder are outlined later in this section.

FIG. 17.15
Click the double-headed arrow to show or hide the left pane.

Left pane of the Binder window; icons representing files will be displayed here

Section pane of the Binder window; data from the files will be displayed here

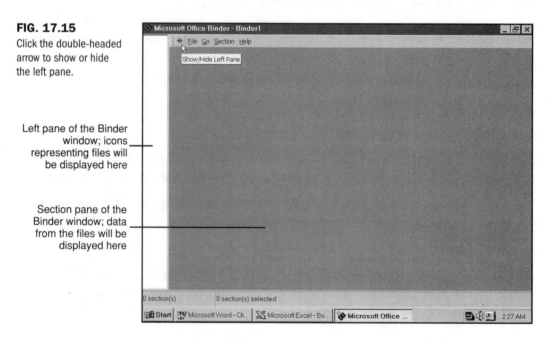

To open a binder that already exists on your computer, first choose File, Open Binder in the Binder window. In the Open Binder dialog box, use the Look In list box to locate the drive and folder containing the binder file. Double-click the binder file name to open the file.

You can add new or existing files to a binder, or even a portion of a file into a binder, by dragging the selected portion from the Office application into the left pane of the binder. Position the pointer in the left pane where you want the file to be placed, and release the mouse button. To add an existing document to a binder, follow these steps:

1. Right-click the left pane and choose Add From File on the shortcut menu. The Add From File dialog box appears.

2. Use the Look In list box to locate the drive and folder containing the file that you want to add to the binder.

3. Select the file, and then choose Add.

4. An icon representing the file appears in the left pane, and a copy of the file itself appears in the section. The file becomes a section in the binder. The menu bar and toolbar for the document's application also appear (merging with the binder menu), enabling you to work on the document from within the binder.

You also can drag a file from either My Computer or Windows Explorer. If the left pane is not visible on the left side of the Binder window, click the double-headed arrow located to the left of File on the menu bar. The left pane should display. Drag and drop the file on the left pane of the Binder window, at the location in the binder where you want the file to be added. To add a new document to a binder, follow these steps:

1. Right-click the left pane and choose Add on the shortcut menu. The Add Section dialog box is displayed.

2. Select the type of document you want to add to your binder from the General tab, or select one of the other tabs to see a list of Microsoft Office templates, and then select a template on which to base your new document.

3. Choose OK.

The new blank document appears as a section in the binder, and the menu and toolbars for the document's application appear. An icon representing the document will appear in the left pane of the binder, with a section name assigned to it. The icon for a section indicates with which application the section's document is associated. You can work on the document from within the binder. Figure 17.16 shows a binder that includes an Excel worksheet and a Word document.

To move or copy a file in the binder, select it from the left pane in the Binder window and drag the icon to the position where you want the file located in the binder. To delete a file in a binder, right-click the icon for the file in the left pane. Choose Delete from the shortcut menu. When the confirmation dialog box appears, choose OK.

If you want to view a file in a binder in its original application, select the file in the left pane of the binder window and choose Section, View Outside. The original application opens, along with the selected file. To return to the Binder, choose File, Close & Return To *bindername*.

Part

V

Ch

17

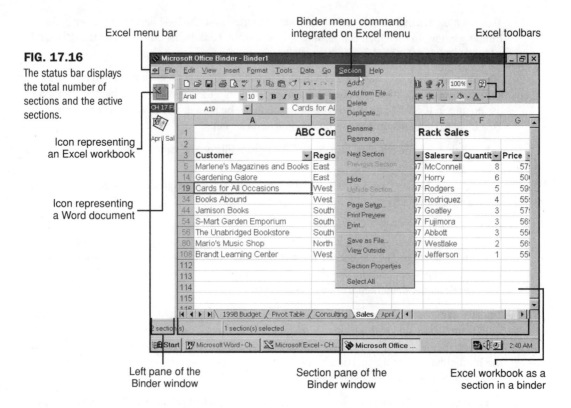

FIG. 17.16

The status bar displays the total number of sections and the active sections.

Excel menu bar

Binder menu command integrated on Excel menu

Excel toolbars

Icon representing an Excel workbook

Icon representing a Word document

Left pane of the Binder window

Section pane of the Binder window

Excel workbook as a section in a binder

Printing and Collating from Multiple Applications

One of the most useful features of the binder is the capability to print all, or selected sections of, a binder. To print selected sections, select the sections you want to print from the left pane. Choose the first file icon, then Ctrl, and then click each file you want to select. To print a binder, follow these steps:

1. Choose File, Print Binder. The Print Binder dialog box appears.

2. In the Print What area, choose the All visible Sections option to print the entire binder. To print just the selected sections, choose the Section(s) Selected in Left Pane option.

3. Specify the number of copies in the Number of Copies box.

4. Choose the Collate option if you want to collate multiple copies.

5. In the Numbering area, choose Consecutive if you want to number the pages in the binder consecutively. Choose Restart Each Section if you want page numbering to start at 1 for each section (file) in the binder.

6. Choose OK.

Exchanging Data over Networks

Companies are finding that when they interconnect employees' computers and give them access to corporate data, the work produced is more productive and accurate. Being able to have virtually instant access to information enables employees to complete projects more quickly.

In addition to interconnecting computers, many companies are rapidly developing their own internal company intranets to publish propriety information for their employees and business affiliates. With the explosive growth of the Internet, you can access a plethora of information on the Internet.

Other chapters is this book focus on retrieving data from databases (Chapter 16), integrating Excel data into other applications, like Word or PowerPoint (Chapter 17), and importing data into Excel from other programs (Chapter 19). This chapter focuses on exchanging data over three types of networks: standard home or office networks, company intranets, and the Internet, which includes the World Wide Web. ■

Working with a Group of People

One of the most productive features in Excel is the capability to share and revise workbooks with groups of people. Frequently, projects involve several people inputting or verifying data in the same documents. Rather than routing paper copies of the files and trying to consolidate the changes, you can use Excel to keep track precisely of who made each change or comment. You then can choose to accept or reject those changes.

Excel includes several features that you can use when you need to coordinate workbook files with groups of people:

- Creating a Binder file
- Sharing workbooks
- Tracking changes
- Highlighting text

If the project you are working on involves documents created by more than one application, use Microsoft Binder to organize related documents and compile them into collated reports.

Microsoft Binder enables you to *bind* documents created in different Microsoft applications into a single, large document—it is a virtual three-ring binder. You can edit any document from within the Microsoft Binder, avoiding the hassle of continually switching back and forth between different applications.

Click Start on the Taskbar and choose Programs, Microsoft Binder, to open the Binder application.

▶ **See** "Grouping Documents with the Binder," **p. 269**

After you have created a binder, you need to allow the rest of the group to access the binder file.

To move a binder on to a network drive, follow these steps:

1. Right-click the Start button on the Taskbar and choose Explorer from the shortcut menu.

2. Locate the binder file; the file name should be displayed in the Contents of list box on the right side of the Explorer window. Binder files have an .OBD extension.

3. Right-click the binder file to display the shortcut menu, and then choose Cut.

4. Locate the shared drive to which you want the files to be moved; the drive name should be displayed in the All Folders list box on the left side of the Explorer window.

5. Right-click the specific folder (directory) to which you want the binder moved. From the shortcut menu, choose Paste.

By moving the binder file to a shared drive/folder on your network, other users now can access it. The next section describes how to share a workbook and track the changes made by other users.

Sharing Your Workbooks with Other Users

A new feature in Excel 97 is the capability to truly share a workbook. One person can edit one worksheet in a workbook, and someone else can edit another worksheet simultaneously. Different people can access adjacent data, such as the formulas on a worksheet or the column headings in the same worksheet. The shared workbook feature replaces the shared list feature found in Microsoft Excel 95.

Before you can take advantage of these features, the workbook has to be set up as a shared workbook. Then, multiple users can view and modify it simultaneously. When one user saves the workbook, the other users who are sharing it will see the changes made by that user. The shared workbook feature is supported only by Excel 97. If some users in your group are still working with previous versions of Excel, they will not be able to open the shared workbook. To set up a shared workbook, follow these steps:

1. Open the workbook you want to share. Make sure you save any changes you have made before you share the workbook.

2. Using the File, Save As command, save the workbook to a shared network drive.

3. Choose Tools, Share Workbook. The Share Workbook dialog box, as shown in Figure 18.1, appears.

FIG. 18.1

From the Share Workbook dialog box, you can set up the workbook to be shared.

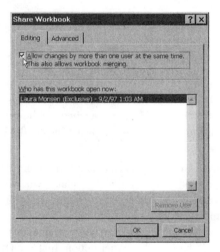

4. On the Editing tab of the dialog box, select the check box titled Allow Changes By More Than One User At The Same Time.

5. Click OK.

After a workbook has been set up to be shared, users can open the shared workbook as they would any other file, by using the File, Open command. When a workbook is shared, the word [Shared] displays in the title bar for the workbook window, as shown later in Figure 18.4. Users save changes to a shared document, just as they would save changes to any other file, by using the File, Save command.

When you share workbooks with others, you need to make several decisions . The Advanced tab of the Share Workbook dialog box, shown in Figure 18.2, and the Highlight Changes dialog box, shown in Figure 18.3, work together to control how changes to the shared workbook are tracked.

FIG. 18.2

The default settings for sharing your workbooks with other users are displayed in this figure.

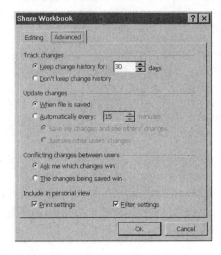

The following list outlines the options on the Advanced tab of the Share Workbook dialog box:

▪ *Track Changes*. By default, Excel keeps a history of all the changes made, for up to 30 days. The history can be viewed by highlighting the cells in the worksheet. When you rest the mouse pointer over a modified cell, the changes are listed. You also can see the changes displayed in a list on a separate worksheet. The settings in the Highlight Changes dialog box control the specifications of when and how you see the changes. Look ahead to the next list for descriptions of the settings in the Highlight Changes dialog box.

▪ *Update Changes*. You have two options when changes to the file are updated: when the file is saved or after a specified period of time. By default, you will see changes to the file when the file is saved. You can view other users' changes more frequently by setting a time interval in the Automatically Every (15) Minutes box. To save the workbook each time you get an update so that other users can see your changes, select Save My Changes And See Others' Changes. The other option, Just See Other Users' Changes, will not save the workbook.

▪ *Conflicting Changes Between Users*. The Ask Me Which Changes Win option displays the Resolve Conflicts dialog box if changes you are saving conflict with changes saved by another user. You can elect to save your changes or keep the changes made by others. The Changes Being Saved Win option always saves your changes automatically, without viewing the proposed changes made by others.

■ *Include In Personal View.* Each user of a shared workbook can set independent view and print options. Whenever a user views the workbook, their settings will be displayed. These settings include page breaks, print areas, headers, footers, and other options selected in the Page Setup dialog box. Additional settings that are saved include zoom percent and options marked on the View tab of the Tools, Options dialog box.

After a workbook has been set up as a shared workbook, you can allow other users to view and edit a workbook, all at the same time, and see each other's changes. Each user of a shared workbook can set independent options for highlighting changes.

 TIP Excel identifies who made what changes when in the shared workbook, based on the name of the user. To ensure accurate tracking, each user should establish his user name before working on the shared book. Instruct each user to choose Tools, Options and click the General tab, and then type her user name in the User Name box.

The Highlight Changes dialog box, shown in Figure 18.3, works with settings on the Advanced tab of the Share Workbook dialog box to control how changes to the shared workbook are tracked.

FIG. 18.3

Changes to a file can be highlighted on-screen, listed in a separate worksheet, or appear in both places.

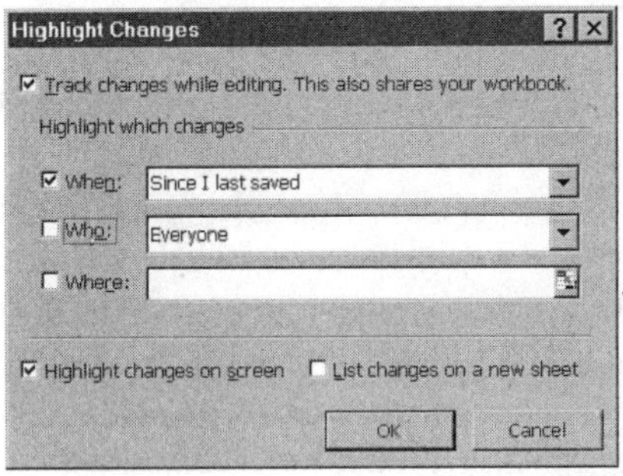

Figure 18.4 shows a shared workbook, with changes and comments added.

Each time you view the shared workbook, you need to specify how you want to review the changes in the Highlight Changes dialog box. The settings are established only for the working session; the next time you view the file, you have to specify your choices again.

■ *Track Changes While Editing.* This setting must remain on for the workbook to be shared. Changes made to cell contents, and inserted or deleted rows and columns, are highlighted. Changes to worksheet names are listed on the History worksheet when you select List Changes On a New Sheet. New or additional comments are displayed when you rest the mouse pointer over the cell.

Certain changes are not highlighted: cell formatting, hidden and unhidden rows and columns, and inserted or deleted worksheets. There are also changes that can't be made to a shared workbook—a list is provided later in this section.

FIG. 18.4

Comment indicators appear as triangles in the upper-right corner of the cell. Cells changed on a shared workbook show a triangular indicator in the upper-left corner of the cell.

Title bar with [Shared] displayed

Triangular and border indicators appear when a cell has been modified

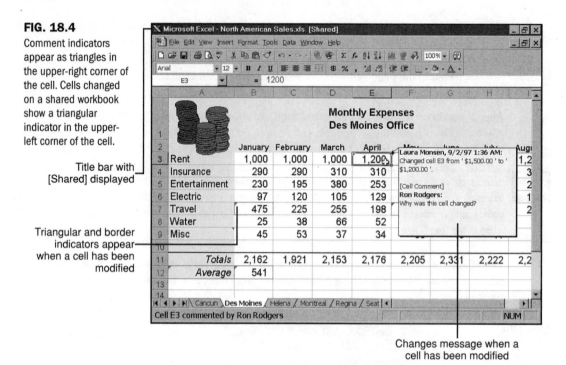

Changes message when a cell has been modified

■ *When.* By default, this setting shows only those changes made to the file since you last saved the file. Alternatives in the drop-down list include seeing all changes, seeing changes not yet reviewed, or seeing changes since a specified date.

■ *Who.* By default, you see changes made by everyone. Alternatives in the drop-down list include changes made by everyone except you, or changes made by a specific person.

■ *Where.* This option is blank so that you can see changes made to the entire file. If you want to see the changes made to only a few specific cells, mark this option and identify the cells. Select non-adjacent cells by using the Ctrl key.

■ *Highlight Changes On Screen.* By default, changes are noted on the worksheet. Cells that have been changed are identified several ways: a triangle in the upper-left corner of the cell, a thin border surrounding the cell, and the row and column headings display a different color to note there are changes in that row or column.

■ *List Changes On A New Worksheet.* If you want to see a list of the changes on a separate worksheet in the workbook, choose this option. The list is based on the settings you have made in the When, Who, and Where options of this dialog box. The name for the new worksheet will be History. The History worksheet displays a complete list of changes, including the names of the users who made the changes, data that was deleted or replaced, and information about conflicting changes. The list displays with the AutoFilter turned on. After you save the workbook, Excel removes the History worksheet. To display it again, you have to mark this option in the Highlight Changes dialog box.

▶ **See** "Discovering the Power of the AutoFilter," **p. 203**

 TIP The History worksheet shows only the changes that have been saved. To include all changes from your current session on the History worksheet, save the workbook *before* you display the History worksheet. The History worksheet does not automatically update during your working session. You have to save your workbook and redisplay the History worksheet.

When you remove a workbook from shared use, the history of changes is erased. When you share the workbook again, a new list of changes is created. For information on saving the history list of changes before you remove the workbook from shared use, see the following section, "Discontinue Workbook Sharing."

When a workbook is shared, some Excel commands are not available:

- *Inserting.* Blocks of cells cannot be inserted, though you can insert new rows and columns.
- *Deleting.* Entire worksheets or blocks of cells cannot be deleted. You can delete entire rows or columns.
- *Formatting.* You cannot apply conditional formats or merged cells after a workbook has been shared.
- *List Manipulation Commands.* The Group and Outline, Subtotals, Tables, and PivotTable Report commands cannot be used when a workbook is shared.
- *Linked or Embedded objects.* Charts, pictures, objects, or hyperlinks cannot be modified in a shared workbook.
- *Macros.* You can only run macros that were created before you shared the workbook. New macros cannot be created.
- *Password Protection.* While a workbook is shared, you cannot create, modify, or remove passwords that protect the worksheets or the entire workbook. Any protection that is assigned to a worksheet or workbook prior to sharing the file remains in effect while the workbook is shared.
- *Scenarios.* This command cannot be used while the workbook is shared.
- *Data Validation.* You cannot modify or create data-validation restrictions while the workbook is shared. Any restrictions that are set up prior to sharing the workbook remain in effect.
- *Drawing.* The drawing tools cannot be used after a workbook has been shared.

Most of these features can be implemented before sharing the workbook, and then are available after sharing the workbook.

Part
V

Ch
18

Discontinue Workbook Sharing

When you no longer need other users to have access to your workbook, or if you want to use an Excel command or feature not supported by shared workbooks (see the previous list), you need to stop sharing the workbook. One thing to be certain of before removing a workbook from shared use is that you are the only user who has the workbook open. Otherwise, the other users may lose their work. To stop sharing a workbook, follow these steps:

1. Choose Tools, Share Document. The Share Workbook dialog box is displayed.

2. Select the Editing tab. If you are the only one listed in the Who Has This Workbook Open Now list box, then you can safely remove the workbook from being shared. If other users are listed, notify them to save and close the file, so that they don't lose their work.

3. After you have verified that you are the only one with access to the workbook, clear the Allow Changes By More Than One User At the Same Time check box.

4. Click OK to stop sharing the workbook.

> **CAUTION**
>
> When you remove a workbook from shared use, the history of changes is erased. When you share the workbook again, a new list of changes is created.
>
> If you plan to remove a workbook from shared use but want to retain the change information, display the information about all changes on the History worksheet by marking the List Changes On A New Worksheet box in the Highlight Changes dialog box. You then can copy the information on the History worksheet to another worksheet in the workbook, print the History worksheet, or save a copy of the shared workbook.

Running a Web Query

Web queries are designed to retrieve data from intranet or Internet Web sites that use the HTTP or FTP protocols. As long as your computer is set up to access the Internet via a modem, or to access a Web site on your company intranet through a network, it is very simple to retrieve data from a Web site by using a Web query. Excel includes several built-in sample financial queries that can be run on the Internet:

- Detailed Stock Quote
- Multiple Stock Quote
- Dow Jones Stocks

These queries are run against the PC Quote, Inc. Web site to obtain current stock market quotes. Figure 18.5 shows the result of running the Detailed Stock Quote query to obtain a quote for Coca-Cola stock.

FIG. 18.5

Whenever a Web query is run, the External Data toolbar is displayed.

External Data toolbar

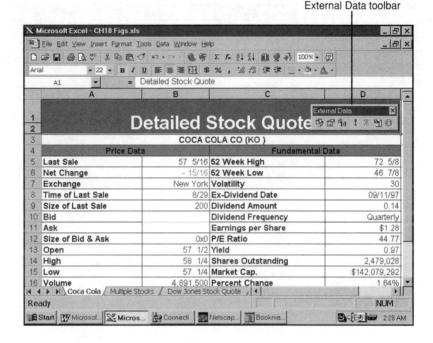

To run one of the built-in queries, use the following steps:

1. Select the worksheet in your workbook where you want the results of the query to be copied.

 TIP Make the results of the query easier to read by turning off the worksheet gridlines. Choose Tools, Options, select the View tab, and then clear the Gridlines check box.

2. Choose Data, Get External Data, Run Web Query. The Run Query dialog box is displayed (refer to Figure 18.5). Select the query you want to run and choose Get Data. Web queries have the .IQY extension. In Figure 18.6, the Multiple Stock Quote query is selected.

3. The Returning External Data to Microsoft Excel dialog box appears (see Figure 18.7). By default, the data appears in the currently active worksheet, starting in cell A1. If you want the data to begin in some other location, select the worksheet and cell where the data should start, or choose New Worksheet to have Excel insert a new worksheet with the data. If you are working from within a PivotTable Report, you can select the PivotTable Report option.

NOTE The next section, "Changing Web Query Properties and Parameters," discusses the options property and parameter options that you can modify with Web queries.

Part
V

Ch
18

FIG. 18.6

Four queries are automatically available in Excel 97, one of which is to get more queries.

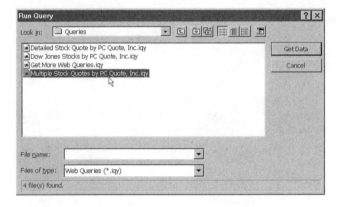

Make a selection in the Returning External Data to Microsoft Excel dialog box, and click OK.

FIG. 18.7

Indicate where you want the data to be returned from the query.

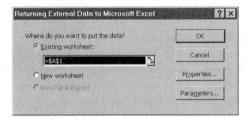

4. The Enter Parameter Value dialog box appears, as shown in Figure 18.8. The parameters for each query will vary. In the text box, enter the appropriate stock symbols. The stock symbols used here are mcd (McDonalds), hwp (Hewlett-Packard), and ko (Coca-Cola).

Select the Use This Value/Reference for Future Refreshes check box if you want to reuse the value you enter for a parameter whenever you refresh the query. This saves you the trouble of reentering parameters that don't change.

After you enter the value in the entry box, choose OK to run the query.

FIG. 18.8

Make sure you enter the correct stock symbols.

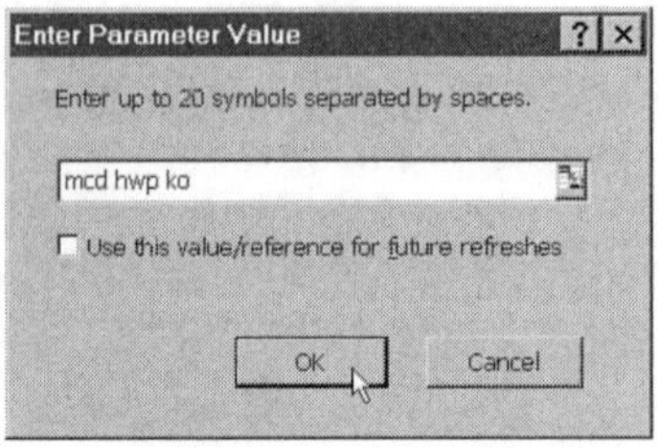

The results of your query are displayed in the worksheet that you designated. Figure 18.9 shows the result of running the Multiple Stock Quote query for McDonalds, Hewlett-Packard, and Coca-Cola.

FIG. 18.9

Use the drop-down arrows in the stock quote to filter the data.

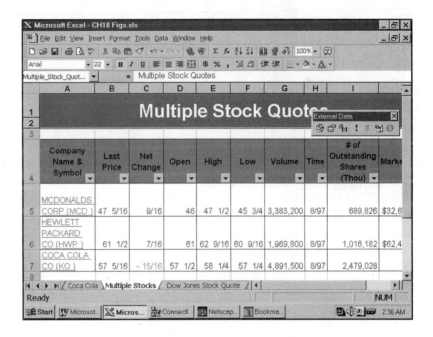

Additional queries are available on Microsoft's Internet Web site. To retrieve more queries from Microsoft, you actually run a query, following these steps:

1. Select the sheet in your workbook where you want the data to appear.
2. Choose Data, Get External Data, Run Web Query. The Run Query dialog box is displayed.
3. Choose Get More Web Queries, then select Get Data. The Returning External Data to Microsoft Excel dialog box appears.
4. Select where you want the data to appear, and click OK.
5. The results of your query are displayed in the worksheet.
6. Scroll down to see the list of queries, as displayed in Figure 18.10. Click the query you want to retrieve. Save this file for quick access to other queries.

ON THE WEB

To learn how to create your own Web queries, download the Microsoft Web Resource Kit from the following Web site:

http://www.microsoft.com/excel/webquery/webquery.exe

Part
V

Ch
18

FIG. 18.10
Use the hyperlinks to access specific quotes.

External Data toolbar

Hyperlink
Mouse pointer

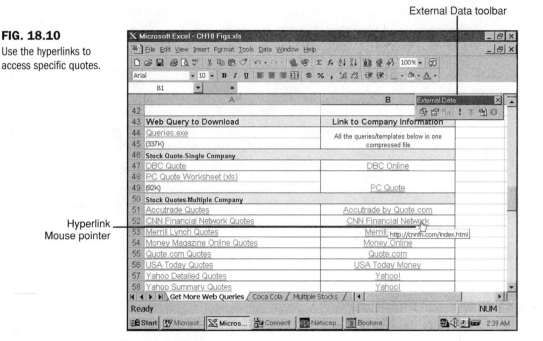

CAUTION

It is always a good practice to save any open files *before* attempting an Internet or intranet connection. If something happens that causes your computer to "hang," any changes made to files that have been saved will be lost if you have to reboot the computer.

When a query is running, a spinning globe icon appears in the status bar. After you have run a query, you can update the results by rerunning the query:

1. Click the Refresh button on the External Data toolbar (refer to Figure 18.10).

2. You will be prompted to reenter any parameters necessary to rerun the query. Refer back to the steps for running a built-in query.

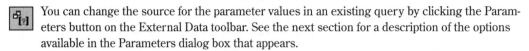

You can change the source for the parameter values in an existing query by clicking the Parameters button on the External Data toolbar. See the next section for a description of the options available in the Parameters dialog box that appears.

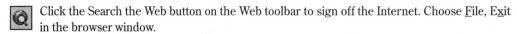

Click the Search the Web button on the Web toolbar to sign off the Internet. Choose File, Exit in the browser window.

Changing Web Query Properties and Parameters

 There are several properties and parameters in Web queries over which you have control. To modify the properties, choose the Properties button in the Returning External Data to Excel dialog box when you first run a query, or click the Data Range Properties button on the External Data toolbar. The External Data Range Properties dialog box appears, as shown in Figure 18.11.

FIG. 18.11

Options that are not available for the current query are grayed out.

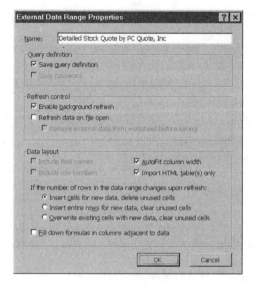

The name of the query you are working with appears in the Name text box. The following list describes each option:

- *Save Query Definition.* Saves the query with the worksheet so that you can refresh the results directly from the worksheet.

- *Save Password.* If the query requires a password (which is requested the first time you run the query), the password is saved so that you won't be asked the password when you refresh the query results.

- *Enable Background Refresh.* Enables you to run query refresh "behind the scenes" so that you can continue to work in Excel.

- *Refresh Data on File Open.* Excel automatically refreshes the data for the query when you open the workbook containing query results.

- *Remove External Data from Worksheet Before Saving.* Removes the data returned from the external data source before the worksheet is saved. Data is refreshed when the workbook is opened again.

Part

V

Ch

18

- *Include Field Names.* Used when you run queries against external databases, such as Access or FoxPro. Not applicable with Web queries. See Chapter 16, "Retrieving Data from External Sources Using Microsoft Query."

- *Include Row Numbers.* Used when you run queries against external databases, such as Access or FoxPro. Not applicable with Web queries. (See Chapter 16.)

- *AutoFit Column Width.* Automatically adjusts column widths for the widest entry in the column.

- *Import HTML Table(s) Only.* Only data stored in HTML tables is retrieved. No other information on the Web page is returned.

- *Insert Cells for New Data, Clear Unused Cells.* Inserts or deletes cells in the data range if the size of the data range changes when you refresh the data.

- *Insert Entire Rows for New Data, Clear Unused Cells.* Overwrites existing cells if the size of the data range changes when you refresh the data.

- *Overwrite Existing Cells with New Data, Clear Unused Cells.* Overwrites existing cells if the size of the data range changes when you refresh the data. Unused cells are cleared.

- *Fill Down Formulas in Columns Adjacent to Data.* If there are columns containing formulas adjacent to the imported data, the formulas are copied into the column to the right if the data range expands when you refresh the data.

 In addition to properties, you have control over several parameters. To modify how the parameters for a query are obtained, choose the Parameters button in the Returning External Data to Excel dialog box when you first run a query, or click the Query Parameters button on the External Data toolbar. The Parameters dialog box appears, as shown in Figure 18.12. Select the parameters you want to modify in the Parameter Name list box. In this instance, there is only one parameter, TICKER. Choose an option for How Parameter Value is Obtained from one of the following three options for the parameter:

- *Prompt for Value Using the Following String.* This option prompts the user for the value for the parameter, using the prompt entered in the text box. Refer back to Figure 18.8 for an example of this parameter

- *Use the Following Value.* Uses the value entered in the text box to run the query.

- *Get the Value from the Following Cell.* Uses the value in the specified cell as the input for the parameter.

When you have finished making changes in the Parameters dialog box, click OK.

FIG. 18.12

Choose one of the three parameter options.

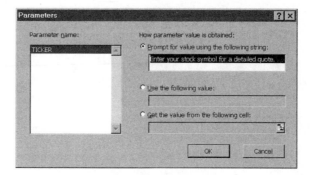

Using Worksheets on Intranets and the Internet

The Microsoft Excel Viewer 97 is a tool that enables Excel users to share their workbook files with people who do not have Excel. The Excel Viewer is a small program, which Microsoft encourages you to freely distribute. This program lets people view and print Excel files. It supports files created in Excel for Windows (version 2.0 and later) and Excel for the Macintosh (versions 2.2a and later). Users will have the capability to view page layout, copy, zoom, AutoFilter, and control cell sizes.

One powerful use of the Excel Viewer is with networks, specifically intranets and the Internet. Generally, tabular data (for example, columnar lists, graphical charts, or financial reports) is not displayed very well when using the Internet tools. More people than ever before are creating and distributing spreadsheets over the Internet and corporate intranets. The Excel Viewer is a tool that is designed to make it easier to view Excel spreadsheet files.

Microsoft Excel Viewer 97 automatically configures itself as a Helper Application for Microsoft Internet Explorer and Netscape Navigator. Users now can view Excel spreadsheets (.xls) that are linked to HTML pages on a local area network (LAN) or the World Wide Web.

TIP Use the Excel help screens to learn more about creating Web pages form Excel worksheets. Type **creating web pages** in the Office Assistant search box, and then press Enter. Select *Create a Web Page From a Worksheet or a Chart* from the list of help topics displayed.

N O T E *Special Edition Using Microsoft FrontPage 97* and *Special Edition Using JavaScript* are books published by Que that provide more detailed information about creating Web pages.

Part
V

Ch
18

CHAPTER 19

Importing and Exporting Data

Previous chapters discuss how to extract data from databases, such as Access, how to copy data to and from other Windows programs, such as Word and PowerPoint, and how to share data over networks, such as internal company intranets and the Internet. In this chapter, you will learn to exchange data with other personal computer programs (such as Lotus 1-2-3, Quattro Pro, dBASE, Quicken, and Project), and to share data with mainframe computers.

Importing, sometimes referred to as reading, involves bringing data into Excel from another program. *Exporting*, sometimes referred to as writing, is sending out data from Excel to another program. This chapter will primarily use the terms importing and exporting. Excel provides several features for importing and exporting data. Excel can read from and write to many different file formats. These file formats are identified in the extension of the filename. For example, Excel spreadsheet files all use the extension .XLS, and dBASE and FoxPro files use the .DBF extension. For those file formats that Excel cannot read from or write to directly, there are several generic file formats, such as .TXT and .CSV (described later in this chapter), that can be used to exchange data between programs.

Understanding file formats

Excel is capable of importing data from, and exporting data to, a variety of programs. Become acquainted with the file formats Excel uses to exchange information indirectly with personal computer and mainframe programs.

Importing data from other programs, including mainframe computers

Use the Text Import Wizard to assist in importing data from programs Excel cannot directly read.

Parsing text

Use the Convert Text to Columns Wizard to separate imported text.

Exporting Excel workbooks to other programs

Send data from Excel to other programs by saving Excel workbooks in a file format from which that application can read.

File Formats

Before learning how to transfer information between Excel and another program, it is important for you to understand file formats. Excel can import and export data directly from many file formats used by DOS, Macintosh, and mainframe programs. When no specific file format is available for Excel to transfer information directly, a generic text file format can be created to transfer text and numbers to and from other programs.

These generic text file formats use spaces, commas, tabs, or other characters, to separate the values in a file so that the values can be placed in individual cells or database fields. The separation of values in this manner is referred to as *delimiting*. File formats that create the separations by inserting spaces, commas, tabs, or other characters, are known as *delimited formats*. For example, files whose values are separated by tabs are referred to as *tab-delimited* files.

In some cases, especially with mainframe programs, the file contains values arranged so that each field or cell has a certain width. These file formats are referred to as *fixed-width* files, or, sometimes, as *column-delimited* files.

The following list identifies the file formats Excel can import from and export to, including notes regarding any limitations:

- *.XLS*   File extension for Excel 2.1, 3.0, or 4.0 worksheets. When opening worksheets from these versions, the worksheets open as the only worksheet in an Excel 97 workbook. When saving from Excel 97 to any of these formats, only the active worksheet in Excel 97 is saved. If the worksheet contains formulas with references to other worksheets in the workbook, you cannot save the worksheet in version 2.1, 3.0, or 4.0 format.

- *.XLW*   File extension for Excel 4.0 workbooks. When opening a bound Excel 4.0 workbook into Excel 97, the bound worksheets open as separate worksheets in an Excel 97 workbook. When saving Excel 97 workbooks into an Excel 4.0 format, all worksheets in the workbook are saved as bound worksheets, chart worksheets, or macro sheets. However, users of Microsoft Excel 4.0 and Windows 3.1 may not be able to open workbooks containing more than 25 worksheets.

- *.XLC*   File extension for Excel 4.0 chart. Use this format to save only the active chart worksheet in an Excel 4.0 format.

- *.XLM*   File extension for Excel 4.0 macro. When saving a macro sheet in Excel 97 to an Excel 4.0 format, the macro code and functionality are saved, but not the Visual Basic code.

- *.XLS*   File extension for Excel 5.0 and Excel 95 workbooks. When saving an Excel 97 workbook to an Excel 5.0/95 format, functionality unique to Excel 97 is not saved with the file. Examples of the new functionality include: text rotation, indention, merging cells, and new chart types, such as pie of pie, and bar of pie.

- *.TXT/.PRN*   File extension for space-delimited files. Sometimes called column-delimited or fixed-width. Columns of data are separated by commas. Each row of data ends in a carriage return. When using this format, only visible text and values in the active worksheet are saved. You may need to adjust the column widths on the worksheet to ensure data is visible. Cells containing formulas are converted as text. All formatting, graphics, objects, and other worksheet contents are lost. If a row of cells contains more than 240 characters, characters beyond 240 are placed on a new line at the end of the converted file. For example, if eight rows of data are being converted, and rows 1 and 3 contain more than 240 characters, the remaining text in row 1 is placed in row 9, the remaining text in row 3 is placed in row 10, and so forth.

- *.TXT*   File extension for tab-delimited files. Columns of data are separated by tab characters. Each row of data ends in a carriage return. In some text files, commas or other characters may be used as delimiters. If a cell contains a comma, the cell contents are enclosed in double quotation marks. For example, if a cell contains 13,000, it appears as "13,000"; and Jackson, Tom appears as "Jackson, Tom". All formatting, graphics, objects, and other worksheet contents are lost.

- *.CSV*   File extension for Comma Separated Value files. Cell values are separated by commas. If a cell contains a comma, the cell contents are enclosed in double quotation marks. For example, if a cell contains 13,000, it appears as "13,000"; and Jackson, Tom appear as "Jackson, Tom". All formatting, graphics, objects, and other worksheet contents are lost.

- *.WKS/ALL*   File extension for Lotus 1-2-3 Release 1.0, 1A, and Lotus Symphony and Microsoft Works spreadsheets. Works files can be opened in Excel 97, but Excel 97 cannot save to a Works format.

- *.WK1*   File extension for Lotus 1-2-3 Release 2.1, 2.2, 2.3, 2.4 spreadsheets. When saving Excel 97 workbooks into this format, only the text, values, and formulas of the active worksheet are saved. Fonts are converted to 10-point Courier font. Column widths are saved, but all other cell and text formats are lost. To save most formatting, use the WK1,ALL or WK1,FMT format.

- *.WK1/.FMT*   File extension for Lotus 1-2-3 Release 2.1, 2.2, 2.3, 2.4 spreadsheets. When saving Excel 97 workbooks into this format, only the text, values, and formulas of the active worksheet are saved. Excel 97 workbooks saved in this format create two files. Data values are saved in a WK1 file, and data formats are saved in a FMT file.

- *.WK3/.FM3*   File extension for Lotus 1-2-3 Release 3.1, 3.3 spreadsheets. When saving Excel 97 workbooks into this format, only worksheets and chart sheets are saved. Excel 97 workbooks saved in this format create two files. Data values are saved in a WK3 file, and data formats are saved in a FM3 file.

- *.WK4*   File extension for Lotus 1-2-3 Release 4.0 and 5.0 spreadsheets. When saving Excel 97 workbooks into this format, the worksheet data and formatting are saved into a single file.

Part
V

Ch
19

■ *.WQ1* File extension for Quattro 2.0 and Quattro Pro for DOS spreadsheets. When saving Excel 97 workbooks into this format, only the text, values, and formulas of the active worksheet are saved. Microsoft Excel 97 can open Quattro Pro version 5.0 for Windows (WB1) files, but it cannot open files created in Quattro Pro version 6.0 for Windows (WB2). First open the file in Quattro Pro version 6.0, and then save the file in QPW (*.WB1) format. Then open the WB1-formatted file in Excel. If you need to work in a file in both Quattro Pro version 6.0 and in Microsoft Excel, save the file in Quattro Pro as a Lotus 1-2-3 WK4 file. Microsoft Excel can open and save files in the WK4 file format.

■ *.DIF* File extension for Data Interchange Format files. This is a common, low-level worksheet format (VisiCalc). When saving Excel 97 workbooks into this format, only the text, values, and formulas of the active worksheet are saved.

■ *.DBF* File extension for dBASE II and dBASE III databases. When saving Excel 97 workbooks into this format, only the text and values of the active worksheet are saved. All cell formatting, page-layout settings, graphics, objects, and other Microsoft Excel 97 features are lost. For dBASE II Databases, only 32 columns can be saved into this format. For dBASE III Databases, only 128 columns can be saved into this format

■ *.DBF* File extension for dBASE IV databases. When saving Excel 97 workbooks into this format, only the text and values of the active worksheet are saved. All cell formatting, page-layout settings, graphics, objects, and other Microsoft Excel 97 features are lost. Up to 256 columns can be saved into this format.

■ *.SLK* File extension for Symbolic Link files Used by Multiplan and Microsoft Works. When saving Excel 97 workbooks into this format, only the values, formulas, and limited-cell formatting on the active worksheet are saved. Use the SYLK format to save workbook files for use in Microsoft Multiplan. Microsoft Excel 97 does not include file format converters for converting workbook files directly into Multiplan format.

TIP Use the Excel help screens to learn more about which features in Excel 97 will or will not convert when saving files to other formats. Type **converting files** in the Office Assistant search box, and press Enter. Select Formatting Features Not Transferred In Converted Files from the list of help topics displayed. In the help screen that appears, scroll down to see the list of file formats, and then click the double-arrow button in front of the file format to see a list of specific items that will or will not convert.

Use a word processor, such as Windows WordPad, to open the saved files, and then see how Excel encloses data in tabs, commas, and quotes.

To see the CSV or Text file formats that Excel can import and export automatically, follow these steps:

1. Create an Excel worksheet with sample data in cells. Make sure some of the data includes commas and spaces, such as **13,000** and **100 Main Street**.

2. Choose File, Save As to save the worksheet. Click the Save As Type drop-down list and select the CSV format.

3. Enter a name in the File Name entry list box and click Save.

4. Choose File, Save As to save the worksheet again, only this time, choose the Text format. Then enter a name in the File Name entry list box and click Save.

5. Open the worksheet using Word for Windows or WordPad. Figure 19.1 shows the same Excel data saved in the CSV and Text formats.

FIG. 19.1

In the bottom window, the text is lined up to the tab marks on the ruler.

CSV file format; data is comma delimited

Text file format; data is tab delimited

Ruler

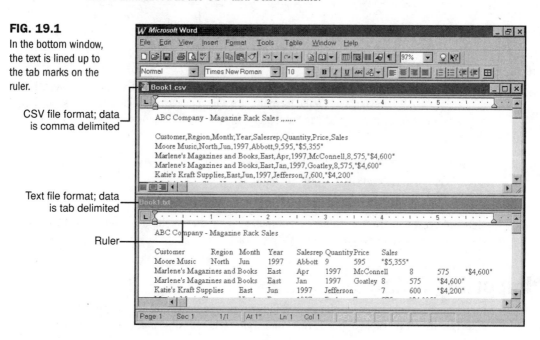

Due to the many enhancements made to Excel 97 workbooks, they are not directly compatible with Excel 5.0/95. When you need to save an Excel 97 workbook in Excel 5.0/95, then in the Save As dialog box, select the Microsoft Excel 5.0/95 Workbook format from the Save As Type drop-down list box. This format assumes you do not need to use the file in Excel 5.0 and Excel 97, or Excel 95 and Excel 97. However, if you do need to use Excel 5.0/95 and Excel 97, then save the workbook by using the Microsoft Excel 97 and 5.0/95 Workbook format in the Save As Type drop-down list box.

One of the terms used in the following sections is *character set*. Different operating environments use different character sets. A character set is a list of numbers, from 1 to 255, that correspond to characters (not just keyboard characters) which may appear in files you import or export. In some operating environments, specific numbers in the character set do not have corresponding characters. Some character-set numbers represent carriage returns, backspace, and linefeeds. Windows uses the ANSI character set. The following are several examples of character set numbers and the corresponding characters.

Character set number	Character
32	(space)
48	0 (zero)
65	A
163	£ (pound currency symbol)
191	¿ (upside down question mark)
233	é (accented letter e)

The file formats tell Excel the type of character set being used so that Excel can convert the data accurately. When you select a file format in the Open or Save As dialog boxes, special operating environments, such as Macintosh or OS/2, are indicated next to the file format name.

- Macintosh programs use the Macintosh character set.
- Windows programs use the ANSI character set.
- DOS and OS/2 programs use the PC-8 character set.

Generally, text data from a mainframe computer uses the PC-8 character set. Some mainframe text files have been known to use the ANSI character set.

Importing Data

You can use Excel to analyze data stored in other programs, taking advantage of features in Excel such as PivotTable Reports, Automatic Subtotals, and Charting, just to name a few.

The quickest and simplest way to import data into Excel is to transfer the data directly, by using one of the many file formats that Excel can read. After the file is opened in Excel, you then can resave the data in the Excel 97 format. Refer to the preceding "File Formats" section for a list of file formats that Excel can import.

To import a file into Excel, open the file by using the following steps:

1. Choose File, Open. The File Open dialog box is displayed.
2. Using the Files Of Type drop-down list box, select the file format that corresponds to the type of file you want to import into Excel. Figure 19.2 shows the .DBF file type selected. This file format is used by both dBASE and FoxPro.
3. Using the Look In list box, locate the file you want to import. You may find it necessary to select another drive or folder to locate the file. Figure 19.2 shows the contents of the Clients folder; the 1997 List is the selected file.
4. Choose Open, and Excel will import the file.

When you import a non-Excel file, Excel remembers the format in which the file arrived. You have the option of saving the file back in the same format, or converting it to the Excel 97 format. In the Save As dialog box, click Save to save the file in its original format. Excel displays a confirmation message to replace the original file, as shown in Figure 19.3.

FIG. 19.2
Use the File Open dialog box to import files created in other programs.

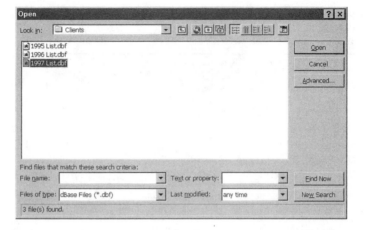

FIG. 19.3
The dialog box indicates the file will be saved as a .DBF, a format used by both dBASE and FoxPro.

The title bar indicates the current file format

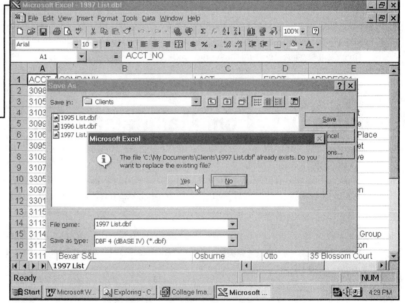

To save the file in the Excel 97 workbook format, choose Microsoft Excel Workbook in the Save As Type drop-down list box.

If you attempt to close an imported file that you have made changes to, Excel asks if you want to save the changes before closing the file, as shown in Figure 19.4. Excel also reminds you that the file is not in the Excel 97 format. Click the Yes button to save changes, and use the procedures previously described to save the file in the original format, or save it as an Excel 97 workbook.

FIG. 19.4
If you don't choose Yes, your changes will be lost.

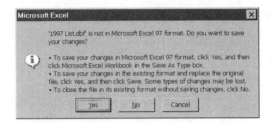

CAUTION

If you have made changes to the file, saving it in a non-Excel format can result in the loss of formulas, functions, special features, and formatting that are unique to Excel 97. Examples include Conditional Formatting, Data Validation, and Visual Basic code.

N O T E   If you need to selectively import data from an Access, FoxPro, dBASE, or Paradox file (or any file laid out in row and column format), use Microsoft Query. You can extract information selectively from a large file by using Microsoft Query, without importing the entire file. Microsoft Query is a separate program that comes with Excel 97. ■

▶ **See** "Introducing Microsoft Query," **p. 247**

Importing Data from Mainframe Computers

If the data you want to import is in a mainframe database, and you can access the mainframe from your computer, check to see if the database supports Structured Query Language (SQL) If so, then you can use Microsoft Query to retrieve the data. Microsoft Query is easy to use. Refer to Chapter 16, "Retrieving Data from External Sources Using Microsoft Query," for more information on using Microsoft Query and Excel to retrieve data from external databases.

However, if your computer is not connected to the mainframe, you have to import the data from the mainframe by saving it from the mainframe into a text file. The text file then can be opened in Excel to import the data.

The three most common text file formats used to download data from mainframes are Text, Formatted Text, and CSV. If the data is in sentences, Excel can separate text lines up to 255 characters long into individual cells in a worksheet. The separation of data is called *parsing*. See the section, "Using the Convert Text to Columns Wizard to Parse Text," later in this chapter, for an explanation of how to accomplish parsing.

Although Excel now can hold up to 65,536 rows (records) of data, this may not be sufficient to import some large mainframe files. Additionally, it may take a very long time to process a file this size in Excel. It is better to import and process selected portions of a large file, if possible.

Excel includes a wizard that is used to convert text files that you import. The Text Import Wizard and its options are described in the next three sections.

Using the Text Import Wizard

Text files are used when Excel cannot import a file type directly. There are three types of text files that Excel can import: CSV, Text, and Formatted Text (sometimes called column-delimited or fixed-width). Most programs can save data to a text file.

Excel automatically separates data fields from CSV and Text formats. Each row of imported data is placed into an Excel row. Comma-delimited or tab-delimited data is separated, and each piece of data appears in its own cell. You can specify the type of delimiter to use in the text file you are importing. Refer to Figure 19.1 for an example of how CSV and Text format files appear before being imported into Excel.

However, with Formatted Text files, each data field (column) is assigned to specific character locations in a line of text. For example, company names may be stored from position 1 to 20, addresses from position 21 to 45, and so on. When the data does not fill the field completely, spaces are added to fill the field, so that all the data lines up in columns of fixed width.

Sometimes, when data is brought into Excel by using the Formatted Text format, an entire row of data must be placed in a single cell. To parse the data, Excel provides the Convert Text to Columns Wizard. Look ahead to the section, "Using the Convert Text to Columns Wizard to Parse Text," for the procedures to separate the data.

To import a text file into Excel, follow these steps:

1. Choose File, Open. The File Open dialog box is displayed.

2. Using the Files Of Type drop-down list box, select Text (*.prn, *.txt, *.csv).

3. Using the Look In list box, locate the file you want to import. You may find it necessary to select another drive or folder to locate the file.

4. Choose Open. Excel automatically opens the Text Import Wizard to import the text file. The Text Import Wizard has three steps. Step 1 of 3 is displayed in Figure 19.5.

Part V

Ch

19

FIG. 19.5
Step 1 in the Text
Import Wizard.

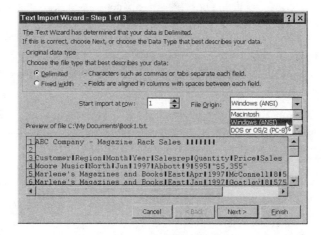

5. In the Original Data Type area of the dialog box, choose either Delimited or Fixed Width.

   Select Delimited if the text file you are importing is delimited with spaces, tabs, commas, or some other character. Select Fixed Width if the text file is space-delimited, column-delimited or fixed-width. Most files using the Formatted Text file format can be imported successfully by using the Fixed Width option.

6. In the File Origin drop-down list box, select the operating environment from which the file is coming (Macintosh, Windows (ANSI), or DOS or OS/2 (PC-8)). This tells Excel the type of character set the file is using. Text data from a mainframe computer most likely uses the PC-8 character set, although some mainframe text files may use the ANSI character set.

   At the bottom of the dialog box, a sample of the text file data is displayed in a preview window (refer to Figure 19.5).

N O T E If the data in the preview window contains odd-looking characters, or appears to be scrambled, you may not have selected the correct File Origin character set. Try using different character sets until the data in the preview window appears correctly.

7. In the Start Import at Row number box, select the row in the text file where you want the importing to start. Use the preview window to assist you; if necessary use the scroll bars in the preview to scroll down to see more rows.

   Because many text files contain titles, or other information, in the first few lines of the file, you can choose not to import this data. In Figure 19.6, the first line contains a title and the second is blank. In this example, you would enter 3 in the Start Import at Row number box.

8. After you select the settings in Step 1 of 3 in the Wizard, choose Next.

   The Text Import Wizard displays a dialog box for the second step of the importing process. The exact dialog box that appears depends on whether you selected Delimited or Fixed Width in the first step. The next two sections in this chapter describe in detail the delimited text import options, the fixed-width text import options, and the final step of the Wizard. Figure 19.6 shows the delimited text import options.

9. When you have finished filling in the Text Import Wizard options, choose Finish. Excel imports the file.

After you have imported the text file, use the File, Save As command to save the file as an Excel 97 workbook. Be sure that you choose Microsoft Excel Workbook in the Save File As Type drop-down list box when you save the imported file.

FIG. 19.6

Step 2 of the Text
Import Wizard.

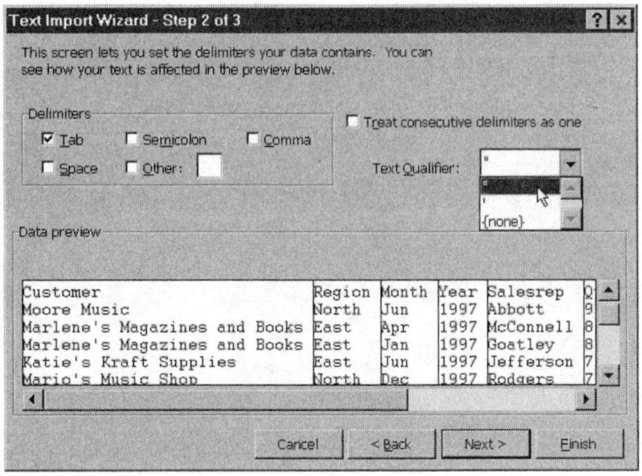

Choosing Delimited Text Import Options

Selecting Delimited in Step 1 of the Text Import Wizard (refer to Figure 19.5) displays the dialog box shown in Figure 19.6.

To finish importing the text, follow these steps:

1. In the Delimiters section of the dialog box, indicate the delimiters in the text file by clicking the appropriate check box. More than one delimiter may be selected, if applicable.

   The Wizard divides each row of text into columns, based on the location of the delimiters. The Data Preview window, at the bottom of the dialog box, indicates where each column begins and ends, with black vertical lines.

2. Select the Treat Consecutive Delimiters As One check box if you want to ignore empty columns of data as the file is imported. Usually, however, you should leave this check box empty.

3. Select the appropriate text qualifier from the Text Qualifier drop-down list.

   The text qualifier is used to enclose numbers or text that include the delimiting character, so that Excel can distinguish the delimiting character from the data containing the delimiting character. For example, if the delimiters are commas and the text qualifier is a double quote, any text that contains a comma will be surrounded by double quotes. Excel ignores the comma inside the double quotes when it imports the data. The most common text qualifier is the double quotation mark.

   Use the Data Preview area at the bottom of the dialog box to verify that the column breaks appear in the correct locations. If they do not, alter the delimiter and text qualifier choice until they do. If you cannot align the columns, choose the Back button and choose Fixed Width as the Original Data Type.

4. Choose the Next button. The Text Import Wizard displays the final step, Step 3, shown in Figure 19.7.

Part
V

Ch
19

FIG. 19.7

Step 3 in the Text Import Wizard.

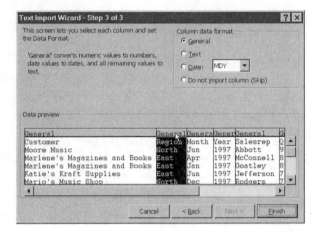

In the final step of the Wizard, select the data format for each column of data. To select a column, click the button over each column. After selecting the column, choose the appropriate Column Data Format options. The options are summarized in the following list:

- *General.* Select this to have Excel convert numeric values to numbers, date values to dates, and all other values to text.

- *Text.* Select this to format all data in the column as text.

- *Date.* Select this to format all data in the column as a date in the specified format.

- *Do Not Import.* Select this if you do not want to import the data in the column. The Text Import Wizard skips the selected column when data is imported.

To import the data, choose Finish.

Choosing Fixed-Width Text-Import Options

Selecting Fixed Width in Step 1 of the Text Import Wizard (refer to Figure 19.5), displays the dialog box shown in Figure 19.8.

Follow these steps to finish importing the text:

1. The Data preview at the bottom of the dialog box shows suggested column breaks, marked on the ruler above the preview window. If the column breaks are not correct, drag them to the correct positions. Create a new column break by clicking the ruler at the top of the Data preview window; delete a column break by double-clicking it.

2. After the column break is established, click the Next button. The dialog box previously shown in Figure 19.7 is displayed.

3. Select the data format for each column of data. To select a column, click the button over each column. After selecting the column, choose the appropriate Column Data Format options. See the preceding bulleted list for a description of the data format options.

4. Choose Finish to import the data.

FIG. 19.8

Even though some of the text is being cut off in the first column, the data for this column is available in the worksheet.

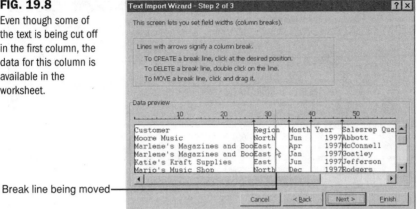

Break line being moved

Using the Convert Text to Columns Wizard to Parse Text

Occasionally, you may need to import a text file that is not properly delimited or is improperly formatted as a fixed-length file. When this happens, you must import the file as a single column. In other situations, you may decide to paste a whole line of data into Excel from another application. It is sometimes easier to paste an entire line than to make several copy and paste operations.

In either case, an entire row of data is entered into a single cell in your Excel worksheet. To separate the long lines of data into individual cells, you must *parse*, or separate, each line into its individual parts. Figure 19.9 shows a worksheet which contains several lines of text. The first line of text is in cell A1, the second line of text is in cell A2, and so forth. The data in the imported text file, as you can see, is not lined up properly for a fixed-width import and must be parsed.

To parse the text shown in Figure 19.9, perform the following steps:

1. If you have just imported the data into Excel, choose File, Save As to save it in Excel format before you proceed with parsing the data.

2. Select the cell or cells of text you want to convert to columns. If you select more than one cell, all cells you select must be in the same column.

   If your file is like the one in Figure 19.9, you cannot convert all the lines at once, because the text is not aligned in columns and does not have delimiters. In this situation, you must convert each line to columns individually. If at least some of the text is aligned in columns, you can select a range of rows to convert all at once.

3. Choose Data, Text to Columns. The Convert Text to Columns Wizard dialog box appears, as shown in Figure 19.10.

Part
V

Ch
19

FIG. 19.9

The data items are not delimited in any way.

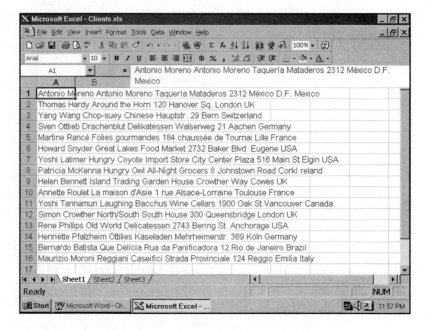

FIG. 19.10

The Convert Text to Columns Wizard is used to separate data in text files.

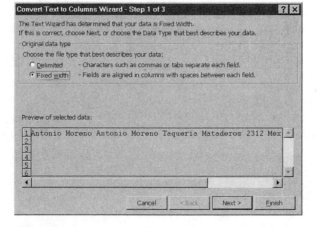

The three steps of the Convert Text to Columns Wizard dialog boxes are exactly the same as the Text Import Wizard dialog boxes, discussed in the earlier section, "Using the Text Import Wizard," but with one exception. In the Convert Text to Columns Wizard, the dialog box for Step 3 of the conversion has one additional option: the Destination text box.

Use the Destination text box to specify a destination for the parsed data other than the cell containing the line you are parsing. If you do not change the destination, the parsed data is inserted, beginning with the cell containing the line you are converting to columns. Fill in the other options in the Convert Text to Columns Wizard dialog boxes. Click the Next button after each step.

When you have completed the three steps in the Convert Text to Columns Wizard, click the Finish button. The text in the selected cell or cells is separated into individual columns.

Figure 19.11 shows the worksheet from Figure 19.9, with the first seven rows parsed into columns, and the column widths adjusted to show the entire contents of the cells.

FIG. 19.11

Parsing is a painstaking process because each line must be converted separately.

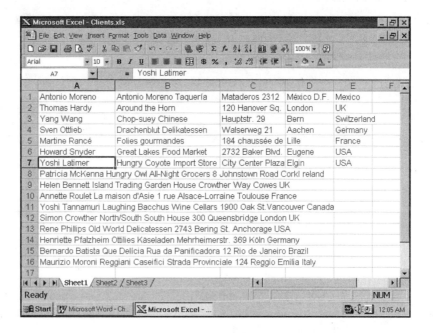

NOTE Be certain that sufficient blank columns exist, to the right of the single column that contains your selected cells, to hold the parsed data. Parsed data overwrites cells to the right, with no consideration for their current contents.

Exporting Data

Export an Excel 97 file to another file format merely involves saving it in a format that can be read by the other program, and then using the tools in the other program to import the file. To save Excel worksheets in a different format, use the following steps:

Part
V

Ch
19

1. Choose File, Save As. The Save As dialog box appears, as shown in Figure 19.12. Type the name for the file in the File Name text box.

2. From the Save As Type list, select the format in which you want to save the file. See the "File Formats" section earlier in this chapter for a complete list.

3. If necessary, select a different folder or drive from the Save In drop-down list.

4. Choose Save.

FIG. 19.12

Use the Save As dialog box to export an Excel file.

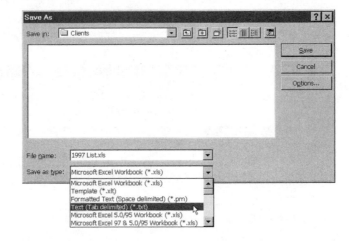

If you save an Excel 97 workbook in Excel 4.0 format, only worksheets, charts, and version 4.0 macro worksheets are saved. If you save an Excel 97 workbook in Lotus 1-2-3 version 3.x format, only the worksheets and chart worksheets are saved. All other formats save only the current worksheet.

You can export data to many DOS or mainframe programs by saving the file in one of the many formats used by Excel. Most DOS or mainframe programs can translate from one of these formats into their own formats. Refer to the "File Formats" section earlier in this chapter for a list of file formats that Excel can export.

Two common file formats for exchanging data with databases or mainframes are CSV and Text. Both of these file types separate the data into worksheet cells with delimiters. Formulas are changed to results. The character set used when saving depends on which type of CSV or Text file you select. Seven different sets are defined in the list:

■ Formatted Text (Space-delimited)

■ Text (Tab-delimited)

■ CSV (Comma-delimited)

■ Text (Macintosh)

- Text(OS/2 or Microsoft-DOS)
- CSV (Macintosh)
- CSV (OS/2 or Microsoft-DOS)

Text files separate cell contents with a delimiter, or arrange the cell data in fixed columns across the page, aligning the columns with space characters. Saving a file with Text (Tab-delimited) format produces a text file with cell contents that are separated by tab characters. Saving a file with Formatted Text (Space-delimited format) produces a text file with the cell contents arranged in fixed-width columns. This second type of text file sometimes is called a fixed-width or column-delimited text file.

Comma Separated Value (CSV) files separate each cell's contents with a comma. Cells that contain commas are enclosed in quotation marks, and then separated by commas. Any text or numbers that contain a comma are enclosed in quotation marks, so that the commas that are part of the cell data are distinguished from the separator commas.

Refer to Figure 19.1 for an example of both Text and CSV file formats.

If you are transferring between Macintosh and Windows versions of Excel 97, you do not need to convert the file. If one computer uses Excel 4.0 or 5.0, and the other uses Excel 97, you need to save files to the older versions before transferring. If the Macintosh version is earlier than Excel 3.0, you need conversion software, which usually comes with the file-transfer software. ●

Part

V

Ch

19

CHAPTER 20

Introducing Visual Basic for Applications

Visual Basic for Applications (VBA) is the programming language that has been used to create user-defined Excel applications since Excel version 5.0's release in 1993. It is the long-awaited fulfillment of a Microsoft goal to provide a rich development environment that is usable throughout the Microsoft Office Suite. This chapter shows how to automate common tasks by using Macros, and how to build upon those Macros by editing them to meet your specific requirements. This chapter also looks at writing your own procedures—independent sections of Visual Basic code—that let you manipulate every facet of the Excel 97 program. Additionally, this chapter explores a new area introduced in Excel 97—events—which enable you to take actions based on which *event* occurs in the spreadsheet. ■

Recording macros that save time and effort

Discover the three-step process for recording macros. Automate those time-consuming, repetitive actions so that you can execute them with a single keystroke.

Discovering the hidden power of Visual Basic

Learn to use the user-friendly Visual Basic Editor to fine-tune your spreadsheets and make them more productive. Create your own Visual Basic procedures by using powerful programming techniques.

Exploring the power of events in Excel

Open the door to automation with Visual Basic events. Make your procedure run the moment you open your workbook.

When to Use VBA

There are some amazing things you can do in Excel 97, but every so often, you need to do more, go a step beyond, to make your application and your time more productive. To accomplish this, you need to record a macro, and *that* means using Visual Basic for Applications. You may be familiar with macros from experience with other products or earlier versions of Excel, but with Excel 97, the increased power to create macros is simply amazing.

Microsoft Visual Basic is the programming system for Office 97. This is the language in which every macro you record is created. You can use this language to write user-defined procedures, and to manipulate Excel objects, such as workbooks, worksheets, and charts. Moreover, with this language, you can create unique applications that combine the power and functionality of every product in the Office 97 suite.

Visual Basic within the Excel environment began with Excel 5.0, providing end-users and developers a rich, object-oriented environment to modify Excel for the specific needs of their organizations. From the start, Microsoft's plan was to incorporate Visual Basic into its other business-related products, which has been realized with Office 97. What does this mean to you, the end-user/developer? It means that by learning how to create and edit Visual Basic procedures in Excel 97, you can transfer those skills and knowledge to other Microsoft Office products, such as Word 97, PowerPoint 97, Access 97, Project 98, the Binder, Outlook, and even the Office Assistant.

Your Visual Basic experience starts with the Macro Recorder. The next four sections of this chapter explain the process behind creating a macro and expanding the recording to meet the specific requirements of your project.

Preparing to Record a Macro

Any task that you perform repeatedly in Microsoft Excel is a prime candidate for automation with a macro. A *macro* is a series of recorded commands that are stored with your workbook, and that can be run whenever you need to perform the specific task the Macro stores. The process of creating a macro is simple: Switch on the Macro Recorder, complete the task the macro represents exactly as you require, and then stop the Macro Recorder.

It's always a good idea to plan the steps and commands that you want the macro to perform *before* you create the macro. If you make a mistake when you record the macro, your corrections are also recorded. Additionally, you need to consider the following items before recording a macro:

- *Activating the Macro.* Consider how you plan to run the macro. You can run it from the menu, a button on a toolbar, a shortcut key, a graphic object in your spreadsheet, or any combination of these choices. Base your decision on what your macro performs, and how often you'll use it.

■ *Storing the Macro.* You can store your macro in the currently active workbook, a new workbook, or the Personal Macro Workbook. The default location is the active workbook. Each macro that is recorded is placed in a separate module sheet, attached to the workbook. This module sheet is visible only in the Visual Basic Editor. Storing macros in the active workbook means you can use the macros only when that workbook is open. Putting your macros in a new workbook begins a new file in which to store them. The new workbook must be open to use the macros stored inside of it. Storing macros in the Personal Macro Workbook provides access to the macros whenever Excel is open. The Personal Macro Workbook is open, by default, as a hidden workbook whenever Excel is open, and it is created the first time you store a macro in it.

■ *Selecting Cells.* If you select cells while recording a macro, the macro always selects those same cell references when it runs. It doesn't matter which cell is the active cell when you choose to run the macro, because macros record absolute cell references. If you want to select cells relative to the position of the active cell, set the Macro Recorder to record relative cell references. On the Stop Recording toolbar, select the Relative Reference button. The Macro Recorder continues to record macros with relative references, until you click Relative Reference again or close Microsoft Excel.

If you want the macro to select a specific cell, perform an action and then select another cell relative to the active cell. You can mix the use of relative and absolute references when you record the macro by selecting the Relative Reference button when you want to use relative referencing, and by deselecting it when you want to use absolute referencing.

■ *Naming the Macro.* The first character of your macro's name must be a letter. Other name characters can be letters, numbers, or underscore characters. Spaces can't be used in a macro name. Name your macros so that you know what function they perform when run. Using capital letters and the underscore character as a word separator makes your macro names more readable.

▶ **See** "Relative Cell Referencing," **p. 21**

▶ **See** "Absolute Cell Referencing," **p. 21**

Suppose you have a number of inventory lists for the various divisions in your company, such as the list for the ACME Computer Products displayed in Figure 20.1. While the data is accurate, the worksheets don't have uniform, polished headings that you can use with a client. You want to change the style and background for each of the worksheets, but instead of formatting each worksheet separately, you decide to create a macro to speed up the process and to ensure consistency in your spreadsheets.

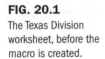

FIG. 20.1

The Texas Division worksheet, before the macro is created.

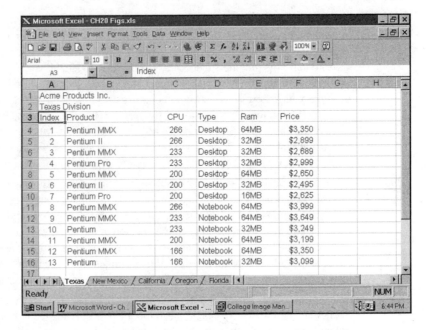

Your first step is to plan the macro. Walk through the steps you want to record several times to make sure you know what to do, and how to do it in the most efficient manner. Remember that the recorder records mistakes as well as corrections; consider writing the steps out on a pad of paper. For example:

1. Select cells A1 through D2.
2. Change the font type and size, center across the columns, and change the background color to red.
3. Select cells A3 through D3.
4. Make the text bold and centered in the cells, and change the background color to blue.
5. Select cell A4.

After you identify the steps you want the macro to perform, it's time to record the macro.

Recording a Macro

Recording a macro involves performing the exact steps you want the macro to perform. It's a good idea to practice these steps several times to make certain your macro can do what you require. If the macro is complex, write down the steps so they're easier to follow and so you don't forget a crucial step. To record a macro, follow these steps:

1. Choose Tools, Macro, Record New Macro. The Record Macro dialog box is displayed, as shown in Figure 20.2

FIG. 20.2

The default settings in the Record Macro dialog box.

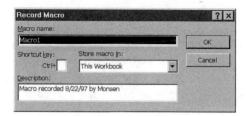

2. In the Macro Name entry box, type a descriptive name for the macro, telling what it does when it runs. The name must start with a letter and cannot contain spaces.

3. The Shortcut Key box lets you select a keyboard shortcut to run your macro. Type any letter into the box, except for numbers and special characters. Use the SHIFT key for uppercase. If no keyboard shortcut is entered, the macro is accessible from the Tools, Macro, Macros menu.

N O T E The shortcut key you enter overrides any default Microsoft Excel shortcut keys during the time the workbook containing your macro is open. ▨

4. Select a location for the macro from the Store Macro In drop-down list. To make a macro available whenever you use Microsoft Excel, store the macro in the Personal Macro Workbook in the XLStart folder, which typically is located in C:\Program Files\Microsoft Office\Office\XLStart.

5. The date you create the macro and the user name listed on the General tab of the Tools, Options dialog box are entered automatically into the Description entry box. The description appears when you select the macro from the menu, or when you assign a macro to a toolbar button. Change the description as desired.

6. Choose OK to begin recording the macro. The Stop Recording toolbar appears.

7. Follow the steps for the macro *exactly* as you laid them out; remember, the recorder records *every* action you take.

8. To stop the recording process, click the Stop Recording button on the Stop Recording toolbar. If, during the course of recording your macro, the Stop Recording toolbar is removed, you can stop recording your macro by choosing Tools, Macro, Stop Recording.

CAUTION

Be aware of *when* you turn off the Macro Recorder, or you may get surprising results. For example, suppose you want to record a macro that creates a colorful default heading for your company, which you can insert on all your older workbooks. You planned everything and started the macro. When the last step finishes, you close the workbook and stop the recording. When you start using your macro, you discover that every time you use the macro, your workbook closes! Why? Because you *recorded* closing the workbook! Stop recording at the point where you want to be in your workbook when the macro is finished running.

Running a Macro

After recording a macro, it's a good idea to test it to make sure it performs the intended steps. While you can run the macro in Microsoft Excel or from the Visual Basic Editor, you usually run the macro in Microsoft Excel. Typically, you run a macro from the Visual Basic Editor when you want to test it during the editing process. The Visual Basic Editor is discussed later in this chapter.

Before running your macro, make sure that you are in the correct place in your spreadsheet to run it. For example, if you are currently working in one of your charts, running a macro designed for a worksheet generates an error. To run a macro, follow these steps:

1. Open the workbook that contains the macro. If your macro is in the Personal.XLS workbook, it opens when you open Excel.

2. Choose Tools, Macro, Macros to display the Macro dialog box, shown in Figure 20.3.

FIG. 20.3

Make sure to select the correct macro by checking the description displayed at the bottom of the dialog box.

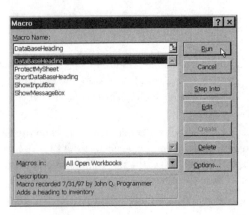

3. In the Macro Name box, select the name of the macro you want to run from the list box. In Figure 20.3, the macro DataBaseHeading is selected.

4. Click Run, and your macro runs exactly as you recorded it.

 You can interrupt a macro before it completes its actions by pressing the Esc key.

Assigning a Macro to a Toolbar Button

Although the menu is a great place to *review* a complete collection of available macros, it is not the most convenient way to *run* a macro. Instead, you can improve access to your macro by assigning it to a toolbar button. The following are steps for assigning a macro to a toolbar button:

1. On the View menu, select Toolbars, Customize Toolbars.

2. In the Toolbars tab, select a toolbar to hold your macro. Because you can place your macro on any toolbar, choose one that matches the purpose of your macro.

3. Select the Command Tab in the Customize dialog box. Scroll down in the Category list and choose Macros (see Figure 20.4).

FIG. 20.4

Use the Customize dialog box to customize your macro buttons.

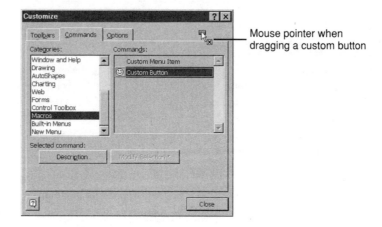

Mouse pointer when dragging a custom button

4. Drag the custom button to the toolbar and drop it where you want to place it.

5. After the custom button is on the toolbar, right-click the button and select Assign Macro from the shortcut menu. The Assign Macro dialog box appears, as shown in Figure 20.5.

FIG. 20.5

The description of the macro appears at the bottom of the Assign Macro dialog box.

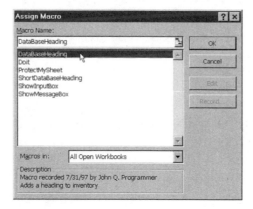

6. Select a macro from the Macro Name list and click OK.

N O T E   While you have the Customize Toolbars dialog box open, you can edit the button image by right-clicking the image and selecting Edit Button Image. The image can't be changed unless the Customize dialog box is open. ■

7. Click Close.

The help screens in Excel provide instructions for assigning a macro to a menu or graphic object. Use the Office Assistant to search for the help screen. Type **run macro** in the Office Assistant search box, and then press Enter to see a list of help topics. Choose Run a Macro from a Keyboard Shortcut, a Graphic Object, or a Toolbar Button.

Editing the Macro

Your macro can do only so much. It's great for repeating the steps of a procedure exactly as you record them. But sometimes you need more flexibility. You might want to apply only some of the steps you record, or you might want to take an additional step that you didn't record. At this point, you need to edit your macro. The editing process takes place in the Visual Basic Editor. One of the Visual Basic Editor's many uses is to write and edit macros that are attached to Microsoft Excel workbooks. Here are the steps to start the editing process:

1. Choose Tools, Macro, Macros. The Macro dialog box displays (refer to Figure 20.3)

2. In the Macro Name box, select the macro you want to edit from the list box.

3. Select Edit. This launches the Visual Basic Editor, with which you can modify the code for your macro.

Now look at how to fine-tune your macros with the Visual Basic Editor.

The Visual Basic Editor

The Visual Basic Editor is a full-featured development environment for Microsoft Excel 97, Word 97, and PowerPoint 97. It provides the means to edit the macros you record and to create new procedures from scratch. Within this environment, you can create new procedures, edit existing ones, debug your code, and run all your code. *Procedures* are independent sections of Visual Basic code that let you manipulate every facet of the program for which they are written. The Visual Basic Editor screen is shown in Figure 20.6.

TheVisual Basic Editor has three main sections. They are the Project Explorer, the Properties Window, and the Code Window.

The Project Explorer Window

The Project Explorer window, shown in Figure 20.7, displays the workbooks, worksheets, and modules within your project. Selecting an item from this window automatically brings up the properties for this object in the Properties window. Selecting one of the two buttons at the top left of the Project Explorer displays either the code or the form for that object. If you recorded a macro, you will notice a Module folder in this window. Each macro you record is stored in a separate module. To edit your code, select the module, and then click the View Code button.

FIG. 20.6

The Visual Basic Editor screen.

Visual Basic Editor · Object Box · Procedure Box · Code Window · Standard Toolbar · Project Explorer · Properties Window

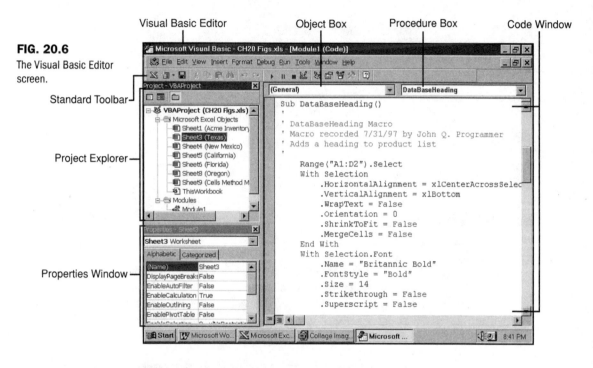

FIG. 20.7

The Project Explorer window in the Visual Basic Editor.

View Code button · View Object button · Toggle Folders button

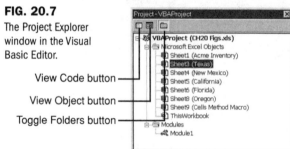

The Properties Window

The Properties window (see Figure 20.8) displays the characteristics of the object selected. You can set these properties to alter the behavior or presentation of the object. For example, the Worksheet object has a DisplayPageBreaks property. If that property is set to True, page breaks are visible; if it is set to False, they are not visible. Each type of object has it own unique properties. Some objects have a good number of properties, while others have just a few.

FIG. 20.8

The Properties Window in the Visual Basic Editor.

Object

Properties

Settings

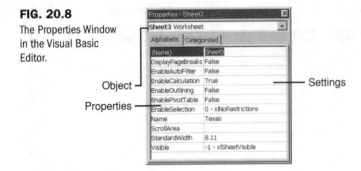

The Code Window

This window displays the code for your macros and for any procedures that you create in your project. This window is used with the Project Window. Select the module in the Project Explorer and click the View Code button at the top of the Project Window. This displays the code for that module in the code window. At the top of the code window are two drop-down lists; the one on the left identifies the object selected; and the one on the right identifies the name of your macro or the selected procedure. An example of the Code window is shown in Figure 20.9.

FIG. 20.9

The Code window in the Visual Basic Editor.

Object drop-down list

Procedures drop-down list

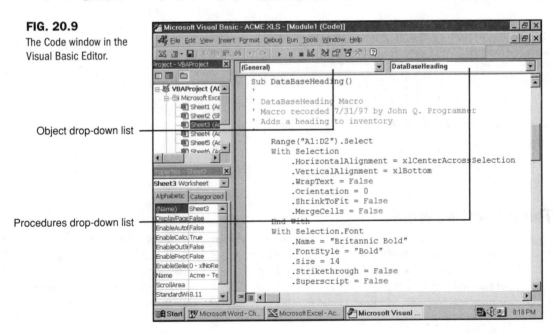

Visual Basic Editor Toolbars

There are four toolbars associated with the Visual Basic Editor. They are the Standard Toolbar, Edit Toolbar, Debug Toolbar, and the UserForm Toolbar. Each provides a different set of tools to create and manipulate the objects and code in your project. You can see an example of these toolbars in Figure 20.10.

FIG. 20.10
Like all Microsoft programs, the toolbars in the Visual Basic Editor display a screen tip when you point to a button.

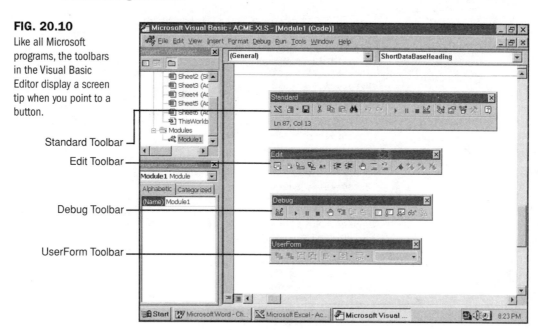

Editing Your VBA Code

Editing your macro involves the same skills that you use in word processing. You can cut, copy, and paste text by using the menu, toolbar, shortcut menu, or keyboard strokes. Inserting new code items is as simple as typing, or even using drag and drop within the code window. Before you start, though, look carefully at the code the recorder generates. Visual Basic is a language that requires a strict syntax for the construction of code lines. Each word, period, parenthesis, and quotation mark has a specific meaning to your macro. If you enter the wrong information, your macro may not run, or worse, it may run and cause some unexpected action in your spreadsheet. Taking this into consideration, look next at how to edit your code.

The Visual Basic Editor can be brought up quickly through the Tools menu in Excel; choose Tools, Macro, Macros. Select the macro you want to edit, and then click the Edit button. This starts the Visual Basic Editor and displays the code for your macro in the code window. Here is the code for the macro recorded earlier in this chapter:

Part
V

Ch
20

```
Sub DataBaseHeading()
'
' DataBaseHeading Macro
' Macro recorded 7/31/97 by John Q. Programmer
' Adds a heading to inventory
'
Range("A1:D2").Select
        With Selection
                .HorizontalAlignment = xlCenterAcrossSelection
                .VerticalAlignment = xlBottom
                .WrapText = False
                .Orientation = 0
                .ShrinkToFit = False
                .MergeCells = False
        End With
        With Selection.Font
                .Name = "Britannic Bold"
                .FontStyle = "Bold"
                .Size = 14
                .Strikethrough = False
                .Superscript = False
                .Subscript = False
                .OutlineFont = False
                .Shadow = False
                .Underline = xlUnderlineStyleNone
                .ColorIndex = xlAutomatic
        End With
        With Selection.Interior
                .ColorIndex = 3
                .Pattern = xlSolid
        End With
Range("A3:D3").Select
        Selection.Font.Bold = True
        With Selection
                .HorizontalAlignment = xlCenter
                .VerticalAlignment = xlBottom
                .WrapText = False
                .Orientation = 0
                .ShrinkToFit = False
                .MergeCells = False
        End With
        With Selection.Interior
                .ColorIndex = 41
                .Pattern = xlSolid
        End With
Range("A4").Select
End Sub
```

The Macro Recorder does an excellent job of recording these procedures, but there are limitations. Take a closer look at a single section of this code. The following section is from the Heading area of the code.

■ `Range("A3:D3").Select`   This line selects cells A3 through D3.

■ `Selection.Font.Bold = True`   This line make the font bold.

- ■ `With Selection`   The `With` and `End With` allow the setting of several properties as a group. The object being altered is the range A3:D3.
- ■ `.HorizontalAlignment = xlCenter`   Center the data in cell.
- ■ `.VerticalAlignment = xlBottom`   Align data to bottom.
- ■ `.WrapText = False`   Do not wrap text.
- ■ `.Orientation = 0`   Data is not angled in cell.
- ■ `.ShrinkToFit = False`   Shrink to fit is turned off.
- ■ `.MergeCells = False`   Cells are not merged.
- ■ `End With`   Completes the `With Selection` statement.

The intent isn't to set all of these properties when recording the macro. It's just that the Macro Recorder doesn't have a choice. It can record only what you do and any associated properties that it notes as you carry out the steps of your procedure. When you use a macro to format cells, this can cause problems. Each cell has a default set of formats—those defaults are recorded as part of the macro code. When the macro was recorded, the only action taken against cells A3 through D3 was to bold and center the data in the cells. Yet the default settings were also recorded with the macro, including the settings that control angling data and merging cells. If the macro is run on a worksheet where the data in cells A3 through D3 is angled or the cells merged, the macro will bold and center the data but removes the formats that angle and merge the cells, because these default settings are included in the macro.

You can fix this by editing the macro and removing the default settings that were automatically recorded, which were not part of the steps you wrote out before recording the macro.

The same snippet of code, after editing the lines you do not need, looks like this:

```
Range("A3:D3").Select
Selection.Font.Bold = True
        With Selection
                  HorizontalAlignment = xlCenter
        End With
```

The code in the Code Window can be edited in the same fashion as text in a word processor; in fact, you will see a flashing cursor when you click in the Code Window. Select the text by dragging your mouse pointer over it. You can cut, copy, and paste the code just as you do in Microsoft Word.

Annotating Your Code with Comments

When you record a macro, the Macro dialog box provides a place for comments to identify what the macro does, who wrote it, and when it was written. Those comments are placed in your code immediately after the initial line of code naming the procedure and are preceded by an apostrophe ('). The Visual Basic Editor enters comments in green:

```
Sub DataBaseHeading()
'
' DataBaseHeading Macro
```

```
' Macro recorded 7/31/97 by John Q. Programmer
' Adds a heading to inventory
'
Range("A1:D2").Select
          With Selection
```

Note that comment lines start with an apostrophe and can be placed in your procedures as you need them. They must be written on a new line, or at the end of an existing line of code. You can be as detailed as you want, because any comments you write are totally ignored by the program and do not interfere with running your procedure.

It is always a good programming practice to document your code with comments. It helps you to keep track of exactly what the procedure is supposed to do and what you were thinking when you wrote it. It makes it easier to understand after several weeks or months what has to be done to modify the code to suit your new requirements. It also makes it easier for others to understand your code.

Referencing Cells

When you record a macro, the identification of which cells are selected is up to the Macro Recorder. The following snippet of code is taken from the macro example recorded earlier in the chapter. This code selects cells A1:D2, and then centers the values in those cells across the selected area:

```
Range("A1:D2").Select
 With Selection
          .HorizontalAlignment = xlCenterAcrossSelection
```

When you select cells while recording a macro, the specific cell references are identified. When the macro is run on another worksheet, the same cell references are used. In the code above, the macro will always select cells A2 through D2. Instead of specific cell references being identified in the macro, you may want to make the macro run after you have selected the cells. Additionally, you change the macro to run relative to the active cell.

There are several methods Visual Basic uses to identify cells when you record macros. The Range method is what occurs when you select cells while *recording* a macro. The syntax for the Range method is:

```
Range(Cell1)
```

or

```
Range(Cell1, Cell2)
```

In the first example, Cell1 refers to the cell or cell range required, such as "A23" , "A23:F33", or "A23, F33". In the alternate syntax, Cell1 and Cell2 refer to the upper-left and lower-right corners of the range.

The `Selection` method is also one you have seen through your recorded macros. If you select cells *before* you turn on your Macro Recorder, the code will reflect the `Selection` Method. This is how you would record macros to apply formatting to whatever cells you have selected. Below is an example of the `Selection` method, which is applying the `Bold` format to the selected cells:

```
Selection.Font.Bold = True
```

The `Offset` method for selecting cells is used to create relative references. You would use this method to refer to another cell, based on the location of the active cell. Below is an example of the `Offset` method, which selects the cell immediately to the right of the active cell:

```
Selection.Offset(0,1).Range("A1").Select
```

`Offset(0,1)` refers to the number of rows and columns from the active cell to move. In this example, on the same row move one column to the right. The reference to `"A1"` does not refer to the actual worksheet cell "A1," but rather to the cell in the upper-left of the newly selected area. This is the syntax that Visual Basic uses as a reference handle to the selected area, regardless of its size. If you select another area, Visual Basic discards the first reference and creates an new one for the newly selected area.

To make the cells in your macro "relative" and not "absolute" (fixed), either select cells before you record the macro or edit the macro and use either the Selection or Offset syntax.

▶ **See** "Relative Cell Referencing," **p. 21**

▶ **See** "Absolute Cell Referencing," **p. 21**

This chapter explored how Visual Basic can be used in Excel. There are several sources of additional information on Visual Basic that you might find useful:

- The help screens in Excel and in the Visual Basic Editor provide many excellent examples of how Visual Basic can be used with Excel. Ask the Office Assistant for a list of examples by typing **macro** in the Office Assistant search box. Choose from among the offered entries in the results list.

- The *Visual Basic for Applications 5* computer reference book, published by Que, offers additional information on working with macros and writing procedures with Visual Basic.

Index

Symbols

error message, 175

#DIV/0! error message, 175

#N/A error message, 175

#NAME? error message, 175

#NULL! error message, 175

#NUM! error message, 175

#REF! error message, 175

#VALUE! error message, 175

$ (dollar sign)
    freezing cell references, 21
    symbol code, 83

% Difference From calculation (pivot tables), 240

% of calculation (pivot tables), 240

% of Column calculation (pivot tables), 241

% of Row calculation (pivot tables), 241

% of Total calculation (pivot tables), 241

* (filter wild cards), 205, 212

< comparison operator, 206

<= comparison operator, 206

<> comparison operator, 206

= comparison operator, 205

> comparison operator, 205

>= comparison operator, 205

? (filter wild cards), 205

100% charts, 107

2-D area charts, 109

2-D bar charts, 107

2-D column charts, 107

2-D doughnut charts, 110

2-D line charts, 109

2-D pie charts, 110

3-D charts, 134-135

3-D View dialog box, 135

A

absolute cell references, 21-22
    converting to relative, 83
    range names, accessing, 65-66

active cells
    Fill Handle, 16
    moving, 14-15

active windows, 48

Add Criteria dialog box, 262-263

Add Data command, 122

Add Data dialog box, 123

Add Scenario dialog box, 167

Add Tables dialog box, 258

Add Trendline dialog box, 134

add-ins, Data Tracking (Template Wizard), 98-99

adding worksheets to workbooks, 36

Advanced Filter, 214-216
    criteria ranges, creating, 214-215

Advanced Filter dialog box, 215

Advanced tab (Share Workbook dialog box), 292-293

Alignment format option
    chart objects, 131
    drawn objects, 132

All category (functions), 63

All filter option (AutoFilter), 208

Complete and Return this Card for a *FREE* Computer Book Catalog

Thank you for purchasing this book! You have purchased a superior computer book written expressly for your needs. To continue to provide the kind of up-to-date, pertinent coverage you've come to expect from us, we need to hear from you. Please take a minute to complete and return this self-addressed, postage-paid form. In return, we'll send you a free catalog of all our computer books on topics ranging from word processing to programming and the internet.

Mr. ☐   Mrs. ☐   Ms. ☐   Dr. ☐

Name (first) ☐☐☐☐☐☐☐☐☐☐☐☐ (M.I.) ☐ (last) ☐☐☐☐☐☐☐☐☐☐☐☐☐☐☐☐

Address ☐☐☐☐☐☐☐☐☐☐☐☐☐☐☐☐☐☐☐☐☐☐☐☐☐☐☐☐☐☐☐

☐☐☐☐☐☐☐☐☐☐☐☐☐☐☐☐☐☐☐☐☐☐☐☐☐☐☐☐☐☐☐

City ☐☐☐☐☐☐☐☐☐☐☐☐☐☐☐☐☐☐ State ☐☐ Zip ☐☐☐☐☐ ☐☐☐☐

Phone ☐☐☐ ☐☐☐ ☐☐☐☐ Fax ☐☐☐ ☐☐☐ ☐☐☐☐

Company Name ☐☐☐☐☐☐☐☐☐☐☐☐☐☐☐☐☐☐☐☐☐☐☐☐☐☐☐☐☐

E-mail address ☐☐☐☐☐☐☐☐☐☐☐☐☐☐☐☐☐☐☐☐☐☐☐☐☐☐☐☐

1. Please check at least (3) influencing factors for purchasing this book.

Front or back cover information on book ☐
Special approach to the content ☐
Completeness of content ☐
Author's reputation ☐
Publisher's reputation ☐
Book cover design or layout ☐
Index or table of contents of book ☐
Price of book ☐
Special effects, graphics, illustrations ☐
Other (Please specify): _____ ☐

2. How did you first learn about this book?

Saw in Macmillan Computer Publishing catalog ☐
Recommended by store personnel ☐
Saw the book on bookshelf at store ☐
Recommended by a friend ☐
Received advertisement in the mail ☐
Saw an advertisement in: _____ ☐
Read book review in: _____ ☐
Other (Please specify): _____ ☐

3. How many computer books have you purchased in the last six months?

This book only ☐   3 to 5 books ☐
2 books ☐   More than 5 ☐

4. Where did you purchase this book?

Bookstore ☐
Computer Store ☐
Consumer Electronics Store ☐
Department Store ☐
Office Club ☐
Warehouse Club ☐
Mail Order ☐
Direct from Publisher ☐
Internet site ☐
Other (Please specify): _____ ☐

5. How long have you been using a computer?

☐ Less than 6 months   ☐ 6 months to a year
☐ 1 to 3 years   ☐ More than 3 years

6. What is your level of experience with personal computers and with the subject of this book?

	With PCs	With subject of book
New	☐	☐
Casual	☐	☐
Accomplished	☐	☐
Expert	☐	☐

Source Code ISBN: 0-7897-1440-X

7. Which of the following best describes your job title?

Administrative Assistant .... ☐
Coordinator .... ☐
Manager/Supervisor .... ☐
Director .... ☐
Vice President .... ☐
President/CEO/COO .... ☐
Lawyer/Doctor/Medical Professional .... ☐
Teacher/Educator/Trainer .... ☐
Engineer/Technician .... ☐
Consultant .... ☐
Not employed/Student/Retired .... ☐
Other (Please specify): _____ ☐

8. Which of the following best describes the area of the company your job title falls under?

Accounting .... ☐
Engineering .... ☐
Manufacturing .... ☐
Operations .... ☐
Marketing .... ☐
Sales .... ☐
Other (Please specify): _____ ☐

9. What is your age?

Under 20 .... ☐
21-29 .... ☐
30-39 .... ☐
40-49 .... ☐
50-59 .... ☐
60-over .... ☐

10. Are you:

Male .... ☐
Female .... ☐

11. Which computer publications do you read regularly? (Please list)

_____
_____
_____
_____
_____
_____
_____
_____
_____
_____

Comments: _____
_____
_____

Fold here and scotch-tape to mail.

Check out Que® Books on the World Wide Web
http://www.quecorp.com

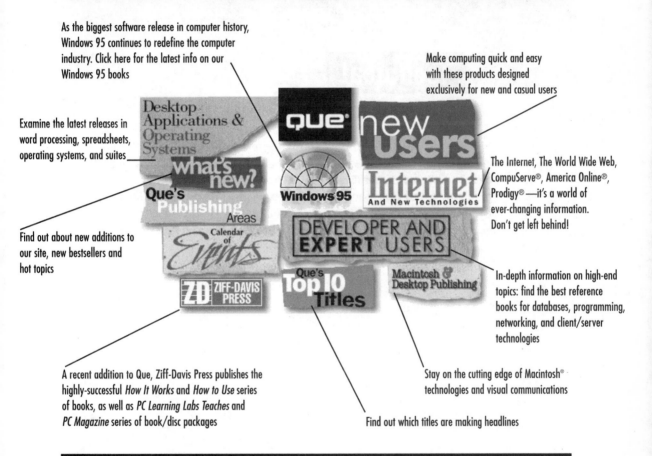

As the biggest software release in computer history, Windows 95 continues to redefine the computer industry. Click here for the latest info on our Windows 95 books

Make computing quick and easy with these products designed exclusively for new and casual users

Examine the latest releases in word processing, spreadsheets, operating systems, and suites

The Internet, The World Wide Web, CompuServe®, America Online®, Prodigy® —it's a world of ever-changing information. Don't get left behind!

Find out about new additions to our site, new bestsellers and hot topics

In-depth information on high-end topics: find the best reference books for databases, programming, networking, and client/server technologies

A recent addition to Que, Ziff-Davis Press publishes the highly-successful *How It Works* and *How to Use* series of books, as well as *PC Learning Labs Teaches* and *PC Magazine* series of book/disc packages

Stay on the cutting edge of Macintosh® technologies and visual communications

Find out which titles are making headlines

With 6 separate publishing groups, Que develops products for many specific market segments and areas of computer technology. Explore our Web Site and you'll find information on best-selling titles, newly published titles, upcoming products, authors, and much more.

- Stay informed on the latest industry trends and products available

- Visit our online bookstore for the latest information and editions

- Download software from Que's library of the best shareware and freeware

MACMILLAN COMPUTER PUBLISHING USA

A VIACOM COMPANY

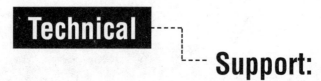

Support:

If you need assistance with the information in this book or with a CD/Disk accompanying the book, please access the Knowledge Base on our Web site at **http://www.superlibrary.com/general/support**. Our most Frequently Asked Questions are answered there. If you do not find the answer to your questions on our Web site, you may contact Macmillan Technical Support **(317) 581-3833** or e-mail us at **support@mcp.com**.